D1554036

DATE DUE

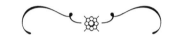

FOUR YEARS

in the

MOUNTAINS *of*

KURDISTAN

FOUR YEARS

in the

MOUNTAINS *of*

KURDISTAN

 1915-1919

AN ARMENIAN BOY'S MEMOIR OF
SURVIVAL

ARAM HAIGAZ

Copyright © 2014 by Iris H. Chekenian

Chekenian, Iris
Four Years in the Mountains of Kurdistan/ by Aram Haigaz
ISBN 978-1-940210-06-3
1. Armenian genocide —memoir 2. World War I—memoir 3. Coming of age—
memoir 4. History of Turkey—memoir 5. Kurdish history—memoir 6. Ottoman
empire—memoir 7. Tales of survival—memoir
Title, jacket and interior design by Laura Klynstra

First Edition

10 9 8 7 6 5 4 3 2 1

1919: Aram Haigaz at nineteen as a Boy Scout in Constantinople, Turkey. Two years later he sailed to the United States and arrived at Ellis Island in May 1921 wearing this uniform.

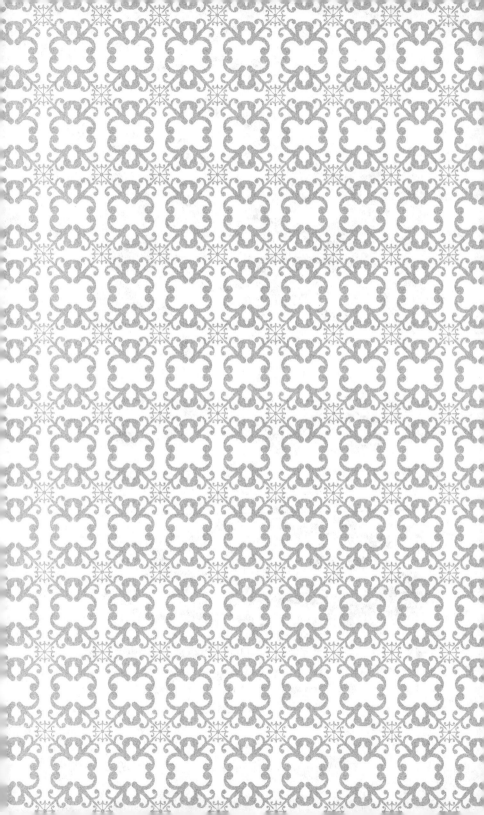

CONTENTS

Four Years in the Mountains of Kurdistan
by Aram Haigaz
A publication of the Kevork Melidinetsi Literary Award
Armenian Catholicosate of Cilicia
Antelias, Lebanon
Published in Armenian in 1972

TRANSLATIONS *from* ARMENIAN

Although he knew English well, my father Aram Haigaz wrote only in Armenian throughout his life. *Four Years in the Mountains of Kurdistan* contains various episodes that he published earlier, in slightly different versions, in his short story collections. Three stories appeared in English translation in *The Armenian Review* during the 1950s and in 1969. He had always hoped to gather the experiences of his Kurdistan years into one volume, and he accomplished that in 1972 with this book. To date, it has not been published in other languages.

His first book was *The Fall of the Aerie*, translated into English by H. Baghdoian and published in 1935. It describes the massacre that demolished his family and the inhabitants of his town of Shabin Karahisar in 1915, leaving him one of a handful of survivors. It is a day-by-day eyewitness account of the Armenian genocide.

In 2006, Armen K. Göllü sent me his verbatim translation of *Four Years in the Mountains of Kurdistan*, which proved to be an invaluable reference for my own research and translation of the Armenian text. I am deeply grateful for his work, and I especially appreciate his knowledge of difficult idioms and his explanations of Kurdish and Turkish words and expressions that are beyond my scope.

THIS TRANSLATION

Years ago, Aram Haigaz and I translated some of his stories together for American publications. During those sessions I learned a great deal about his style and preferences. He disliked pretentious language, and deliberately avoided big words in favor of a simple, seemingly effortless narrative. He did not seek a literal translation but aimed more for the essence, and when it came to passages that were "too Armenian" or might not interest the American reader, he would say, "Cut it," even when I protested. That experience helped me immeasurably to take on the challenge of translating and editing *Four Years in the Mountains of Kurdistan.*

During the translation process, some Kurdish and Turkish proper names and words were transposed to the more readable English spelling. The names of some of the characters were changed to avoid repetition. Lengthy digressions were cut when they interfered with the pace, and further deletions were made to trim the original 512-page volume to a comfortable length. The book was organized into eight chapters to clarify the passage of time, which replaced the original seventy-four story titles. The chronology of events was retained throughout.

The first four paragraphs of this translation were adapted from Aram Haigaz's other writings, and from conversations with him, in order to set the scene in 1915—familiar to Armenians of the past— for today's readers. The narrative itself, being an autobiographical memoir and true account, remains as written. Whenever possible, I tried to retain the author's sentence structure, in hopes of providing some feeling for the beauty of the original language.

IRIS HAIGAZ CHEKENIAN

INTRODUCTION

BACKGROUND

Four Years in the Mountains of Kurdistan tells of four years in the life of Aram Haigaz, who was born in 1900 in the Armenian town of Shabin Karahisar, in the northeastern part of present day Turkey.

In 1915, when the story begins, the surge to exterminate the entire Armenian population of Ottoman Turkey was at its peak. The strategy of the Turkish government was to arrest and kill the men in the villages and then deport the women and children on the pretext of "temporary relocation," a well-documented prelude to annihilation.

The historically Christian Armenians were considered infidels by their Muslim rulers, and although some survived by converting to Islam, or in other ways, the number of Armenian deaths is generally put at 1.5 million.

Aram Haigaz was fifteen when Shabin Karahisar was attacked, and was with his people as they fought to defend themselves against the Turkish battalions for almost one month (June 2-30, 1915) until famine forced their surrender. His brothers, father, other relatives, and most of the townspeople were killed. He and his mother survived and were consigned to a caravan, as those moving herds of humanity were called. Their group consisted of about 350 captives, but there were thousands of such units throughout Turkey, many larger, with the deportees marched without food or shelter to the Syrian deserts to perish en route or be massacred. Such mass expulsions required manpower: the Kurdish tribes, along with some 30,000 convicts released from prisons throughout the country, and other outlaw gangs, were called upon to help the government carry out the killings. By the end of World War I, three out of four Armenians living in Turkey had been slaughtered.

THE STORY

This memoir begins on the fourth day of the author's deportation march. How he survived—his adoption by a Turkish master, conversion to Islam, years of servitude, rise from shepherd to trusted servant and secretary—is described in flowing and often lyrical passages, ending with his escape to freedom.

Surprisingly, *Four Years in the Mountains of Kurdistan* is not a litany of pain but the story of a young man's rich and adventurous life in an ancient society and culture.

Survival in the mountains meant being isolated from cities and other developed areas. It was a land of beys and tribal chieftains, a land without telephones, trains, or automobiles, a land of nomads and illiterate peasants, when Turkey was still the Ottoman Empire. The dramatis personae are not great military or state leaders but the people Aram Haigaz lived with; we get to know them in bad times and good, and in the small moments of everyday life as he grows from boyhood to a young man.

Although World War I was raging at the time, it remains in the background. Yet the tragedy of the genocide and the immeasurable losses that resulted are conveyed in unexpected and subtle ways.

The narrative ends one year after the armistice and the virtual end of the Ottoman Empire.

ABOUT KURDISTAN

When the events of this book took place, Kurdistan was not a country, nor is it today. The word "Kurdistan" refers to geographic areas inhabited mainly by Kurds—in Turkey, where about half of the world's Kurds live, as well as in Iraq, Iran, Syria, and other lands. It is said that the Kurds are the largest ethnic group in the world without a country of their own. They have struggled for an independent state for almost a century. However, after the First Gulf War in 1991 and further political changes in 2003, the Kurds have succeeded in establishing an autonomous regional government in northern Iraq, which today is the closest they have come to their dream for independence.

IRIS HAIGAZ CHEKENIAN
November 2014

Adapted from CIA map: openlearningworld.com

CHARACTERS

ALI BEY — the author's first Turkish master
Ali Bey's household was a microcosm of rural life in Ottoman Turkey.
At the top was the ruling class of Turkish Muslims; below them were
the Kurds, who were also Muslims but looked upon as inferior; at the
bottom were the Armenians, the Christian infidels.

Ali Bey's three wives
Fetiye - the Turkish senior Hanum
Laz girl - from Laz region of Turkey
Kamile - Armenian, 15, converted

Ali Bey's Armenian servants and ages

REAL NAME	CONVERTED TO:
Aram	Muselim, 15
Khoren	Haji, 14
Mendoohi	Minireh, 12
Anoush	Kamile, 15
Mariam	Melike, 14
Krikor	Shukri, 12

Ali Bey's Kurdish servants
Chako, Gazin, Guelo, Hakkuh, Musto, Rustem,
Sabriye (Sulo's wife), Sehel (Rustem's wife),
Shevku, Suleyman, Sulo

Others
Osman - Turkish head shepherd
Arev - Osman's Armenian wife, renamed Gulizar

NAZUM BEY, the author's second Turkish master
Nazum Bey is Ali Bey's youngest brother, appointed a *mudur*, the
governing official of a district and its surrounding villages.

Nazum's wives
Naileh Hanum - his senior wife, Turkish
Merouze - his second wife, Turkish

Nazum's daughters
Kadriye, 17
Farieh, 10

Nazum's uncle
Mehmet Bey of Roosku
Lutfiye, Mehmet Bey's wife

FOUR YEARS

in the

MOUNTAINS *of*

KURDISTAN

CHAPTER 1

Our Cross, 1915

We felt safe. Our town of Shabin Karahisar was sprawled along the slopes of a rock mountain that rose up to an enormous black fort, protecting us like an eagle's nest. Although troubles had come in previous years under the tyranny of Sultan Hamid and other rulers, we had grown up hearing our parents say, "This storm, too, shall pass."

But in 1915, we did not know that orders to annihilate the entire Armenian population of Turkey had been transmitted in code throughout the land. That spring, when I was barely fifteen, hundreds of our men were imprisoned and shot, and soon after, we heard of widespread massacres in many of the other provinces. Horsemen came to us almost steadily with news that the surrounding villages had been destroyed. Our leaders told us to mobilize. We would be next.

We turned to the mountain to defend ourselves and to the fort that stood at its peak, a mighty, centuries-old castle that still bore Roman markings. We set fire to the entire town, and our citizens baked as much bread as possible in ovens fired with wood torn from their homes. Everyone headed for the fort, taking with them only food and animals. Like my schoolmates, I ran up and down the rocky mountainside several times with supplies as our 5,000 townspeople fled the raging conflagration below and started climbing up.

From June 2 to 30, our poorly armed men, women, and children fought the relentless onslaught of the Turkish battalions until, overcome by famine, they crumbled and hoisted the white flag of surrender. Like the untold thousands of valiant Armenians throughout the land, they fell in blood, shattered before the mighty Ottoman Empire.

Now we, their remnants, were on the path to exile, walking with anguish and fear pressing upon us. I was with my mother in a group of about 350 women and children who survived after the handful of our remaining men, including my father, were executed at the surrender. We did not know where the police guards were taking us, or why, nor did we know where our forced march would lead.

On the fourth day of deportation, spent and hungry, we approached a large village that seemed to be thriving. Even from a distance, we could see the movement of people and hear the sounds of animals and carts in the streets. Smoke curled from the chimneys and the surrounding fields were thick with crops.

Perhaps we might find bread here, and, brightened with hope, we walked faster than expected, faster, and then started racing ahead, but the soldiers pushed us back into a semicircle and herded us into two empty stables near the outskirts.

"We've reached Aydzbuder," someone said. Our hearts shuddered with fear. It had been an Armenian village of about 300 families, but what had happened to them? They, too, must have been massacred or deported, and it was the neighboring Turks who had taken over their homes and fields.

"But why did it take so long to get here?" a woman asked. "Aydzbuder is only seven hours from town."

"We were zigzagging," someone replied. "It's another scheme to wipe us out."

"Our job is finished," announced one of the guards. "A new police troop will come to take charge of you. Pray God they will protect you as well as we have," he added solemnly, seeming to believe his words.

It was almost noon and no one had come. Perhaps the village officials had not been notified that we were here. The police watched us closely while we continued to stand, shuffling, waiting. Soon the reason for the delay became clear as we were ordered to regroup and pile into a single stable—which at first seemed impossible but was managed with shoving, crushing, threats, and ample profanity. Then the guards pulled us out and searched us again one by one, mocking the shy women and jabbing bayonets at expectant mothers, all the while cursing their meager haul.

When the thievery was done, they turned us over to the next troops and rode off.

We spent most of the afternoon in the stable, explaining to the new soldiers that we had already been robbed several times and nothing remained, but that did not quell their anger: apparently they thought we were flour sacks—anytime we were shaken, something was bound to spill out.

"When we get to the village, you can complain to the *mudur* [district administrator]," barked one of them. We promised to do that despite knowing that redress was not possible.

Eventually we were led to the village square. We piled into the stable of an inn where we spent the night battling mosquitoes, fleas, bedbugs, and parasites left by the previous rounds of deportees. The suffocating, wretched atmosphere was saturated with the stench of sweat, excrement, and poisonous filth.

Almost all of us were suffering from headaches and sunburn, but that did not mask, or allow us to forget, our overpowering hunger. Vigilance by the guards was relatively slack, so a few boys were able to slip out and search through some of the abandoned Armenian houses. Several even managed to buy some bread and yogurt—with what, I do not know. One returned with flour and salt, and another brought a pot of honey from a deserted kitchen. We found some water and, for better or worse, had something to eat.

We learned that deportees from other towns were being held in barns and on threshing floors elsewhere in the village, but we had no way to communicate with them. It was getting dark, so we tried to sleep, anxious to renew our energy for tomorrow's hardships, but it was impossible when we were choking with dust and heat, bones and muscles pounding in pain.

Just before midnight the police soldiers came in. They closed the doors, searched among us with torches in hand, and pulled out eight beautiful girls.

Begging, pleading, shouting, arguing was futile.

"She is a mother with two small babies!" cried a woman trying to save her daughter from being taken. The rapist's response was so foul that the other women buried their faces in their hands and hung their heads.

Early the next morning five of the young women were brought back, red-eyed, tormented, their shoulders stooped. I was surprised that their worried mothers did not seem happy or relieved to see them; it was as though the girls who returned after the night's absence were shamed, tarnished forever as women whom nobody would ever touch or love.

"I wish you had not been born, my unlucky child," moaned one of the mothers, stroking her daughter's head in her lap. "I wish my womb had dried up and I had not given birth to you." Everyone understood their grief, but nobody knew how to console them.

Later that morning a group of women went to the mudur to complain. Some even managed to renounce their Christian faith and convert to Islam, enabling them to remain in the village. A couple of seamstresses and several small boys were accepted as potential workers and also were permitted to stay. The rest of us started off.

This time no mountains or valleys were in sight. Ahead of us was a vast plain, sometimes green but always tinged with yellow, undulating, flat, and endless. No one had to say it; we knew that the plows of industrious Armenians had sown these fertile fields, extending all around and spread before us in geometric perfection like huge square quilts. Beyond, the sky and land came together into an expanse that vanished in the distance, gold and green blurring the horizon.

Beneath our feet the soil was hot and brittle, and the sun was a flaming helmet on our heads. Our eyes burned with tears from the scorching heat and blinding light. Here and there we encountered the remains of a village buried under mounds of debris and broken roofs. We walked farther and passed empty stables, huts, water mills, and rows of abandoned houses.

There was no movement, no sound, no songs, not a wisp of smoke rising from a single roof, not even the bellowing of an animal to rend the grief, the all-pervasive grief. We heard only the incessant chirping of crickets and the shuffle of our steps raising dust on the plains where Armenian villages had perished.

We walked, walked, and walked on; our bare feet were scorched and as we walked farther, the dark line of our caravan, dotted with colors, grew longer and thinner amid the fields as many faltered and fell.

Hunger, thirst, uncertainty, and exhaustion tormented us. We might endure the hunger by crushing some wheat kernels in our palms and swallowing them, but what to do with the thirst that swelled and cracked our tongues, made our hearts throb in our chests, and dried up our throats and veins? The awful, corrosive lack of water in our bodies prevented the trickle of sweat, the blessed, cooling sweat that tried to flow under the maddening heat of the sun but could not, so it stung and pricked our flesh dry, itching, stinking, anointing us with putrefaction.

Suddenly the police troops were alerted. They whipped their horses and came together to confer about something, then scurried forward and back, riding up and down the line.

We sensed danger. The vanguard stopped and waited as the others quickened their steps to reach them. A little beyond, at a hillock, some of the deportees were milling about in confusion. Perhaps it was fear of an attack that had agitated them. Our women clutched the children to their sides. My mother and I tried to move closer to each other for protection, but many of our fellow travelers were not agile; some were old, some were carrying babies, there were pregnant women, sick, tired, weak, so the caravan remained disordered despite efforts to tighten our positions.

Just then the soldiers cut through our midst, splitting us into two groups. They ordered the first group to clear out of the way and move ahead as fast as possible. But what about the others? They were to come along gradually, under the protection of the guards left to watch over them, and would join us later.

Terror enveloped us. Some families were now separated, with loved ones left behind in the other caravan—mothers, children, wives, sisters, and relatives. How careless of us not to protest strongly! What would happen to them? When would they be able to join us? Where were they being taken?

"My daughter is in the other group...my child..."

"I lost two of mine at the same time. Were they not my precious little ones?"

"My baby remained there," lamented another, her voice rising high. "I saved my left breast for later. I thought if I fed him tonight, he would sleep better....May I go blind, my sweet baby, if I had known, I wouldn't have saved it, I would have given you all the milk, my baby.... What am I to do now?"

Finally one of the guards came over and asked what all the noise and wailing was about. I do not know if he pitied her, but he asked her name and, swinging his horse around, sped back. But it was too late. The police officers who had stayed behind with the second caravan were riding toward us, rifles laid crosswise across their knees, jauntily spurring their horses, alone.

After indescribable hardship we arrived at Aghvanis. It was the county seat, a populous and fertile town where many Armenians once lived. Low, earthen, one-story houses were crowded together on a hillside, and above them was the church with a white school building tucked under its eaves. Everything we could see was deserted and forsaken, like the other Armenian villages we had passed.

Yet the main square in town was noisy and busy; it had been transformed into a military post and crossroads for soldiers en route to the battlefront.[1] Convoys were hauling food and ammunition, and a large barracks and warehouses were under construction. Horses, wagons, and peasants had been brought from elsewhere to do the work. Most compelling for us, though, was the smell of bread in the air, the unbelievable, unmistakable essence of fresh bread being baked.

The guards piled us into a barn at the edge of the village and allowed us to rest, something we sorely needed. We spread out on the hot ground and started thinking about possible ways to find the bread. Supervision was lax, almost nonexistent. A few boys and I came together and, following our noses to the savory aroma, we found the hearths.

Women were baking fantastic loaves of white bread on large metal pans, and oh! to our great surprise they wanted only a quarter penny a loaf. We loaded up with as much as we could carry and returned to the caravan.

A young Armenian boy, accompanied by a policeman, had come to visit our group. He was smartly dressed in clean new European clothes. He told us that the mudur of Aghvanis was his new father, a

---

1 The Ottoman Empire (Turkey) entered World War I in October 1914 on the side of the Central Powers against the Allies.

good man who did not harass the caravans passing through and punished only wrongdoers. He added that he was satisfied with his new life, his new religion and his new father.

My mother was fascinated with his story. She called me to her side and whispered, "If he has managed to stay, then you also have a chance to be saved. Anyway, with that foot of yours [I was limping badly], you won't be able to walk for long. I do not want to give you up to these villagers either—working in the fields will kill you. Let us try to find someone here to take you. You must renounce your religion…deceive, lie, imitate, feign, only try to stay alive until this storm passes. Just look around you. Not one other boy your age is left."

"But what about you, my brothers' wives, and the children?" I asked.

"Do not worry. Your presence is of no help to us, and when the Lord calls us," she crossed herself, "we shall die with our faith and courage." She started to cry. "My daughters-in-law have poison with them, they will die before giving up their honor. And I am old anyway, what can they do to me?"

"Mother!"

"Now go, my son, go and find some way to stay here."

I left for the village, not knowing what to look for, but stopped when I met some police officers along the way.

"Sirs," I said to the group, "I would like to become a Muslim and accept the true religion. Whom can I see about this?"

"Where are you from?" asked one of them.

"I am from Shabin Karahisar."

Instantly the man's expression turned brutal. He must have known about our town's resistance against the Turks and was enraged.

"*Gavur* [infidel]!" he shouted, putting a hand on his belt and cursing in Turkish: "Filthy infidel, enemy of the state, nonbeliever, traitor, devil, son of a—"

Luckily we were on an open street. With one leap I turned the corner, then another, and after circling a large area managed to return to my mother, panting and spent.

"I am at a loss, I don't know what to do," she said.

We decided to take the obvious solution—deny my birthplace.

I returned to the village to try again, but this time made sure to go by a different route.

Before long I met a boy pushing a cartload of sand and started a conversation with him, cautiously. He said he lived with his mother and sister about three hours away. His father and brother were at the front.

"Do you need somebody to help out at home?" I asked.

"Of course," he said excitedly, "we need a man very much. If you become a Muslim, we can live together like brothers. And don't worry, we have plenty to eat."

"Yes, I'll do it," I agreed. "When can we leave?"

"After sunset when my work is finished."

It would be madness to wait that long. He was sorry to lose me, and we parted. I returned to our group. Barely half an hour later another caravan joined us, this one a true caravan, with donkeys, horses, baskets, trunks, cases, and neatly dressed deportees who apparently had not experienced any hunger.

We jumped at the chance to mingle with them. We talked and asked questions, and we were in turn questioned.

They were from Giresun, on the shores of the Black Sea ("So even the sea was not enough to save them," my mother murmured). They had traveled so long that they'd lost count of how many days. Most of their men were killed along the way, and others had been rounded up and executed at the start. They had endured so much, and "now we go, we know not where." En route they had passed near Shabin Karahisar, which was totally in ashes except for the stone church, and they blamed its citizens for angering the Turks. "May the people of Karahisar go blind for causing this catastrophe. If only they had not gone up the mountain to fight…"

Oh, the naiveté of my people, who believed that self-defense was a God-given right and could not conceive of the diabolical scheme that awaited them.

Some found relatives or friends in the caravans and hugged each other, tears blending with joy. They spoke of those who were gone and shared the details of their final days, ending always with the dreaded question: "Where are they taking us?"

Soon the caravans were merged and we started out together, an arrangement that my mother thought might be favorable for me. If we were robbed, I could say I was from Karahisar, peeled like an onion and left bare; otherwise I would say I was from Giresun and had no ties at all to those "enemies of the state" and their kind.

To be perfectly honest, though, we envied the Giresun group, with their fancy clothes and good looks; our tattered wretchedness seemed even more glaring as we walked beside them, and we were ashamed.

We covered the distance between Aghvanis and Chobanle in an hour. At the edge of the village, we came to a stone bridge that was not yet finished but passable. Soldiers and construction workers were sprawled out in the sand pits on their rest break.

We were barely halfway across the bridge when several women threw themselves into the river. Others followed; swaddled infants fell in, children, screaming balls of flesh, skirts fluttering, curses, tears, prayers.

Below, on the riverbank, some Turkish women waded into the water and pulled the Armenians out of the current. Amid the screams and noisy commotion, the stone breakers grabbed their hammers and struck the caravan, attacking the people from Giresun. The policemen and the entire labor battalion joined them, and within moments the villagers, the guards, and the field workers followed as a mob. There was no opposition and nobody to stop them, for the opportunity for plunder was incomparable.

How many people and possessions were lost at this ill-fated bridge,

I do not know. But when we finally reached the open plain, the caravan was much smaller, and the absence of men in the Giresun group was especially noticeable.

Once again we were weaving along a path that led through the fields. On both sides were expanses of heavy-headed yellow wheat ready for harvesting. The sun was a fire over our heads and the air was still. The soil was like desert sand, burning our bare heels. The field was panting and the concert of crickets was loud, unending and enveloping.

The guards drove their horses into the fields, plowing furrows through the wheat. At times we heard the whistle of a whip in the air followed by sounds of pleading or a cry of pain. A horse charged through us, leaving screaming women and children in its tracks.

We started to walk fast, like a flock of sheep sensing an imminent storm. A lad from Giresun was walking on the left side of the road. He must have been close to twenty, because his upper lip was the color of lead in the sun; the chief guard rode up beside him.

I could not hear them, but it was clear that the young man was trying to show, with his arms spread apart, "I have nothing," as he faced the threatening guard. Now the guard raised the butt of his rifle over his shoulder. The boy let out an inhuman scream and rushed headlong into the crowd. No use. The guard pursued him as the women parted to make way for his horse. He reached him and could easily have crushed his head with the butt of his rifle, yet he continued to badger him for loot.

We waited, not breathing. The lad turned here and there, appealing to his acquaintances, relatives, anybody, in vain. He collected nothing. Everyone had already been robbed. Once again the guard lifted his rifle. The young man saw him and fled into the field, but he had not taken four steps when the gun went off. He fell on his back with a hole in his throat, gasping hard for air as a bright red stream flowed from his mouth.

Trying not to move, I searched all around me. I was the oldest

surviving male in the caravan. Not a single man from Giresun who
had joined us a few hours ago was left, and there were no men in our
own group to start with. [The Turkish strategy was to execute the men
in each village before launching an attack.]

I tried to make conversation with one of the soldiers accompanying
us on foot. I walked by his side and started talking.

"Sergeant *efendi*" [a title of respect; sir], I said, elevating his rank,
"where are you from?"

"I am from Kangal," he said.

"That is in the province of Sivas, I think."

"Yes."

"I learned that in school."

"You mean they taught you about our little village in your school?"

"Who says little? Isn't your hometown the government seat of that
region?"

"You infidels, you know everything," he said smugly. "Too bad you
turned out to be traitors."

"Sergeant *efendi*," I said, snatching the moment, "how can I become
a Muslim?"

"By reciting the Islamic Creed, our ritual prayer."

"That I know…but where do I get permission? To whom do I
appeal?" I kept talking. "Today I saw the light, do you know how? God
is one for all the civilized nations and people, right? He is the one
that created us and the universe. The only difference is that some people recognize Jesus as the prophet and send their prayers to heaven
through Him, some do it through Moses, and some—and they are the
fortunate ones—recognize Muhammad, the last and greatest of all the
prophets. For centuries my forefathers and I called upon Jesus Christ.
But see what has become of us! Today we are left homeless, hungry,
and thirsty. From now on I am going to call the Lord 'Muhammad.'
Even if I die, I want to die a Muslim."

"You are a very smart infidel."

"I owe it to the Prophet Muhammad," I replied piously. "He is the one who opened my eyes. And now I feel I am a true Muslim."

"I believe that to be so. Keep walking beside me and no one will touch a hair on your head."

Elated, I walked alongside him. He was tired from the weight of his rifle and heavy cartridge belt. He panted with each step and scratched his thick beard often. He was sweating.

On the left side of the road, beyond the fields, flowed a silvery river. Up farther, a waterwheel was half hidden among the willows and birches. We passed some women reaping wheat. They paused to watch us, sickles dangling from their hands. Several of them, faces covered up to their noses, approached to see where we were from.

We moved on. It seemed another village was nearby—already some barns and vegetable gardens with thistle borders were in sight, but when the flat-roofed houses came into view, we were forbidden to approach.

"Aren't we going to stop here?" I asked anxiously.

"No, we will go to Kanlutash."

"Is it very far?"

"No, half an hour away," he said, quickening his pace to join the guards up front.

We walked for a very long half hour and once again were prodded and threatened. We were exhausted, thirsty, and suffered sunstroke. A few women left their babies in the tall wheat grasses and walked off, while others fell with their offspring along the way. The gendarmes picked up several of those wailing spheres of flesh and thrust them at one or another in the group, but no one wanted to carry the infants.

Eventually we reached the outskirts of Kanlutash, a large village where we were allowed to rest. We sank to the ground and tried to soothe our blistering feet. Later we went into town to search for water and food.

By now the size of our caravan was greatly reduced. Very few of the old folks and children were left, and at every town we had passed, several of our women and girls had been seized as mementos.

"I threw my little one off the Chobanle bridge," said one woman.

"I was able to carry mine until Aghvanis," said another. "He was heavy...if it were not for this..." she flicked her eyes to her swollen belly. "Toward evening, I went to the river with my baby and since the village was nearby, I thought perhaps someone would see him and take him. I cupped my palms together and gave him some water, kissed him and fled."

"May I go blind!" cried another woman. "Why didn't I think of that! I left mine in the river. Had I left him on the bank like you, perhaps someone might have seen him and taken him home. May I go blind! How could I have been so stupid!"

She looked about beseechingly, expecting somebody to respond, to say something, curse her or console her with a word to relieve her misery. But no one spoke; each had her own sorrows and troubled conscience. Who could do anything upon hearing this woman's all-too-common plight? All the while, the mother wandered from one to another in the group, lamenting that she wasn't able to feed her hungry baby. "You tell me...mothers, sisters, what could I have done? You tell me...."

LA ILAHA ILLALLAH

We were sprawled out on a patch of stubble in Kanlutash to catch our breaths. We stretched our tortured legs and paused to look over our family. En route we had lost two cousins; now there were nine of us—my mother, daughters-in-law and their children.

Despite the methodical searches, we had managed to hide one five-penny coin and a silver ring. We also had a medium-sized bottle—our most valuable possession—for dispensing water, drop by drop, to whomever among us was weak and unsteady.

After a brief rest my mother asked if I had enough strength to fetch some water. I started out with the bottle and heard her loving voice calling after me: "Be careful, don't go too far, do not drink too much water at once, wash yourself and wash your feet. Don't be late…"

Fortunately the fountain was close by and water was abundant. I drank so insatiably that when I straightened up, my flooded stomach gurgled.

A dozen or so Turkish women were gathered around the fountain, surveying the scene.

"He is a good-looking brat," said one of them, nodding toward me. "He must be a city boy."

I looked at her with inquiring eyes and smiled. She was a wrinkled, fuzzy old woman, but this was no time to be critical.

"Aunt!" I said, moving toward her, "if I become a Muslim, would you adopt me?"

She took my hand into her withered, earth-colored palm and, somewhat bewildered, glanced around at the others questioningly, seeking advice.

"Oh, he is still a child," said a red-haired woman in a Laz dialect. "His upper lip is still bare." The old woman and I breathed in relief, and I was ready to embrace that lady from Laz.

"Nimet, said the old woman, "let us have him recite our Creed." Nimet looked at me sympathetically, took my hand, kneeled at my side and, with a smile, told me to repeat:

"*La Ilaha Illallah.*" [There is no god but Allah.]

"La Ilaha Ill Allah."

"*Muhammadur Rasulullah*" [Muhammad is the Prophet of Allah.]

"Muhammad ur…" [Muhammad is…]

"*Rasulullah.*"

"Rasulul-lah."

"*Al hamdulillah.*" [Praise be to Allah.]

"Al hamdulillah."

"*Muslumanum.*" [I am a follower of Islam.]

"Muslumanum."

"Now that you are one with Islam," said the old woman, "come with me."

"I have to see my mother," I replied firmly. "I have to say goodbye and receive her blessing."

"Good," she agreed. "I will go with you."

One of the local soldiers left his comrades and came toward us; I could see a long whip stuck into the top of one of his heavy boots as he approached.

The old woman greeted him. "Brother-in-law, this boy has become a *Müslüman*; I am going to keep him."

He scrutinized me with a steady, unwavering gaze as he measured my height. His eyes moved down to my bare, bleeding feet. He shook his head with a look of resignation and said, "Take him to the gate of the mosque, you will see others waiting there as well. You must get permission from Nedim Bey."[2]

At the entrance to the mosque, Turks from different areas were milling around. Among them were several Armenian boys waiting for Nedim Bey, but nobody knew where he was. The old lady was impatient and urged me to see my mother.

"Come," she insisted, "I will take you to her."

Breathlessly I explained everything. My mother's eyes were brimming with tears.

"I won't go."

"No, my son," she said, upset. "I am not crying…these are tears of joy. Go, you will be saved. Go!"

I promised to return and followed the old woman.

---

2 Bey, pronounced *bay*, title of respect after a personal name, is the equivalent of "mister" in English. In the Ottoman Empire the title was given to tribal rulers and important officials, and meant "great" or "lord."

In a cool, entirely carpeted room, the first military officer we saw was seated on a large pillow with his legs folded under him, dining on honey and butter. A white-bearded old man, about sixty to sixty-five, sat across from him at the table. He had small, kind eyes, and did not eat but talked continuously. Boys of various ages came and went, looking anxious and sad as they moved back and forth. A beautiful bride, wearing a transparent veil and headdress studded with gold pieces, was serving the table.

"Ali Bey," said the woman who brought me, directing her words to the officer, "permit me to take this boy."

He did not respond, but the old man spoke to me, "Sit, sit my son. Are you hungry?"

I nodded.

"Bring some food," he ordered.

The bride disappeared.

When I bent to sit down, my eyes darkened, blurry shapes all around moved back and forth, ripples of colors and vibrating circles clouded my head, and all the while the sound of a distant waterfall was rushing toward me. But it did not last long. Gradually I recovered my senses, although my forehead was sweating profusely and fatigue engulfed me.

"Eat," came a voice.

Before me, on a large plate, were fresh bread, bulgur pilaf, and yogurt.

"May I take this bread to my mother?" I asked.

"Take it, my son, take it," said the old Turk. He turned to stare out the window. It seemed to me that his voice was sad. A while later he looked back into the room, troubled, and gestured toward the field where our caravan was spread out, and said, very slowly: "Ali Bey, we must see that their curse does not stay with us."

Nothing was said for a long time.

I finished eating and waited for the next move.

"Where are you from?" Ali Bey spoke for the first time.

"From Tamzara."

"What are you doing in the caravan from Karahisar?" he demanded. "Tamzara was cleansed [deported] twenty-five days ago."

"I was in the city to learn a trade when the fighting broke out," I lied. "I couldn't return home."

"Were you in the fortress?"

"Yes."

"How many Turks did you kill?"

"I was so frightened I didn't poke my head out of the hole."

This last answer seemed to end the matter.

"What trade were you learning in the city?" the old man asked.

"Shoemaking."

"Can you make a sandal?"

"Yes."

"Elder sister," said the officer, turning to the old woman, "this city boy is of no use to you. You will send him to the fields and mountains, but he cannot manage harvesting or chopping wood in the forest, and forget plowing or threshing…he has never done such things."

"But what are you going to do with him?"

"What else? I will keep him for myself and make him my personal servant, or maybe I will send him to school."

Then, addressing me, he asked about my family in the caravan.

"My mother, relatives and their children."

"How old is your mother?"

"In her forties."

"Is she willing to become a follower of Islam?"

"Never."

"Ali Bey," interrupted the old man, "leave this boy to me. He can grow up with our children."

"No. I need him."

"Before leaving I want to see my mother," I said in a bold voice.

"Go, but do not be late, because we have to see Nedim Bey."

"Look, I am not crying now," said my mother, who was kneeling before me. Her lips brushed rows of kisses on my forehead and her caring hands surrounded my ruffled head with endless loving and meaningful touches. Her palms stroked my hair, wiped tears from my eyes, they caressed my forehead and paused on my cheeks as though to fix the image of my face, so that even if her memory were to lapse, her hands would retain the sweetness and warmth of their impression.

"See, I do not cry any more," said her wet voice, "my little, my unlucky son, see, I don't weep any more...do not cry, my baby, it is enough. I bless you with all my soul, with all my heart. Be brave and endure it when they call you the son of an infidel. Now I say, look after your health. Try by any means, and work with all your strength to stay alive. Someday this storm too shall pass. And when that day comes, remember us, your religion, your nationality, your faith....Do not worry about us, we will manage. Do not cry, I am crying because I can't help it. How can a mother not cry over her son? You are the fifth and my youngest one, how can I stop crying?"

The tears pouring from her eyes flooded her sun-beaten, tired, sweet face.

"I am not going, Mother. I will not go and leave you alone," I wailed, wrapping myself around her neck.

Instantly she was alarmed. Her tears stopped, she wiped her face, and gripping my shoulders, she looked directly into my eyes and said: "No, my son, staying means certain death: you have to go. You are old enough to remember everything; you have to go and live. Kiss us all and go. I bless you, and may the milk I gave you be blessed....Come, let me kiss you once more, just once more, and again for the last time, my sweet boy, my unlucky baby, my baby being left to strangers, my...my...do not cry. See, I am not crying either....Let me kiss you once more, once more, don't cry...Go...

CHAPTER 2

My First Master

The officer named Ali Bey took me to his superior, Nedim Bey, and requested permission for me to leave the caravan.

Nedim Bey was a short man in a lieutenant's uniform. He had completed his assignment to deliver the remains of the caravan and was anxious to leave. He looked at me silently and turned to Ali Bey: "He is a bit tall..." hesitating, "but..."

"Oh, he is still a child. Please, I will make a good Muslim out of him."

"All right, take him." Nedim Bey turned on his heel and hastened to his horse.

Ali Bey touched his fingers to his forehead in gratitude and said: "Come, we are going home. Are you tired?"

Not just tired, I was shattered, yet fearing that any complaint or hint of weakness might cast a negative impression, I answered, "No."

He proceeded slowly on horseback and I walked behind him until we met the members of his raiding party at the edge of the village. They were resting on the grass alongside a spring while their horses grazed in the field.

Ali Bey dismounted and handed me the reins. He approached the group and checked that all nine were present. One of them spread a large, colorful scarf on the ground and each man emptied the day's loot over it. The spoils were measured and shared, including one part for Nedim Bey, although he had not contributed to the items on the scarf. Farewells were said and the men left on their horses, riding past the field, their backs fading into the setting sun.

Before we started out again, Ali Bey decided to find a name for me. He began, pronouncing aloud: "Hasan, Kadir, Ahmed..." Not satisfied, he tried again. "Shevku, Osman, Tevfik, Muselim...Muselim..." He liked the last one and repeated it. He turned to me.

"My son, now that you have accepted Islam, you must break the ties with your past. You must forget all of that and bear an Islamic name. Your name is Muselim, Abdullah *oghlu* Muselim [Abdullah's son Muselim."]

I knew that I would never have trouble remembering that name because I had many things to forget, but only one thing to remember.

My name, my new name.

The key to my salvation.

We proceeded in silence.

"Do you want to ride on his rump?" he asked unexpectedly.

"I can still walk."

We passed over the same mournful roads that I had crossed in the morning. I saw the corpse of the boy from Giresun, half naked and thrown aside. Other corpses were all around, dark and starting to decompose. Was it the heat of the day that hastened their inevitable misery? I did not know.

It was dark when we got back to Chobanle. We stopped at a barn.

The houses of the village peered from the darkness with half-closed eyes. Strange sounds and an unusual humming noise were all around. Fearing that the village might be a meeting place for plunderers and soldiers, I moved closer to the horse, trembling.

The night filled me with terror. I thought of my mother and the others, and my eyes filled with tears. I regretted leaving them. I was alone.

"Rustem!" Ali Bey shouted from the barn.

A shadow appeared, silent and swift as a cat in the dark.

"*Efendim!*" [My master, sir!]

"Rustem, I brought another boy today, he is right here, his name is Muselim. Take him home, I will be a little late."

To me, he said: "Go, my boy, go home with Rustem."

Rustem was a black man. His white teeth were lustrous and shiny even in the darkness. His eyes seemed as big as apples, constantly darting about. He was tall, agile and young.

"Come, *peej* [bastard]," he said.

I did not know where we were headed or how far, but we walked along a steep, winding, perilously narrow trail on the mountainside. The sky was so clear I could see the movement of Rustem's hands under his coat as he trudged in front of me, and my heart pounded with fear.

Every time we passed a gorge, black, half concealed in the darkness, I imagined corpses down there, piled one upon the other, oozing bloody red wounds, their eyes open. I dragged myself after Rustem, aching, exhausted, fearing that at any moment his right hand would burst from his jacket to fire at me.

Then his dreaded voice: "Come, *peej!*"

The moon rose behind a hill and spread a candle glow over the fields, the trees, and the river that we had followed since starting out. Far off, it seemed that people were calling to each other, their voices prolonged and overlapping in echoes. Suddenly the loud creaking of a wagon splintered the air.

"Asum is carrying hay to the barn," explained the black man. "Do you hear that sound? The shaft of his wagon is made from cherry wood, it's the only one in the village."

We heard dogs barking, animals bellowing, and the dull rattle of a water mill. At the base of a hill were some houses, their windows dimly visible. "This is my mother-in-law's village," Rustem boasted. Hearing that, I wondered how on earth any woman agreed to marry this man. "Our house is a half hour away."

We bypassed the village and proceeded on the path along the river-bank. Rustem, lighting a cigarette, asked if I smoked.

"No," I replied, not sure whether he was trying to be friendly or if he was testing me. So far as I knew, smoking was for grown-ups, and it was better for me to be taken for a youngster.

We walked around a grove of poplars and climbed a hill that revealed the peaked, irregular stones of a cemetery. The village must be close.

The land was plowed, and we passed a vegetable garden that smelled of garlic. I tried not to stare at the rows of gray cabbages, side by side, looking like bald heads in the darkness.

Just ahead, almost hidden in the woods, was a two-story house and close by, eight to ten small huts. As we moved forward I felt uneasy, but I was so tired I couldn't think anymore. A cool breeze came from the woods, and I imagined how pleasant it would be to lie down and sleep in that freshness…what beautiful reverie…

"Aha! The palace," exclaimed Rustem. "We're here."

The dogs at the house snarled at me viciously.

"Chalum, Bogar, shoosh!"

"Stay at my side," he warned. "If they get you, they'll tear you apart!"

The bulky animals growled to themselves, sniffed the air, examined me with droopy eyes, and scornfully obeyed Rustem.

We walked halfway around the house and came to a covered porch that led into a wide hallway. The smell of fire and cooking followed us as we stepped through a door into a room lit with candles. Two women were seated cross-legged on a large cushion, eating. The aroma told me they were having green beans cooked with meat! They turned their heads, trying to identify us in the shadowy light.

"I brought you another boy," Rustem announced.

"What boy! He is a big fellow, a guy!" said one of the women, raising her scarf above her chin.

I knew that I would be executed before dawn. If not for the dogs outside, I might try to flee and disappear into the woods. I could not foresee what might happen later, but I had to escape now, since the woman thought I was a guy and any Armenian male old enough to be *that* had no right to live.

But alas, the dogs were there. I wiped my cold, wet forehead with my hand and, exhausted, leaned against a wall and slid down to the floor, shrinking my height as much as possible.

I prayed that Ali Bey would come soon because if left here, I was lost. Rustem called me a *peej* and this woman thought I was a grown-up.

"Where are you from?" asked the other woman, speaking for the first time.

"From Tamzara," I lied, remembering what I had told Ali Bey.

"Tamzara near Karahisar?"

"Yes, *Hanum* [lady, a title of respect]."

The hanum scrutinized me carefully, eyes squinting, not covering her face like the other woman, nor did she close the flap of her shirt, which was open to her bosom.

"Minireh," she called eagerly, "Minireh, Kamile, girls, come here!"

A beautiful girl, barely twelve years old, entered, smiling.

"Hanum..."

"Quick, my girl, call Kamile!"

Soon Minireh returned with an older, red-cheeked girl, serious and inquiring.

"Kamile, the bey sent one of your compatriots today, see if you recognize him."

I looked at Kamile, pleading, terrified, anxious. If she only...

She came over to examine me in the flickering, dim light. Trying to remember, she moved closer, searching.

"No," she said, "I don't know him." Feeling certain, she added, "This boy is not my compatriot."

My throat tightened. I tried to swallow but my mouth was dry. At any moment, Rustem would glare into my eyes and bellow, "Liar! Traitor! You were up at the fort fighting with the rebels, the enemies of the state! Come outside with me and..."

As always, Turkish was spoken until Kamile asked, "Are you Armenian?" in our mother tongue.

"Yes," I replied hastily, my words racing: "Please back me up, I can explain later. I am from Tamzara, but I went to school in town, that's why you don't know me." And I gave her the name of a relative who lived there as my own.

Kamile woke up.

"Oh," she said, turning to them, "I remember now, how could I forget? I know his family very well, and their house, too...ever since he was a child. He has changed so much! I remember him playing in the streets. They used to live in our neighborhood, and later they sent him to school in the city. How much he has changed!"

I was saved. My mind raced: "Kamile, I want to embrace and kiss you. I am grateful to you forever. I will feel most fortunate to live under the same roof with you and Minireh."

Minireh spoke up: "If we had known from the start, we would not have doubted you. Anyway, that is past. Are you hungry? Don't be afraid, these are good people. My brother is here too."

The neighing of a horse and the sound of approaching hooves came from the open window.

"The bey is here." They all rose.

I followed them into the hall to meet him.

Tired from the long ride, Ali Bey strode into the house. He threw his leather hat and gun on a cushion and turned to one of the women:

"I will not go again, woman," he grumbled. "This was the last time!"

WHAT WAS YOUR ARMENIAN NAME?

It was dark when Haji came in. He was a good-looking boy from a wealthy family, and full of life. I guessed he was about fourteen. He burst in, brandishing a heavy stick and shouting, "I'm hungry!" His sister excitedly rushed into the kitchen, calling out that her brother was back from grazing the animals and he was hungry! Then she introduced me to him.

"My name is Haji," he said, smiling. "I am from Aydzbuder." He took my hand firmly and shook it for a long time.

We ate together. Haji and his sister, Minireh, had been brought here two weeks ago and already considered themselves members of the household; they knew every nook and corner and felt at ease.

We went out and Haji explained that we were to sleep in the tent, which we would share that night with two Kurds, Musto—short for Mustafa—and possibly Shevku, unless he'd gone to his father's village.

"He comes from across the way," he added, "a village of about thirty homes. He is okay. But Musto...Musto is a terrific man, wait until you see for yourself."

Out of nowhere he produced a quilt, saying, "Put half of it under you and cover yourself with the other half. Soon you will get used to sleeping without a pillow, it's healthier anyway. Tomorrow my sister will sew up the holes so the wool won't spill out. It belonged to Armenians. The Turks brought it here and tore it apart, looking for money. Some Turk found fifty gold pieces sewn into a quilt so now they think there's money in every quilt, and when they rob a caravan the first thing they do is take the quilts. Fools."

He paused and asked: "What was your Armenian name?"

"Aram."

"Mine was Khoren. I even miss my Armenian name. Fortunately my sister still calls me Khoren when we are together, and when we are alone with nobody to hear us, we speak Armenian."

I do not know how long we talked that night, but it was enough to tell each other everything that mattered about ourselves. With nothing more to do, we went to bed.

"My mother told me that for…"

"Our Father who art in Heaven…"

"…boys like us, God was merciful."

"Hallowed be thy name…"

"Good night, Khoren."

"Good night, Aram."

He turned on his side and was soon asleep.

Under the large black tent of goat hair, I stayed awake for a long time. A pleasant breeze came from the opening at the front end, and, lying on my back, I saw dim stars blinking in the summer sky and long trails of falling stars disappearing into an ocean of deep violet.

Watching them, I remembered my mother saying, "Every time a star falls, somebody dies." Who died now? I wondered, and cried silently a little. If a star fell for every Armenian who died, I thought, it would be raining stars now.

Fireflies drifted into the tent and drew shadows on the walls. The wind rustled the trees and rippled the wheat fields. My eyelids grew heavy. A hound bayed at the moon, on and on.

⟿ ✦⊛✦ ⟾

I bolted awake in the early morning—something was trying to chew my ear! It was a young kid. There were goats all over the tent, on my quilt, above my head, left and right, black, mischievous and agile. They wiggled their little tails, they sniffed, defecated, jumped, and chewed on everything in sight.

Khoren appeared, sack on shoulder, chatted a little, rounded up the goats and left, following them uphill through the woods until he disappeared from view.

I left the tent and washed myself at the lush, flowing fountain.

Fields, sunshine, and woods were all around. The village was called Aghullar and it belonged entirely to Ali Bey; its ten houses were inhabited by tribal Kurds and their families. The senior shepherd, who was Turkish, also lived here.

Without exception, everyone in the village worked for the bey—they sowed, reaped, cleaned the stables, grazed the animals, made butter and cheese, baked bread, watered the crops, and cut down the woods to clear the land for new fields.

The bey had three wives. Fetiye Hanum, the senior, was Turkish, and had no children. The middle one, called the 'Laz girl,' from her Turkish homeland, was ugly and crude, also childless. The third wife, Kamile, was the Armenian girl who had identified me. Her real name was Anoush. She was a new bride of fifteen days, brought here to bear children for this barren family and thereby remedy Ali Bey's humiliation. They all lived together.

Also in the household were black Rustem, his wife, and their one-year-old son. Next came the converted Armenians: Khoren and me; his sister, Mendoohi; and a family of four that arrived the day after me—mother; daughter Mariam, fourteen years old; son Krikor, twelve; and the little girl, Vartuhi, about four. Although the family had given Ali Bey a considerable sum of money to save their lives, the grandmother was considered useless and had been taken off and killed by Rustem.

Fetiye Hanum, the head of our household, was beautiful and somewhat plump, with smooth white skin. She did not consider us adults and did not cover up in our presence; we were free to come and go throughout the house, provided we were working.

Every morning she leaned from an open window on the second floor and called out the day's orders: "Haji, take the animals grazing with Osman. Guelo, Musto, go to the fields for reaping. Suleyman, you gather the clover. Sabriye, light the stove. Chako, make up the barn. Shukri, feed the turkeys..." The litany continued without pause until everyone, depending on his or her strength and experience, was assigned a job.

I was excused the first day because, not knowing the routine, I did not appear below the window with the other workers and servants. But Musto explained the rules, and so, early the next morning, I waited with the others to receive my instructions.

I learned to bring water from the well, fetch dry branches for the stove, free the hens, feed them, collect eggs, take food to the field workers, chase goats out of the kitchen, water the oxen, churn the milk to make butter, and prepare the sacks for straining cheese. In time, after falling off the thresher several times and disengaging the oxen, I finally learned how far to lean, to stay balanced while circling, and to order them to pull—"Ho!"—without falling.

None of these duties prevented me from eating because I was always eating, day or night. I ate anything I could find, and whenever I had the chance. My mouth and throat were scratched and swollen from barley chaff but I did not mind. My pockets were always stuffed with pieces of dark bread, dry, hard as bone, collected from the fields, the kitchen, from drawers, from everywhere. With the greatest pleasure and appetite I would crush the crusts between my teeth because I was always hungry. I say 'always' because, in truth, I *was* always hungry; it was only the degree of hunger that changed: starving, very hungry, less hungry.

Guelo, one of the Kurdish servants, ridiculed me, claiming that I was like a hen with no satiation. He even displayed his wit to Ali Bey, saying, "He eats like a bull but works less than a hen," relishing his words. "What an appetite *Allahum*, my God!"

"You wait," said Musto, looking on. "Give him a couple of days to fill his marrow, then we'll see who is the glutton. After all, what does he eat? Just barley bread."

Guelo shook his head skeptically and said something in Kurdish to Musto. I did not know their language yet because all of us spoke Turkish,[3] but I assumed his words were unfavorable. Feeling no offense, I took a piece of bread from my pocket and started chewing.

We had three meals a day, all similar: a very large bowl of soup and three small loaves of bread for each of us.

The first day I joined the workers at mealtime, Guelo protested. He refused to sit at the table with a "dirty infidel." News was carried to Fetiye Hanum. She came in, stopped, flicked her eyes over each person at the table, then glared at Guelo, who was standing, and said: "Sit down and stuff yourself. If *he* sits at the table without complaining, you sit too, and if you don't want that, you can collect your belongings and go."

Guelo sank down like a beaten cat, glanced menacingly at me, took his share of bread, and moved away.

My pockets bulged with bread and my stomach was swollen with soup when I headed to the threshing floor, where I had been assigned to operate the thresher. It was not easy to circle around all day under the hot sun, but mine was not to choose. When the time came to rest the oxen, I ran to the spring and washed my face, arms and mouth. I would have liked to take a dip in the refreshing, cold river but I was still afraid. Khoren had said that the river was walking distance from our house, "just long enough to smoke a cigarette."

I smiled at his way of measuring time and distance.

It seemed I was almost not hungry.

One day I asked Khoren how old he was and whether he had any brothers or sisters besides Minireh, whose real name was Mendoohi.

"I will be fourteen soon. I had no other brothers or sisters, it was

3 Under Ottoman rule, minorities living in Turkey (Armenians, Greeks, Kurds) had to speak Turkish. Until recent years, speaking Kurdish in public was a crime.

just the two of us," he replied.

"I am one year older than you. Your sister, how old is she?"

"Twelve."

"Do you like shepherding?" I asked.

"Very much. Osman, the senior shepherd, is not a bad guy, and even though he's a Turk, he treats us all well. I am his helper. I like taking the animals out with him because it keeps me away from the gendarmes and the gangs that pass through here, always up to no good.... Why be in plain sight? There is an evil one among them, Mad Shero, bloodthirsty, worse than a wolf....Then there are our dogs. I've gotten quite close to them. Would you believe it if I tell you that when I am up on the mountain, I talk to the dogs in Armenian? That way I won't forget my language and I can pour my heart out about the merciless Turks and what they've done. I tell them about my mother and father, and the others in my family.

"Sometimes Chako is sent in my place to help Osman. There is no set routine. Now, with you here, you might also be ordered to go with the herd. Just be sure to take good care of the dogs; that is very important. Having a good dog is an honorable thing for the Kurds, like having good weapons or a horse.

"The other day we heard that Mehmet Bey's dog in Roosku had nine pups, all in one litter. We were told that the mother and father of the litter were both shepherd dogs. Osman, his father, and I went to visit them."

"Visit the dogs?"

"Certainly. We conveyed our bey's greetings and took some gifts to his wife. Mehmet is our bey's uncle. When the puppies are a little bigger, he will let us choose one for us."

"How do you choose between puppies that are so small?"

"To see if one is a fighter, a guard dog."

"How would you know?"

"You and I would not know, but Osman's father is a fantastic shepherd…he will know."

My eyelids grew heavy. I was tired and thought that Khoren was trying to entertain me to take my mind off sad memories. His effort was useless. I said, "Good night," and he was silent. It was some time before I could sleep; I kept trying to guess where my mother and the others were and what they were doing. Had they been allowed to rest peacefully for the night? Or had the Turks again, like savage wolves, fallen upon the young girls and women?

"Dear God be with them," I pleaded from the depths of my soul, and I was aware of the sound of thousands of crickets everywhere around us. Back home, the crickets sang like this. In the fall, when dew settled on the rows of yellow squash in the fields, a couple of them would hide in a warm corner of our house and chirp until winter came, sweetening my childhood sleep.

Remembering those days, I wept silently so as not to wake Khoren. It was the first time in my life that I was separated from my mother. I would never be in the same room with her again, I would never sleep under the same roof with her again.

Through the triangular opening of the tent, I gazed at the dark blue sky, the stars shimmering like the reflections in deep well water. I heard the distant barking of a hound and wept and prayed again.

⌐•⊛•¬

The black kid on my quilt escaped when I reached out to hug him in the morning. Soon Khoren was up, and so were a couple of farmers who had come into the tent after we were asleep. With Khoren leading the way, we went to the spring, splashed icy water on our faces, and cleaned up. I was wiping my face with the edge of my shirt when a Kurdish boy about our age came over. He looked at me and said to Khoren: "Osman is sick. You and I are taking the animals to graze. Who is this one, is he an infidel?"

"Yes, he is Armenian, but not infidel anymore, he has converted to

Islam, and he lives in our house now."

"Let's ask the hanum if he can come with us, we can train him."

Fetiye Hanum was easy to find, with her sleepy head conspicuous at the window. We waited below until she gave her permission, saying to me: "Go with Haji [Khoren] and Chako and do what they say. They are experienced."

We fed the dogs and started out.

"Are we going far? Is it dangerous?" I asked Haji.

"Don't be afraid. Once we say that we are Ali Bey's shepherds, nobody will touch us. Besides, there are no Turks where we are going, not one soul, not even a fly. We will reach Kel Dag before noon."

"If it's very far, I don't have moccasins. The Turks took my shoes, and all I have on my feet is cloth. Every thorn pokes through."

"Why didn't you say so before we started? We could have managed something at home. It's too late now, we can't do anything today. When we get back tonight, I'll talk to Musto. I am sure he will help." Then, a moment later: "Don't worry. I will see that you get a pair of moccasins."

"Can we buy them?"

"No more. Since the Armenian deportations, it's impossible to find anything like that. Otherwise we could ask the bey to buy a pair for you."

Just as Khoren had promised, we spent the entire day roaming the mountains and swimming in the river. We gathered blackberries and wild strawberries; we sat by the fire and had milk and toasted bread, and we were content.

It was then I felt a deep guilt, thinking of the caravan of deportees and my family. Fighting tears, I ran behind a bush and spat out the swollen lump of bread in my mouth. A few yards away, Chako was lying naked on the sand, singing a carefree folk tune.

Eight days later, when the barns were readied for the grain and the sacks of barley were brought in from the fields, I was handed a whip and sent to the threshing floor where, under the burning sun, in clouds of dust and perspiration, I led the oxen circling round and round all day.

Guelo, my teacher and supervisor for this, told me that the two yellow oxen turning the thresher were confiscated from Armenians. "When we looted the bull house, we took three asses, these two oxen, and a young water buffalo for our share," he explained indifferently, as if saying, "I plucked a berry and ate it." Then, with a mocking smile, "When you are alone, you can talk to them in Armenian."

I said nothing. But I decided never to be harsh with these animals, to feed them well, not to tire them, and never to muzzle their mouths during threshing.

That evening, after we'd released the oxen and taken them to the water hole, we returned to a household that was agitated. Khoren's sister was worried because her brother was delayed.

"I know something bad has happened," she cried. "He is never this late; he must have met up with bad people, thieves…"

The bey came in and peered out to the woods.

"Do not be afraid, Minireh, nobody would dare raise a hand to one of my shepherds."

She was not calmed; she pleaded for everyone to go out and look for her brother.

"If my brother's life does not matter to you, why don't you go and search for your animals—the flock, the goats, the cows?"

"Don't worry," said Musto, placing his big, affectionate hand on her head. "We are hungry and need to eat. If he has not shown up by then, we'll take our Martini rifles and go after him."

Fortunately, it was not long before we heard the bellowing sounds of animals coming from the woods and Khoren's cheerful voice. His sister and I ran to meet him.

"Where were you, why are you so late?"

"We had the place all upset. If you hadn't come now, everybody would be out looking for you."

"Hold on, don't jump at me! How late am I, anyway?" Then, lowering his voice: "I brought moccasins."

We looked at his shoulder pack. It was empty.

"Where are they?"

"On the calf's back."

"You mean to say…?"

"Yes, I brought a whole calf. I took the animals to the grazing grounds at Kayu village and met some Turkish shepherds. There was an Armenian boy in their group and we spent the day together. Toward evening as we were separating, it was shadowy—there was this well-fed calf in their herd that I had an eye on all day—I managed to get him mixed in with our herd and brought him here. See, there he is," he said, pointing at him.

Once our animals were led into the stable, it was easy to spot the young, healthy calf standing near the edge, confused, his eyes darting about in unfamiliar surroundings.

"Where are the Kurds?" asked Khoren.

"Inside, eating."

"May they eat poison! Go and call them."

I ran as fast as I could toward the dining hall, calling their names.

"Guelo, Musto, Hakkuh, Shevku, come!"

"What is it? What happened?"

"Haji [Khoren] brought a calf, we are going to skin him!" I shouted joyfully.

They all hurried out.

"Allah be praised, Haji is a remarkable boy," said Sulo, stroking his mustache. "We are going to feast on meat!"

We circled the bewildered calf. In the light of the moon, his skin was smooth and shiny and his eyes were flashing sparks. As if ready to attack, his head was raised and he was breathing hard, snorting.

"What are you waiting for?" asked Khoren, annoyed. "The people from Kayu will be looking for him! They could be here any minute and take him, do you want that?"

Sulo, who was a huge calf himself, the greediest and most emp-ty-headed Kurd I have ever met, a strong and tireless worker, approached the calf and started talking to it in Kurdish, coaxing with sweet words, enticing tones, and slowly, slowly, moving closer and closer. Then he grabbed one ear in his thick hand. The other Kurds fell upon him and, urging and threatening, managed to force the animal into the adjacent baking house. There, they shouted for Sulo, cheering him on to display his skills. Sulo, who had waited for this moment, threw off his jacket, tossed it aside, and grappled the animal's head in his iron grip. With one hand he grabbed a horn and with the other jammed the animal's mouth and blocked its nostrils with his thumb and forefinger. When the calf strained to free itself, Sulo locked his heavy arms around him and tried to topple the animal by twisting its head. So began the battle between man and beast. All the calf's efforts to escape were useless. Both were exerting their utmost strength. The animal, forelegs planted wide, was trying to keep its balance. He wheezed, snorted, gasped. His black, shiny hide was completely wet. Sulo was sweating and cursing, the veins in his neck and forehead swollen, almost ready to burst. He was panting hard. The other Kurds cheered and shouted encouragement.

"Come, Sulo, smart Sulo, lion-hearted Sulo, twist it, twist his neck, twist it again…"

"Don't let go, don't let go, more, just a little more, a little, only a hair is left, just a hair, only—a—hair…"

With a loud thump the animal fell to the ground. His head and nos-trils were now free from Sulo's grip and he could breathe, but the other Kurds rushed forward and sat upon its full length. They tied the calf's legs together with a piece of rope and, bending its head back, put a knife to its throat. Hot blood spurted forth and gushed to the ground.

I ran out.

"Muselim! Where the hell are you going? Bring the dogs in to lick up the blood!" Osman shouted after me.

I pretended not to hear.

When I returned to the baking house, the calf had stopped trembling and was motionless. They had untied its legs, fired the oven, brought in some dirt to dry up and cover the pool of blood, and started skinning the animal.

Before they were able to finish, Chako, who had been left outside as a watch, rushed in shouting: "The Kayu people are coming! Put out the lights!"

The men dropped their knives. Some rushed to wash the blood from their hands, the others shut the doors of the bake house and hastened out.

Three men from Kayu approached with the customary polite greetings.

"*Merhaba*, hello, good evening."

"*Merhaba*," replied our people in unison.

"Was there a calf in your herd that did not belong to you?"

"A what?"

"A young calf."

"No, not that we know of, but if you wish, we can light a torch and go over to the stable and look."

They lit a gummy branch and entered the stable to "search" for the lost calf.

The Kayu group, sad and dejected, hands beneath their sashes like mourners, turned away. We, pushing and jostling, rushed back to the bake house.

That night we devoured more than half of the tender animal, some parts barely cooked, licking our fingers and eating noisily. We would take a roasted chunk from the oak fire, brush off the char, and gulp it down with limitless gluttony. If the meat was not cooked enough, not properly salted or not tender, we would toss it behind us to the dogs that waited silently with wagging tails. Then we'd grab a new piece.

Sulo was the only one who chewed every morsel without reservation, although he kept eyeing us, resenting our every bite, even what we threw to the dogs. Unable to contain himself, he roared: "Eat dirt! Eat poison! Damn it, you have a feast of meat, and you are scrutinizing every piece! Is this one fatty? Is that one lean?"

"It's not that…we only want to see if it's tender or tough," Khoren explained.

"What does that mean? Are you old? Don't you have teeth? Is it hard for you to swallow?"

Finally we'd had enough. A pale light appeared in the east and the first faint chirping came from the woods.

We all went to the spring to wash up and quench our thirst. Sulo put his mouth to the flowing water and drank until his body swelled. He loosened his waistband, sat back against an oak tree, and fell asleep. We were still there when he turned over and started to snore, his mouth half open, his cheeks working like bellows.

We returned to the bake house, cleaned it up, and stuffed the remains of the animal into the oven to roast. We spread the hide flat on the ground, salted it well, then rolled it up and placed it in a corner where it would remain to cure properly.

Eight days later we took it outdoors and unrolled it to dry under the summer sun.

Not long after, Musto declared that the time had come to cut up and distribute the hide. He sharpened his knife, sank down on his knees, and used a string soaked in red soil to draw parallel lines on the inner side. Then he straightened up, turned to Khoren, and said, "Haji, my son, all this belongs to you; tell me which part you want for your moccasins."

"The back," said Khoren. "One part for me, one for my sister, and one for Muselim. You share the rest among you."

And he sniffed. Anytime he was very sad or happy, he sniffed; he must have been very happy now, because he sniffed three times.

That night, after we finished our field chores and sat, weary, in front of our tent to rest, Musto asked us to build a fire.

"I need some light to sew your moccasins," he said.

The night was tranquil. From a distance came the splashing of water in the fountain, and from a bed of clay in a brook, the croaking of two frogs, perhaps courting or fighting, filled the air.

Mariam, Krikor and Vartuhi were now orphans. Their mother, who had been ill since they had arrived, died.

In her last moments, despite the urging of the local women, she had murmured "*Hisus Kristos* [Jesus Christ]" instead of the Islamic creed, and so she was branded "infidel" and denied burial in the cemetery.

When morning came, clear and bright, two of our Kurdish servants, Guelo and Sulo, placed her body on a flat board that was used to carry manure from the stable, and took her out of the house. Because the "stretcher" was short, her legs and long black hair dangled at each end. She had no shroud, no funeral. Her thin face was ivory, and the clothing that she had worn during her long illness clung to her bones, dirty and soggy.

The body was taken to the gorge at the eastern side of the village and rolled down the bank. Sulo first removed some of her clothes, which he took home. Her bedding was put out to air under the sun, and also left overnight in the frost. The entrance hall where she had slept was rearranged; the children's straw mats were pushed against the walls and everybody felt relieved.

Several days later her children started to appear, stepping out slowly, but Vartuhi, the four-year-old, could not move. Her legs were paralyzed below the knee. I wondered why Mariam, the older sister, seemed unconcerned. When the little one was carried outdoors and left under a tree, I asked Mariam why she was not taking care of her sister.

"Why should I?" she said, her voice shaking with venom. "My mother is dead! May she die too, the thief!"

"Thief?"

"Yes, the thief. My mother had saved some raisins. As soon as she died, that one stole them and ate them."

"How do you know she was the one?"

"I know because she has diarrhea. She dirtied her bottom so much that they threw her out of the house."

"But she can't help it, she cannot walk!"

"She could walk enough to reach the raisins! Why shouldn't she…"

I did not let her finish. She must have been crazed, otherwise how could she be so heartless?

When one of the girls had a chance, some food was taken to the child—a couple of spoons of yogurt, a cup of new milk, still warm. But she seemed doomed. Her face had shrunk to the size of a palm, her bones protruded at the joints, her knees were red and twisted. She was covered with dirt and lice, and reeked badly.

"If she didn't smell so bad," said Musto, "perhaps we could carry her to our tent and…" He stopped there. He lowered his voice: "Muselim, try to stay close to the village for a while. You are tall and your face has the look of a city boy, an Armenian. Who knows if you might run into trouble."

"Musto, tell me the truth, have you heard something?"

"Yes, but don't be afraid. The Armenians are being rounded up again, but the bey has influence and connections. He will not give you to the government."

"Thank you, Musto, you are a good man."

"Try to get rid of your clothes as soon as possible," he continued. "Get a simple shirt and loose pants so you won't be noticed."

Suddenly, Krikor's tearful voice was calling. We rushed from the tent. On the stubble in the moonlight, we saw him with his sister, two silhouettes clinging to each other. We ran to them.

"Let me go, let me go and weep over her a little," begged Mariam. Two of us could hardly hold or calm her. With her untidy hair and worn face, she seemed a strange, lost creature.

"If you want to cry over our mother, go tomorrow in the daylight and cry as long as you want. I'll come with you," her brother pleaded.

The poor boy did not know the horror of his suggestion—his mother's body was exposed in the gorge and probably had started to decompose.

We returned to the tent.

"I'll go there tomorrow morning and throw some dirt over the body," said Musto quietly.

I stayed awake for a long time. The night was mild and the air calm. I thought about my mother and the others. Where might they be? What are they doing? Are they alive, sick, dead? Have they had anything to eat? I wanted to know.

When Krikor returned to the tent, we asked about his sisters.

"The little one, Vartuhi, won't last long, and the older one fell asleep, exhausted," he said. Sitting on a stool, he sobbed uncontrollably.

"Let him cry until his grief is spent," said Musto, drawing a box of tobacco from his belt.

The next morning, when Fetiye Hanum was assigning the daily chores as usual, she looked at Guelo, the most heartless of all the villagers and the one who most hated the Armenians, and said, "Guelo, on your way to the field, would you throw that nonbeliever girl into the river?"

Guelo started to nod his usual assent before realizing that she meant four-year-old Vartuhi.

"I cannot do it, Hanum. If you order me to strangle the older ones or twist every one of their necks, Allah be praised, I swear to do it with one hand as easily as ripping off the head of a chicken." He glared at me. "I'll show you right now as a test—if I don't break his neck in one motion, you can spit at my face. But that little one…God has already doomed her, I cannot do it."

She turned to the older, thickset Kurd, "Sulo, you take her."

Sulo did not answer. He smiled and continued hitching the animals to his cart.

At that moment Musto was saddling the asses. He had handed a newly sharpened axe to Krikor and was showing him how to fasten it.

"Musto!"

"Yes, Hanum."

"Musto, yesterday you said that you are out of tobacco."

"Yes, Hanum, I have none left."

"I will give you a couple of pounds of good tobacco if you throw that girl into the river."

"No, Hanum, I can't, my hand would not…" Muttering softly to himself, "Even for that much in gold, I cannot do it."

"Okay, you lamb hearts, do you expect me to do it? It should be on my head! Why do I keep you here? I feed you, I dress you, I take care of your aches and troubles, I keep you out of military service! Tell me, for the love of Allah, for the sake of the Prophet, do you want me to take the blame? Tell me…"

"Muselim!" she turned suddenly. "*You* take her!"

Like Sulo, I did not respond and moved out of sight.

Krikor was dumbstruck, his big eyes open so wide that he was more to be pitied than his sister. Luckily, Musto went over to him, took the axe from his hand, tied it to the saddle together with a sack of bread, and said to the terrified, shaken boy, "Let's go."

Krikor hesitated, afraid that someone would drown his sister in his absence. Perhaps he felt guilty to leave her, or realized that she was already doomed, or thought of his mother and regretted that he was ever born. I do not know. He stopped for only a moment, and started after Musto.

"You wait and see. I'll get rid of all of you in the fall and bring in

Turks to replace you. Then you will know what it means to be Fetiye," threatened our Turkish hanum, and left.

Later we heard from one of the servants that Ali Bey was annoyed with the hanum for her behavior.

"For God's sake, woman, leave those who are dying to their own fate," he had said. "After all, they too are born from mothers. It is a sin."

While Haji was ordered to work elsewhere, Fetiye Hanum told me to "be sure to get some sleep" in the afternoon because I was to replace him and accompany Osman to graze the herd at night. That was the start of my shepherding with Osman—a learning experience that, I did not know then, would become an enduring part of me.

The villagers expected us in the morning before the sun was too hot, and were waiting when we returned with the goats to the dairy grounds, gathering them under the big oaks.

Milkers, with buckets hanging from their bare arms, made their way to the herd. Two other servants and I joined the workers and helped them. Our job was to hold the heads of the goats so they would not squirm while being milked.

Every goat had a name, and there were well over one hundred. I wondered how it was possible to differentiate one from the other, as all of them were black and looked alike. But the Kurdish peasants, with ingenious sight and memory, knew if any goats escaped being milked, and called out their names: "I didn't milk Chakur or Geig today!"

We walked up to the house exhausted, with the milk-laden buckets hanging from our arms.

During these few days with Osman, I was almost happy. But on this afternoon, when we returned home, one of the servants met us to report that the little girl had been thrown into the water.

"Who did it?"

"Sehel."

"Is she dead?"

"No, Haji pulled her out."

"Where is she now?"

"There, under the tree."

She died the same day. Sulo's Kurdish wife, Sabriye, placed the wasted corpse on a small plank and carried it to the nearby woods. I followed with a spade. I dug a small hole under an oak tree. "Our Father—" My voice choked. I covered the spot with dirt and put a marker over it.

When we returned home, Mariam was crying and exhorting her mother to "rise up and see their condition."

I ran to find Musto.

"Did you throw dirt on that woman's body?" I asked.

"Yes, I covered her up very well. She is buried."

I found Khoren and said to him, "Tomorrow, if Mariam wants to visit her mother and weep over her, don't stop her. Let her do it. Our mothers did not have anyone to weep over them...let hers have somebody."

"Muselim, it is time for the cattle to be grazing, prepare the food for the dogs."

It was Osman's father, whom we all called "Uncle Hussein," walking toward me on a cool afternoon.

"Where is Osman?" I asked.

"He is away on business. You and I are taking the herd to the mountains today."

I was happy at the prospect of being with Uncle Hussein through the night. The old man had problems with his eyes, and bright sunlight bothered him. But he was a superb flute player. When he played, my heart swelled, and the sheep would leave their grazing to gather around him, peaceful, ruminating.

In the morning when we returned to the village, Osman was there to greet us, grinning broadly.

"Muselim," he bubbled, "I have become your brother-in-law."

I did not know what he meant.

"Don't you understand? I am telling you that I married an Armenian girl! Come, come home with me so I can introduce you."

On the way we met Khoren and gave him the news. He joined us.

Osman's mother was at the door.

"Come in, come in. Wipe your feet well. Osman brought you to see the bride?"

"Yes."

"And he told you that she is one of yours?"

"Yes."

"Did you clean your sandals properly?"

"Yes, we did."

"Come, come in."

We entered. No one was there.

"Where are you, Gulizar? See who has come to see you."

A head peeked out from behind a curtain at the corner of the room and a hand was pulling a scarf to cover her face.

"There is no need for that, come, come out. These are your brothers, your kin," said Osman, smiling.

Gulizar was a shapely, beautiful dark-haired girl with blue eyes. Seeing us, she laughed and wept at the same time.

Khoren and I introduced ourselves with our Armenian names.

"Mine was Arev," she said, "they changed it to Gulizar."

"You are Muslims now! You are not to speak the infidel tongue," scolded Osman's mother.

Gulizar started to cry.

"Come," said Osman, "why are you crying?"

She sobbed even louder and her shoulders shook.

We'd caused her to be upset. We were confused. What should we do? Leave? We looked at each other.

"Sit, sit down," urged Osman's mother.

"Where are you from?" the girl asked, wiping her tears.

We each told her. Khoren added that his sister was also here and that her converted name was Minireh.

"Your mother, what happened to your mother?"

"They took her away."

"Mine, too," she said. Then to me, "And yours?"

"Mine too."

We grew sad.

Seeing this, Osman prompted us to leave. "She is your sister, you will have a chance to see her often."

We were on our feet when his mother said, "Let me give them a yogurt drink."

"Yes, yes," urged Osman.

"May your marriage be long and happy," said Khoren, raising his glass.

"Amen."

The yogurt drink was good and thick, and just cold enough. We each downed it in one gulp. We bid the bride good night and went out.

"Did you like my wife?" asked Osman.

"What is there not to like?"

"That's what I thought, so I married her."

"If you wanted to be married, why didn't you look for a Turkish girl?" I asked.

"Where would I find such a pure and beautiful girl?"

Osman was captivated with Arev, now called Gulizar. He was deeply in love with her, and his tender feelings for the Armenian girl even transferred to us and made us happy.

Sometimes he invited us to his house for dinner. We joyfully accepted the invitations and devoured the tasty meals prepared by Arev, a far cry from the nameless soup that was served to us every day. We felt happy being together and consoled, and for a brief time we forgot our sorrows.

Osman asked us to teach him some Armenian words, and occasionally he slipped them into his conversation, smiling and gazing into Arev's eyes.

His mother would be annoyed. "They are Muslims now! Instead of forbidding them to speak their infidel tongue, you learn their language!"

"My dear mother, speaking a word or two in Armenian will not make me an infidel, nor will they become good Muslims by never speaking an Armenian word."

"Do you mean that we are not good Muslims?" I protested. "Do we not recite the creed? Did we not keep the Fast of Ramazan?"[4]

His mother replied for Osman. "My children, do not pay attention to what he says. I know you are good Muslims."

"May God forsake you! Die! Keep thinking that we would renounce our enlightened faith," Arev hissed in Armenian.

"*Al Hamdu Lillah* [Praise be to Allah]" I intoned piously.

"*Al Hamdu Lillah*," repeated Khoren.

"You just wait," said Osman, gazing at her affectionately. "A few months more and I will have learned enough Armenian to understand whatever you say."

"I didn't know you were so clever," she remarked sarcastically.

"There are many things you do not know yet," replied Osman, smiling with pride. And to us: "My wife is incomparable, isn't she?"

"Our sister is an angel, a true angel."

"I am a lucky man," Osman murmured as we bid them good night.

---

4 The Islamic holy month of Ramadan is Ramazan in Turkey.

CHAPTER 3

Life as a Shepherd

Days drifted into each other with little to tell them apart. But one afternoon, when I had freed the oxen and Sulo and Guelo were poking their staffs over the threshing floor, I noticed Ali Bey watching them from the upper level. I fetched a chair and took it to him.

"Bey, please sit."

He looked surprised and flicked his eyes to me, then to the chair. "Thank you, my son."

It was the first time I ever heard the words "thank you" from him.

I had forgotten about it when Kamile, the bey's Armenian wife, came to me the next day.

"What did you do to the bey yesterday?"

"Who, me?"

"Yes, you."

"What could I do to the bey? I didn't do anything! You must be mistaken."

"It seems you offered him a chair when he was watching the workers on the threshing floor," Kamile said, smiling. "It pleased him very much. He came home touched: 'I am forty years old. Throughout my life, I have been surrounded by all kinds of servants and workers and in those forty years, nobody ever brought me a chair without my asking,' he said. 'But this boy, whose mother, father, countrymen, we put to the sword or threw into the sea, did so....Allah bear witness, as of today, he is my son. When the war is over, I will take him to the city and prepare the documents to make it official.

"'From now on, I want all of you to look upon him with new eyes. Do not treat him as an ordinary servant. Be attentive to his food and clothing. Do not give him heavy chores. In the name of Allah...and to think we cut their throats or dumped them into the Euphrates.'"

When the bey's words got around, the other servants turned against me—except for the Armenians—taunting and mocking, saluting, bowing before me with formal gestures.

Before long the bey called me to the guest room where the entire household was gathered.

"Muselim, my son, in the presence of all of your hanum mothers, I hereby promise that when the war is over, I will adopt you officially and declare you heir to everything I have. You, in turn, will care for my lands. You will protect the hanums always and make certain that they lack nothing. You will see that the Kurds do not rob us. And that is not all...I want you to search for a beautiful girl. Now get going, let me see you do something! I dream of a wedding, and on that day I will get drunk!"

I reddened. I was dumbstruck. I could not face him. I had been taught that it was shameful and impolite to speak of a girl or marriage in the presence of my elders.

Ali Bey noticed. "All right, go to your duties, but do not forget what I said."

Toward evening, when the weather had cooled and Osman and I were taking the herd out, I told him what had happened. He listened, smiling, and said: "In that case, pray that the war is over soon. As for the beautiful girl, I know a girl in Roosku who, believe me, is out of this world—tall, her shape, her eyes, brows, unmatched. There is no one like her in all of Kurdistan. Some time ago I asked for her hand but her parents refused. If they had given her to me, though, I would not have married Gulizar, so in the end it was lucky for me."

I listened to him without interrupting. We walked side by side until twilight dimmed to almost darkness. The sun, whose golden rays touched only the highest mountaintops, slowly lifted her skirt and disappeared behind the western clouds. Soon a few stars appeared and the lingering swallow-tails returned to their nests, leaving us to ourselves.

We came to a high, wide gorge with a creek running on one side and carpets of tall grass, still green, all around.

"We can graze the flock here and we will also sleep here," Osman said.

I went to the creek to fill his water jug, and when I returned we had our meal and kept an eye on the animals until Osman determined that they were fully fed.

"They're already on their knees, chewing their cud. What do you say, shall we sleep?"

We bundled up in our felt coverings as the moon rose behind a hill and flushed the surroundings with a honey-colored light. Osman was already asleep with his staff beside him, and in that mottled darkness his shape was like a heap of earth, a newly covered grave.

The sight sent shivers through my spine. I remembered seeing thousands of bodies left on the ground like that, unburied, the same brownish mound in the moonlight. I could not sleep. Dear Lord, when will I be free of these memories and the parade of horrific scenes? When?

I silently recited the Lord's Prayer and was almost asleep when Osman lifted his head: "Find the guide goat and tie a rope from his horn to your arm, just in case we oversleep and are not awake when they start moving."

I tried to sleep. Chalum came around a couple of times, sniffing my face and touching my cheek with his cold, wet nose. I caressed his head, whispered for him to go away, and turned on my side.

ALI BEY AND THE WOLVES

When I awoke in the morning, Osman was sitting up and blinking the sleepiness out of his eyes. On the eastern horizon, where earth and sky met, traces of yellow were like golden fish swimming in a sea of ink.

Everything was wet as I moved through the tall grass, my feet, the shrubbery, the damp wool of the sheep. Osman came up close: "Stay alert and keep your eyes open. Something's going on, the dogs were growling all night."

"Where are they? I can't see them. Last night Chalum came to me and groaned in my ear," I told him.

I had barely uttered the words when panic startled the sheep; they rushed toward us, scrambling in chaos.

"Wolves!" shouted Osman, and pulling an old pistol from his belt, he ran toward the animals, firing point-blank.

The dogs, swifter than any falcon, ran ahead of us to the edge of the woods and disappeared. Osman followed them and I, frightened and confused, stopped to kneel down beside a soft, bloody heap under my feet. It was our one and only Angora goat, almost all white, with long fine hair, pale yellowish horns, and shining, crystal-blue eyes. We had nurtured him with special care and hoped that he would breed and multiply. The wolves had torn open his belly and devoured his heart, liver, lungs, and kidneys in an instant. They were in a hurry, and it is easy to swallow those organs without chewing. The rest of the animal was still warm, trembling and steaming.

I was shaken. I could not decide what to do—leave the flock and follow Osman, or stay and guard the animals as best I could. What if the wolves returned? Once a wolf tastes blood, it loses all reason. What to do if they came back?

The sheep were frightened, and it took a while for them to calm down and resume grazing. Some of them, mouthing a blade of grass, ears back, gazed steadily at the spot where the wolves had disappeared.

I decided to turn the flock toward home. From afar, very far, came the ugly sounds of dogs yelping, mingled with Osman's shouts. A few minutes later Bogar emerged from the woods, sniffing the trails, and came to me.

"Hey, where are the others? Why are you here?"

He crumpled down, tongue out, panting. I was baffled. Bogar seemed to have avoided any sort of fight. There were no signs of blood and no wounds on his shiny coat. But what happened? Where were the others? The animals were already moving toward home, so I decided to leave them and look for Osman.

Fortunately, just before I got to the woods I saw Chalum and Osman in the distance, side by side, the dog limping and unsteady, coming toward me.

I ran to meet them but I could not speak. I knelt in front of the dog. His wounds were terrible. Very carefully and tenderly, I took his soft head in my hands.

"Chalum, poor Chalum, what has happened to you?" He started to lick my hands.

I turned to Osman, distraught. "What happened? How did it happen?"

"Have you seen Bogar?" he asked, ignoring my question.

"Yes, he is here. He came a little while ago."

"Call him! Call him to come."

I raised my voice and called him. He came and stood in front of me, head up, tail wagging.

Osman, shepherd's stick in hand, got behind the animal and, holding its tail securely in his left hand, raised the huge club and slammed it down with all his might on the dog's back. The animal curled over, writhed, squealing with pain and trying to defend itself. This time the stick found his head, his right side, left side, hitting wherever, not stopping.

"Osman, what are you doing? Are you crazy?"

"Go away or you'll get it too!"

"Osman, stop! It is enough!" He did not listen.

"Osman!"

"I will teach this deserter not to quit and run away in the middle of a fight."

"Fine, teach him! But this beating and teaching are enough!"

Finally he let go of the dog's tail. Bogar escaped to safety, howling, and crouched down to ask himself why humans have crazy whims; either they love them or beat them fiercely.

Osman sat on the ground beside Chalum and started to cry. I said nothing to try to console him. I let him alone.

"Forgive me, take no notice," he said finally, wiping his tears with his red handkerchief, "and do not tell anyone I wept. If my mother died, I would not cry, if I lost my father, I would not cry. But this betrayal stabs my heart deeply. At the most critical moment of the fight, he left me and his brother alone and ran off with his tail on his back."

Osman was justified. Chalum's condition was horrible. One of his big, heavy paws hung limp, totally useless. Apparently one of the wolves had succeeded in locking it in his iron jaw and crushed the bones. It was a miracle that it was not completely torn off.

That was not all. There were open wounds on the dog's face, ribs, and thigh. A deep gash on his neck was bleeding steadily. All our attempts to stop the bleeding did not help, until I remembered an old peasant remedy. We burned Osman's head covering and pressed the ashes into the wound and wrapped it around his neck. For the moment, our hearts were relieved. We lay the dog down on the grass and we sat beside him.

"Did you check around? What damage did they do to the herd?" asked Osman.

"They caught the Angora and lapped up his insides, heart, and lungs. They did not touch the flesh. He's over there under the juniper tree."

"I would have preferred they killed a couple of sheep or another goat rather than harm the dog."

Silence.

"Osman."

"What."

"Are you angry at me for not following you?"

"Good thing you didn't come. That would not have been smart."

Silence again.

"Osman, if I ask something, will you answer?"

"Ask."

"What happened there? How did the dog get like this?"

"What could happen? It's obvious! Chalum went after them and forced them off into the water, and they fled across the river. But then they got courageous and turned back all together to attack the dog. By the time I reached Chalum, this is what they left."

He leaned over the dog and, very carefully and tenderly, stroked his head.

"How many were they? Could you count them?"

"There were seven to start with, but Chalum got one, so it was the other six that he had to fight later. On our way back, we passed the one that was down; his back was broken and he could not walk, but he was still alive. He dared to snarl at us so I crushed his skull with my club, hitting hard, hitting…hitting…until his teeth fell out." As he spoke, he was pounding the earth with his club.

"Is it still there? I would like to go and see," I said, rising.

"Stay here. You can see him later when we go to skin him."

"I hope the others don't come back and eat the carcass."

"No, they only do that in the winter when they're starving. During this season they do not eat each other."

By now the sun was up and the hills were warm. It was past time for the animals to be watered and taken home for milking. But the dog could not walk. The wolf remained where it had fallen, and the Angora was under the juniper tree.

"The best thing is for me to skin the wolf, take the pelt to the village, and send a couple of people to help you," Osman decided. "That way the bey will be told in advance."

Half an hour after he left, Khoren and Chako appeared. Their faces paled when they saw the dog. "Oh oh!" cried the Kurd, "what will the bey say when he sees this?"

"We did whatever we could," I said.

Soon, Guelo and Musto arrived with a stretcher that was used to carry dung from the stable. We lifted the heavy dog onto it and started on our way.

When we neared home, the villagers were waiting at the fountain, gasping and lamenting the mishap as they gathered around us.

The bey had sent for Hussein, Osman's father, who lived in the adjacent village, to drop everything and come to save his cherished dog. The old shepherd arrived early that night. He examined the animal carefully, squinting his weak eyes, and said: "There is no need to worry about the wounds that he can reach with his tongue, his licking will heal them all. His neck will mend. Do not use medication. As for the paw..." He pressed his lips together in a thin line and, wiping his forehead, continued, "As for the paw, if there were no open wounds, I could position the bones and bind it until it healed, but with those wounds, I cannot. We must leave it as is and to his fate."

Ali Bey, who had listened intently to the old man's words, turned to Osman. "Go to Roosku tomorrow and bring back the puppy my uncle promised."

"But they are still suckling," Osman protested.

"I said go and get him." the bey was annoyed. "Let him grow up on sheep's milk."

Then, to me: "Muselim, go with him tomorrow. When you return with the puppy, you will care for him and be responsible for him. I relieve you of all other duties."

"As you wish, Bey. I have never raised a dog, but with Osman and his father to guide me, I can do it."

Very early the next morning, old Hussein came to the tent and we started off. Although the hint of fall was in the air, it was still summer and harvesting was not yet over. We passed by the water mill where many carts, laden with bulging sacks of grain, were gathered, and the rattle of the heavy stone, turning fast, thundered through the flour-whitened door.

"Where are you going so early in the morning?" shouted one of the Kurds.

"Across the way," Uncle Hussein replied. "Wolves attacked Ali Bey's flock yesterday and left his dog in tatters. We are on our way to get another one."

In a half hour we reached Roosku, a village of about fifty houses clinging to the skirts of two hills forming a valley. We communicated with people there easily from our side: when one of their animals strayed into our fields, someone would shout the news across to them, hands cupped to his mouth, and we in turn did the same. We finally arrived and stopped at Mehmet Bey's door. The servants led us directly to the stable.

It was a large building with separate partitions for horses, oxen, and cows, and in one corner a heap of hay reached to the ceiling. We expressed the usual courtesies and greetings on behalf of Ali Bey, and then Uncle Hussein explained the reason for our visit.

"What is the hurry?" asked Mehmet Bey. "The puppies are still suckling on milk!"

We recounted the unfortunate events of the previous day. He nodded: "That explains his impatience. Ask my son to show you where the puppies are. Choose the one you like and take it home."

The mother dog was lying on her side in the hallway, eyes closed. Hearing our footsteps, she raised her head, sniffed, and put her head down again. Covering the full length of her massive body was a row of puppies hanging onto on her brimming breasts, their eyes closed, their mouths immersed in milk foam.

We waited until they stopped feeding and were completely sated. The mother dog finally got up, abandoned her brood, and drifted to a corner, settling against the wall to watch the puppies chasing, bouncing, nipping ears and necks.

"Which one, Uncle Hussein?"

"I have not decided yet, wait. That one, the smallest, seems the most curious; he does not play, he does not fight, he sniffs the air and looks around continuously." He bent down and, with the wary mother dog watching, he took them in his hands, one by one, and examined them.

"No, not this one, not this one either, not this one either..." he murmured to himself, and put them down again. When he came to the fifth puppy, the smallest one, his face brightened.

"Aha! This one."

"Is he an attacker? Can he kill a wolf?"

"Yes."

"How do you know?"

"Be silent." He tucked the puppy under his coat and we went to see Mehmet Bey.

"Let me see, which one?"

The old man took out the puppy and lifted him up.

"That puny one? How? You chose the smallest, most helpless...but it is yours to decide. Give my best regards to Ali and his wife."

We thanked him and started on our return. I was filled with joy about the puppy that was to be my protégé. When we were halfway down the road, nearing the water mill, I could wait no longer and stretched out my arms, pleading: "Uncle Hussein, please give him to me so I can hold him. After all, the bey said I was to take care of him. Let him get to know me as soon as possible."

He opened his coat and handed me the puppy. He was barely as heavy as a cat, a round bundle of soft fur.

"Uncle Hussein!"

"What is it?"

"How did you choose this one? How do you know he will be a guard dog, a protector?"

"That is it. I chose him."

"I know, but how do you know that when he grows up, he will be able to—"

He stopped me.

"I will tell you, but you are not to repeat it to anybody. Last night I cut a piece of the wolf skin that Osman brought back and hid it in my sleeve. When I was examining the puppies one after the other, he was the only one that sensed the smell and started poking for it."

When we arrived home, the air of happiness entered the house with us. We went directly to the guest room where the bey was sitting on the settee, smoking.

I held out the puppy. "Bey, Uncle Hussein liked this one."

"Well, my son, you know what to do."

Holding him in my arms, I ran to the kitchen and put a big bowl of milk before him. He drank more than half of it. With his belly fully rounded, he found a suitable corner and fell asleep.

A little later, Osman and Khoren came to see him, picking him up and stroking him.

"What are we going to name him?" asked Khoren.

"I hadn't thought about that."

"Hmm…Gobul, Komo, Koorchul, Chalo…"

"Komo is a good name," said Osman.

"Let's go and ask the bey," I said.

The bey said that if we liked that name, to let it be. And so his name was Komo. From that moment on, I spent my days with Komo. I protected him, fed him, brushed his coat, and kept him clean. During his first night with us, a surprising thing happened. As it grew dark, he became anxious and restless and started to cry. He did not sleep until I tucked him to my side. I told Uncle Hussein about it in the morning, and in his wise, experienced way, the old shepherd explained: "From the day he was born, and perhaps even before he was born, he was accustomed to his mother's heartbeat, and when that was missing he could not sleep, and cried until you took him to your side."

"You mean he slept because he was able to hear my heartbeat?"

"Correct."

Komo liked Chalum as much as he liked me, and maybe even more. He would cuddle between Chalum's long legs and sleep peacefully or, feeling safe there, would threaten passersby with a high young bark. On the day we gave him a large bone to exercise his new teeth, he dragged it to Chalum, wagging his tail and barking "Here, it's yours!"

Chalum soon recovered, but something was missing from the once splendid, powerful shepherd dog with split-second reflexes and lightning speed. He had become a half dog. Just as Osman's father had predicted, his wounds healed but the bones did not knit properly, leaving one leg short. He accompanied the herd, limping, but if wolves were to attack again, he would not be able to overtake them.

When he and Komo stood side by side or walked together—and they were always with each other—Chalum looked like an old man taking his grandson out to play.

Barely one month after Komo had come to us, Osman ordered his ears to be cropped.

"Why do you want to cut them?" I protested.

"Have you ever seen a gamper (a Caucasian shepherd dog) with its ears uncut?"

"Many."

"Where?"

"Everywhere," I lied.

"It is for his own good," Osman explained. "If the ears are cropped close to his skull, the wolves can't get hold of his head in a fight."

"I know."

"Then why do you object?"

"He will be ugly."

"The ears of all the others are cut—are they ugly?"

"Well, don't cut them when I am around," I said. "Tell me the day before, so I won't be here."

"We'll let you know."

Four days later, Osman came to me: "Tomorrow morning we will cut Komo's ears. Do as you wish."

I had planned to go to the mountains, but changed my mind and stayed home. Perhaps I could be of some help—at least I could console him. If I was not by his side when he most needed a friend, then what kind of friend was I?

The morning was cool and bright when Uncle Hussein, Osman, Haji, and Chako came together. Hussein pulled from his belt a folded knife that had been carefully sharpened the day before. Each of them took a palmful of salt before calling Komo. He scampered over, trusting and confident.

I ran off.

Moments later, even with my hands pressed tightly over my ears, I heard Komo's howls and heart-rending cries. I knew they had cut one of his ears and poured salt on the open wound. Then the other one. Too much! I ran to them and took the dog into my arms. He was rubbing his paw over the bleeding wound, over and over, as though an insect was stinging his ears.

How could he know?

The following week the cuts were healed, but he had become an ugly dog. Part of his identity was gone. When he focused on something, fully attentive, he looked as though he did not have the ears to listen. As the days passed, his body started to evolve and change.

When he was a puppy, his torso was round as a stovepipe, especially when his belly was full, which it always was. His short legs were thick and fuzzy, and his neck met his body with soft curves. Now that pleasing harmony was lost. His legs were longer, his belly recessed, his ribs showed like the wires of a cage, and he had the appearance of a starving dog. All of the symmetry and everything appealing about him were gone.

Ali Bey followed these changes closely, aware of every sign, and would nod his head, truly pleased.

Finally, one day, Uncle Hussein declared that it was the time for Komo to give up snoozing under the shade trees and go with the other dogs to protect the herd. I recalled my own first day at school and did not know whether to be sad or happy for Komo.

The next morning, when he joined Bogar and Chalum to accompany the animals, I felt that my duty as caretaker was over.

It was not yet noon when Komo came running back. I knelt beside him and, taking him in my arms, explained that what he had done was very wrong, and it was unforgivable to return. What would others say if they saw him? What would they think of him?

I walked him back to the grazing grounds. Fortunately, he knew where the herd was and led me there. No one had yet noticed his shameful conduct. We ended the day together.

Early the next morning, he devoured his food as never before and left with the herd. This time he did not come back.

I was relieved. He had become a shepherd dog.[5]

⌁ ⊛ ⌁

We did not know the three Kurds who rode into the village one

---

5 Shepherd dogs (gampers) are heavy, meaty dogs, with big paws to negotiate the rough terrain and lightning-fast reflexes. Their job is to guard the flock, not move it. They are fearless, and one dog will fight several wolves at the same time. They require no special training; they hide within the herd and defend it against any threat.

afternoon, bringing with them a woman. They left her at the house and departed.

We learned that the young woman was Armenian. This was the busiest season in the fields, and most of the servants were helping outdoors, so Fetiye had put her to work in the house. She was a beautiful girl, about twenty-five, with black eyes and white skin. She worked enthusiastically day and night without tiring, chewing gum continuously. She cleaned indoors, swept the halls and the courtyard, wiped the porch, tidied the storerooms, and set everything in order.

"That infidel girl has polished the house enough for a wedding," said Osman's mother. "She is as fastidious as a new bride."

Hearing that, Fetiye's efficient mind started churning.

"Muselim," she said to me, "I am going to have you married."

I stared at her, astonished. Thinking it was a bad joke, but worried, I went out.

By the next day word had spread through the village and everybody was talking and wondering. It was rumored that someone had been sent to fetch a *hoja* (a wise man, a minor cleric). The villagers spoke of the "bride" and eyed each other while smiling at me.

Fetiye Hanum ordered a section of the storeroom to be cleared out and scrubbed; the ground was wetted and swept clean, a carpet spread, and bedding and quilts were set up in the corner. I met Sehel in the hallway; she was taking a small oil lamp to the storeroom. She smiled knowingly and whispered into my ear: "It is your honeymoon room!" A pause, then, "Come home early tonight so you can have a bath."

Siran, the newly arrived Armenian girl, had already bathed and combed her long pretty hair. She was dressed and surrounded by women, all fussing and helping her. There was great joy in the house.

Almost in panic I ran upstairs to the hanum's room. She and Ali Bey were seated face-to-face on the divan, talking.

"What is it, my son?"

"Bey, are there any deportee caravans passing this way?"

"No, my son. Why do you ask?"

"I would ask that you send me to join one of them."

"Why? What has happened?" He looked concerned.

I was biting my lips to keep from bursting into tears.

"Aren't you happy in this house?"

"That's not it!" I could not go on.

"Don't you want to be married?"

"No, I do not."

"Very well. Do not cry. When you are older, I will find a girl of Islam to be your bride."

That ended the matter for me. But later, Mendoohi told me that the bey and the hanum had argued about it for a long time.

Finally, when Siran's belly was swollen enough to disrupt her work, the shepherd Michig was summoned from the village of Huni to marry her. When the couple returned home, Michig sent two rams as a gift to the hanum to show his appreciation.

Fall strode in with bold steps and embroidered our mountains and valleys with a thousand colors. Golden ripening and fullness dominated everywhere. Migrating birds crossed the skies day and night, and plump starlings practiced hovering exercises before our eyes.

Guelo was sent to the meadow for autumn sowing, where he was to remain all week to prepare the soil for the forthcoming crop.

The sheep wool, like the dog fur, grew thicker every day, and beneath the stiff black hair of the goats, a fine, delicate fuzz was peeking through.

Komo was grown now. He was able to keep his tail rounded on his back and I was sure that if the barbarians had not cut off his ears, they would be pricked straight up.

When the cold mist settled over the village we shivered, but it did not bother Komo. He would extend his muzzle toward the mountaintops, sniffing the air intently, expectantly. What preoccupied him I did not know—perhaps the scent of the wolf, his eternal enemy. Who knows?

By nightfall a thin layer of ice formed on the yellow grass and glistened like molten silver. The stars sank low, close to the earth, and it made one think that if he could climb up the opposite hill and reach out, he might snatch a few and give them to his sweetheart for earrings. The villagers did not see the beauty of all this, and when I babbled on, they looked perplexed. They thought I was crazy.

Autumn was in a stubborn and lasting struggle with winter, and the latter was about to win. We repaired and renewed the roofs, the doors, and narrow windowpanes, and cleared away the spiderwebs.

"The winter here is harsh," said Musto. "Our mountain storms are like no other. We need to prepare well ahead."

When anyone mentioned cold, shelter, or hunger, I thought of my mother and relatives who were taken to the desert, and my heart went to pieces. They were gone and I remained here at the mercy of strangers. Coward, turncoat, I had changed my faith and I was a deserter. I was ashamed. Who could forgive me? Was there anyone who had the power to pardon my sins and ease this burden?

One day, the sun that had left our mountains suddenly returned, shining bright and blazing. We all tumbled outdoors and the village was revived. It was during those unexpected sunny days that a group of horsemen, riding along the road by the river, came near and dismounted at our house.

"The beys have come, the beys have come!" shouted the Kurds, running to take their horses.

Alishan Bey, Haidar Bey, Mahmoud Bey, Izzet Bey, Ihsan Bey, Haji Bey, Dursun Bey. So many beys, my God, descended from ancient dynasties and noble tribes. They had once led an empire.

As to their servants and helpers, there were more servants than beys; Izzet Bey alone had four attendants; his party was the largest and most splendid. One of his men rode like a king, guiding his horse with one hand on the reins, and with his left hand covered in a leather glove, he held a reddish falcon with yellow eyes and long claws.

"Please come in. Welcome, salutations."

"The partridges must be fattened by now. We came for a hunt."

"Welcome, one thousand welcomes."

We opened up the guest room and lit a fire. The guests sat cross-legged on the colorful carpets, recounting the journey as their fingers combed through mustaches and beards. We offered cigarettes and served generous tumblers of raki.

Haidar Bey was young, slender, with polite gestures and a beautiful face; Alishan, his brother, looked like a teacher or an intellectual; Mahmoud Bey was round, lumpy and lazy, his face was a big O with eyes and eyebrows on it; an ugly black mole was the first thing one saw on Ihsan Bey's cheek—he was voracious, noisy and boastful. The others were crude, harsh men. Perhaps only Hadji Bey stood alone; his smallpox-scarred face was stern and fearful; an inner voice told me that he had a major part in the massacre of Armenians. Now all of these beys were together in our guest room, noisy, unruly, hotheaded, with no interest in listening to each other.

Sulo was skinning a sheep on the porch. The guests' servants gathered to watch him work, taunting him with gibes, trying to intimidate and mock him. But Sulo paid no heed. Every so often, wielding his sharp knife, he shaved a piece of fat from the animal's still-warm tail and downed it raw.

A Kurd would give his soul for meat, but unless an animal was terminally sick or died accidentally, he would not kill his animals for food. Occasionally he might steal a goat or sheep from a neighbor and eat that. If caught, he had to repay the owner with a comparable animal, and give another of equal value to the Turkish official governing the village if he hoped to escape punishment.

I was sure it was only fear of their beys that kept the Kurd servants, eyeing Sulo on the porch, from disarming him and devouring the sheep.

Izzet Bey's falcon, forgotten in the excitement, had smelled fresh blood. He was agitated, squawking, flapping his wings. Finally his master came out and ordered that a piece of meat be thrown to the falcon to calm him.

Indoors, the other beys were on their feet in the guest room, looking about and admiring the display of guns, daggers, and weapons covering the walls.

I remembered an afternoon before 1915 when my parents had taken me with them to visit a patriarchal family. On the wall of the large guesthouse hung bundles of onions, peppers, mint, and wheat, and also a picture of the supreme Armenian Catholicos Khrimian, known as "a saintly man."

Now I wondered, if only our people had hung something on their walls other than onions and peppers, perhaps our fate would have been different.

⤙⤙ ⊛ ⤚⤚

The night the guests arrived, the saz (a type of lute) was played, folk songs were sung, and the raki flowed. The visiting horses, sated with barley, dozed outside the stables, and the last time I saw it, the falcon was perched on a stump, biting the head of a chicken.

The beys and their servants left the next day, but they were back toward evening and the revelry started anew. Most of their talk was about women and prostitutes in the different villages, and eventually it turned to shepherds and their dogs, which was not unusual. Ali Bey described Chalum's heroic battle with wolves and told me to show the new dog to the beys.

Komo was outside the front door, his tail swishing left and right, watching a boy chew on a piece of dry bread. He ignored me. Gripping the nape of his neck, I led him into the guest room. Some of the beys politely rose to their feet and surrounded him.

"*Mashallah* [God has willed it], he is a fine dog: *mashallah!*"

Mahmoud Bey, who had remained seated, turned to his host: "Ali, do you still have the wolf skin that your shepherd brought back?"

"Of course."

"I have an offer. Tomorrow, have it filled with hay and hide it somewhere in the field. Then let us see if your much-praised dogs will go after it and find it."

"Mahmoud Bey, my friend," said Ali Bey, his voice calm, "here is an easy way for you to win some money. I say that my dogs, young or grown, are brave, but apparently you think otherwise. Come, let us make a bet. I am ready to bet not just you, but all the others who agree with you. What do you say?"

They all started shouting, half drunk.

"Hold on, one at a time," said Ali Bey, and to me: "Muselim, get a piece of paper and start writing."

"One ram!" announced Mahmoud Bey.

Izzet Bey followed: "One colt."

From the next: "Six milking goats."

"Two young lambs," said Hadji Bey.

I was about to write when Ali Bey cut in. "Stop, do not mark that. Hadji Bey is rich; two lambs are nothing for him. Let him bet six, let him bet ten..."

"No, two are enough, we did not come here to rob you."

There were no other bidders. We were happy, but I was anxious. What if Komo was not the dog we imagined? After all, so far he had shown no special ability other than eating.

"Go and call Osman," said Ali Bey to me. I went.

"What does he want with me in the middle of the night?" he grumbled.

We walked to the guest room and Osman, drawing together the sides of his jacket, greeted the bey and eyed the visitors.

"You still have the wolf skin, don't you?"

"Yes, my bey, I salted and dried it."

"Wet it and sew it up, fill it with straw and make it look like a real wolf as much as you can. Finish it tonight. Take Musto to help you, he is good at such work. In the morning lock the dogs indoors, then take the filled skin to the thorny stubble and hide it in the bushes. That is all. You will understand tomorrow."

Osman and I left. I told him about the wagers, confessing my fears.

"Chalum was torn apart by wolves, and the young one has never seen a wolf in his life."

"Don't worry," Osman replied. "What will be, will be."

We went into his house to work on the skin. I asked him whether Alishan and Haidar beys were rich or poor, because they did not make any bets.

"They are rich. Even their goatherds are richer than our bey," Osman explained. "Their herd grazes with eight shepherds and sixteen dogs. Their baking oven is fired every day to make bread for at least forty guests around their table at mealtime." He stopped, took a deep breath, and, forgetting what he'd said a moment ago, went on, "Hell, they have more dogs than we have animals in our herd."

He lifted the wolf skin off the wall and soaked it in water for softening. I returned to the beys.

The night passed until, semiconscious from drinking and eating, the beys settled down to sleep.

Osman had sent word for his father to come. It was close to midnight when Uncle Hussein appeared. After hearing our story, he pulled out his purse and emptied it—a few silver coins—on the floor:

"Osman, my son, this is everything I have. Tomorrow, put it all on our dogs."

I was elated. But just then Musto, who was helping Osman, straightened up and said to me: "If your sidekick leaves us red-faced tomorrow, they will not keep him here much longer."

I thought he was joking or trying to frighten me, but I could not sleep. Early in the morning I ran to see Osman.

"What happened?" he asked, eyeing me closely.

"Nothing yet, but thinking of what might happen…"

"Do not believe everything Musto says."

It was not until after the animals were milked that the beys streamed out of the house, slowly, like worms emerging from their holes. They drank abundant water to soothe the night's hangover and, after a noisy breakfast, declared it was time for the test.

We put all four dogs, Chalum, Bogar, Komo, and Abbas's dog, Chomar, into the barn and closed the door.

Osman carried the wolf skin to the stubble and hid it behind a bush. The beys lined up and announced that they were ready.

Ali Bey told me to let the dogs out, one by one.

"Release Abbas's dog first!"

Coming suddenly into the bright sunshine from the darkness of the barn, Chomar blinked his eyes, grumbled, and went directly to the trough of dog food and sank his nose into it.

His master, abashed and somewhat startled, spit on the ground, cursed, spit again, and moved off mumbling to himself.

"Muselim, release Bogar!" called Ali Bey.

Bogar appeared and shook himself like an animal coming out of water, sniffed the air, and ran like the wind toward the stuffed wolf. But halfway there he stopped, spun around, and returned to us.

"Get lost! You gave up! You…"

We chased the dog off.

"Release Chalum!"

Chalum came out snarling and barking—even from inside the barn, he had detected the enemy's scent. In an instant he knew the source and ran toward the wolf, but he was lame, and it was almost pitiful to watch his attack. When he finally got there, he toured the carcass and determined that it was a fake. We held our breaths, waiting to see what he would do. When the dog had no doubt that the wolflike thing was harmless, he lifted his right hind leg and urinated on it.

Osman could not contain himself. He called Chalum to him and, wrapping his thick arms around his neck, toppled him as they started to tumble over and over and play on the ground.

"Muselim, now Komo!"

I went into the barn and spoke my last words to the dog I loved so much. I opened the door and we went out together.

"Komo, brave Komo, go and get him!"

It took barely a second for Komo to set his direction and, just as Chalum had done, he dashed toward the makeshift wolf. I say 'dash,' but no, he flew like the shadow of a hawk in the sky, now here, now gone. Once there, he attacked the thing with great fury, biting, snarling, ripping and shaking it apart.

Osman and I ran to him and fell on the ground, all three of us.

"Komo, Komo, Komo, brave Komo!"

When we got up, I held him face to face.

"You fool! Crazy! Didn't you see that it was a fake? Dead? Filled with hay?" His instinct told him he had done a good thing, and he was just as happy as we.

Ali Bey ordered Osman to choose a young lamb and slaughter it.

"Let them eat and go," he declared. "Let this be a farewell dinner. I do not want any of their goats, or the foal, or anything else. Let them eat and go."

While Ali Bey was busy with the preparations, the other beys gathered under the shade of a big oak tree, going back and forth over the test. Even Alishan Bey, who was usually stern-faced, was talking and laughing, gesturing with his hands. The most enjoyable part of it was Chalum's urinating on the wolf, he decided.

"God knows, even a human could not find a better way to express his contempt," he said, shaking his head side to side. "It was astonishing, really amazing."

AREV

Sometimes, sitting by our tent in the quiet of night, lulled by a soft chorus of nightingales, I could hear the screeching wheels of an oxcart from across the valley.

When I was growing up, I had listened every Monday morning to the singing squeaks of the oxcarts laden with timber and produce from our orchards and bound for market. Now in the mountains of Kurdistan, time and distance vanished and I was back home. I did not know: Was I a crybaby, or was it because I was young that I could not hold back the tears flowing constantly from my eyes?

Happily, I was not alone. There were cattle that had been seized from Armenians, and also the other orphan boys and girls. I loved them all equally, and, as Guelo said mockingly, I even talked to the animals.

Then there was Arev, Osman's bride, so patient and brave. She had milky white skin and sweet, blue-green eyes. If she happened to meet me on her way to fetch water or do some other chores, her lovely face brightened and her eyes smiled. She and the other Armenian girls looked upon me as their big brother and protector.

What irony—me, a protector? Amid these scoundrels?

One day when Arev saw me outside, she said: "I am baking bread tomorrow and my mother-in-law will be at the other village. Come and have something to eat."

"It is dangerous. I do not fear for myself, but it may not be good for you. They do not starve us. Yes, we get only barley bread, but there is plenty of it and it fills us up. Arev, we are not starving!"

"I know, but..."

"But what?"

"When I think of you boys, I can't eat." Her eyes were wet.

"Don't cry," I said, touching her shoulder affectionately. "We are not as bad off as you think. After all, we are under the bey's protection."

"Damn their protection! They can keep it for themselves. Even

God forgot to protect His faithful believers!"

"Wonderful sister, I am so happy you are here."

"You will come tomorrow, won't you?" She smiled weakly, and we parted.

Occasionally after that, she would stand a broom against the outside wall, a signal for me to go into the house where her freshly baked bread, soaked with butter, was mine to take.

Often I was sent to accompany Osman with the herd late in the day, and although we did not talk about it, his attachment to Arev heightened my appreciation for him. Very early the next morning, we would bring the animals home for milking and catch up with our interrupted sleep. Toward evening, we would take our rations and again drive the herd to the grazing grounds.

The goats would be out front, running, fighting to take the lead, snatching a blade of grass from each other or nibbling a leafy twig. They had the stupid notion that foliage growing in easily accessible areas, that held no challenge, was not palatable. A leaf clinging to the high branch of a tree, dry and yellow, was far preferable to anything on the ground. But when they came upon a rugged hill or a bare cliff, their gluttony was forgotten for the joy of clambering over one rock to another. The sheep always followed the goats on level ground, but when it came to dangerous climbing, they were cautious, totally lacking a spirit of adventure.

As the animals became sated, they moved more slowly. They were calmer, and many sank to the ground on folded knees. Osman sat on a rock, took out his pipe, and started to play.

The shadows grew thicker and lengthened. Darkness settled into the valleys as crimson clouds streaked across the western horizon. The birds gathered and slowly drifted to the comfort of their nests. Flycatchers hung in the air. No light remained on the ground, but up above, very high in the sky, an eagle soared on wings tinged with gold—the sun was still there.

Now darkness like a blue veil wrapped itself around the world and the stillness became deep. Stars brightened and spread over us like gems on black velvet.

Before we turned in, Osman milked a ewe into a small tin cup, and we ate, sitting side by side—bread with fresh warm milk, passing the cup back and forth between us.

The dogs, as always, chose their own sentry posts to guard the herd. The two of us, some distance from each other, tied one end of a rope to the horns of the lead goats, and with the other end wrapped around our wrists, we lay down to sleep.

It seemed to me that the farther we were from civilization the larger and brighter the stars became, hanging so low I could almost pluck one from the sky; even the Milky Way was not vaporous and blurry, but a shining river of lights. It must be frigid up there, I thought, because it is cold down here.

Before long a misty fog blanketed our surroundings and nothing more was visible. The dogs were quiet, the night, tranquil.

⚶

To our surprise and disappointment, Khoren and I realized that Osman had stopped inviting us to his home for dinner. And Arev, who went often to the fountain to fetch water, a colorful shawl over her head in accord with Islamic law, had not been seen. I waited for the right moment to ask Osman.

"I thought you already knew," he said despondently. "Gulizar is not feeling well, she is a little sick."

"What is the matter with her?" I asked, concerned.

"She is going to be a mother."

"What's that to worry about? All women get pregnant sooner or later."

"You don't understand!" he blared, stabbing the ground with his staff. "There are some women who are like animals, like our workers.

They get pregnant and lo, one day, while carrying hay in the fields, they feel pain and go off to a corner and give birth to a crying baby as easily as a hen laying eggs. But Gulizar is not like them. As her time comes nearer, she is melting away." He started to cry.

I could not help thinking that these people killed tens of thousands of our men and women, threw them over steep banks into raging waters, starved them to death, and now he cries over one girl. I said nothing. That evening, after Khoren brought in the herd and we were sitting in front of our tent, I told him what Osman had said.

"I already knew all that," he said.

"How did you know?"

"Oh you city folk! Until you grow mustaches, you remain children!" He began to explain the signs of pregnancy in humans and animals and the mystery of conception, enlightening me with details.

"But how do you know all this? Who told you?"

"Nobody. I learned it from life, from the animals, and from my own experience."

When I smiled over his so-called "experience," he grew serious and continued. "Remember a month ago, when I was sent to Huni for fifteen days to replace Rufet Bey's shepherd because he was sick? Do you know who they gave me as a helper? Michig's daughter, Merchan."

"I do not know who she is."

"Too bad, you've missed a lot."

"Missed what?"

"How to explain so you can understand? Well…as I said, Rufet Bey borrowed me from his brother to work until his own shepherd was feeling better. When I got there, they asked if I knew my way around their fields and grazing lands. How would I ever know? So they decided: 'Michig's daughter will come along to help you.'

"We took the flock out together and back for several days. The Rufet Beys took really good care of me; they fed me well and even gave me a pair of new moccasins! But little did I know that luck was yet to smile at me.

"One day Merchan said, 'Haji, would you like to take the flock
to the Yayla highlands?' What was I to say? She was the one who
knew every inch of the surroundings, where to find the best grass, the
streams…'Okay let's go,' I said. We set out at daybreak and drove the
flock into the forest. The grass was knee high. We went farther until
we finally reached a clearing. At the top of a hill were a few meager
huts and a fenced area for the flock.

"'Is this what you call Yayla?' I asked.

"'Yes. We bring the herd here on the hottest days of summer.' We
drove the animals under the trees to rest. We put the dogs on watch
and stretched out on our backs, side by side. Merchan was chewing
the tip of a blade of grass and she started to tickle my neck with it,
then my ear. At first I pushed her hand away like brushing off a fly, but
when I lost my patience, I grabbed her wrist and twisted it. She turned
on her side and her breasts fell out of her shirt, milk white, firm and
beautiful. I stared with wide-open eyes, almost out of my mind. She
was as black as a gypsy, yet her body was white as milk. Who would
have thought…?

"'What are you looking at with your mouth open?' she said. 'If you
want to, you may kiss them!'"

"Did you kiss?" I asked, excited.

"Sure, I kissed…and that was not all. We hugged and tumbled
around on the grass. I used every trick I knew to prolong our 'fight.' I
got so much pleasure from touching her soft, hot skin, the roundness
of her thighs…I was trembling and afraid of her, but I couldn't stop
playing with her. I experienced such delightful feelings in my body
that I had not known until that day. Finally came a moment when
I said to myself, 'Let whatever happens, happen,' and took her in my
arms and…"

He stopped.

"Then?" I said, breathlessly. "What happened then?"

"That is all. If you want to know what happened, the next time a replacement shepherd is needed for Huni, you go and take the herd with Michig's daughter."

I tried very hard to make him talk, but he would not give in. He said not a word more and fell into his reveries, gazing into the green woods ahead.

"You know, Khoren, you lied," I said.

"How?"

"If they ask for a shepherd from Huni again, you won't give me a chance. You will go yourself."

He did not reply.

I thought of Michig's daughter day and night. Sometimes I even imagined taking her in my arms, kissing her neck, her cheek, and her breasts. I kept wishing that the Huni shepherd would get sick so they would have to call for help.

While I waited and hoped, the threshing was over and the wheat was brought in from the rooftops where it had been spread to dry. Flocks of migrating birds glided across the sky like caravans, and the trees turned bare. The winds rushing down the valley brought winter's calling card.

October. Vintage colors, overcast sky, rain. Sun rarely seen. Frost on rooftops and manure piles.

November. The smell of decaying leaves, fog, mold, wind, snow.

December. Blizzards, ice. Crackling fire. Oxen chewing their cuds outside the feed stalls.

January. A near-starving wolf howling from the top of a snowy hill, his snout pointed toward the village.

Arev was dead.

Osman came to us in tears one morning, saying: "Boys, my hearth is extinguished. Your sister has died."

Merciless God! Arev was dead from the pains of childbirth, and

Osman was weeping and pulling his hair.

"Boys," he said, wiping his tears repeatedly with his red handkerchief, "what does *Anoon Hor* mean? Those were the last words she uttered. My mother was with her, kneeling over her pillow. She knew that Gulizar was dying. She knelt beside her and told her, 'Gulizar, my beloved daughter-in-law,' she said, 'my soul, recite with me, *La ilaha ill-Allah* so that you will die a Müslüman and the gates of paradise will open before you, so that you will find peace after death. Gulizar, my daughter, my baby, say your prayers with me, *La ilaha ill-Allah…*'

" 'Anoon Hor,' she sobbed, turning her head right and left on the pillow.

" 'Gulizar, my baby.'

" 'Anoon Hor…'

"And she died. Boys, I kiss your feet, what is *Anoon Hor*? What does it mean?"

Khoren and I looked at each other, our eyes moist. What to say? How could we translate the words from our church that meant "In the name of the Father"? Arev had wanted to die a Christian, in a Turkish bed, while giving birth to a Turkish child, and with her last breath sighing "*Anoon Hor*" so that they would not, could not think, up there in heaven, that the Armenian girl had forsaken the faith of her forefathers.

But what to say to Osman? Now that we knew what had happened at Arev's deathbed, it was up to us to see that she was buried as a Christian and with a Christian prayer. We were quiet and wept a little more. I suppose we cried not only for Arev, but for all the other Armenian girls who had suffered the same fate.

"What can we do?" asked Khoren finally.

"A lot," I said. Then to the grieving shepherd: "Osman, my friend, do you really want to hear the truth? *Anoon Hor* is the Lord's Prayer of Armenians. Gulizar wanted to die with the prayer of her ancestors, that is, by reciting *Anoon Hor*.…If you respect her memory, do not bury her in your cemetery where she cannot rest, and where, so far as I know, she would not be permitted by the religion of Islam. Bury her in a quiet spot, perhaps under the shade of a tree, so her tortured body can rest in peace."

—⟶⊛⟵—

A few months later, when I was about to leave that village, I visited Arev's grave for the last time and repeated the prayer I'd recited at her burial. In my mind I pictured a corner of Osman's dimly lit house and the dying Armenian woman who, despite the urging of those around her, refused to die a Muslim and with her last breath murmured "Anoon Hor."

My eyes were wet and my heart was in turmoil remembering. I was holding a green branch. I tossed it over her grave and said: "Arev, precious sister, pure as the mountain snow, if you are able to see me or hear my prayer, please help…help me to be half as brave and faithful as you, because the road before me is long and thorny."

—⟶⊛⟵—

February. Winter was unleashed, deep and awesome winter. The snow crowning the high peaks moved down to the fields and the village, and the leaden sky, unwilling to be left behind, also descended to the earth. The wind howled with snow-laden breath, unending, slapping the glass panes of our windows and shaking the houses. Soon the hills beyond were obscured, leaving a white panorama stained only by the bluish shadows of the evergreens.

Weeks before, some of our workers had cleared their accounts with the bey, loaded their belongings on horses, and gone to Dersim. I had heard about the Kurdish city of Dersim, with its high summits and rebellious people, fearless and brave. How much snow had fallen there? I wondered. Those grounds had probably never been marred by the footprints of tax collectors or the Turkish police.

At rare moments, miraculously, when the wind stopped, the silence was so pervasive that one could hear the cracking of ice on the river and the whisper of snow slipping down through the evergreens. Deep in the earth, though, the springs did not freeze; our fountain steamed continuously and gave us comfort.

Finally the southeasterly wind brought longer days. Everything started to melt, only to freeze again at night and glisten in the moonlight. But by morning, after the sun was up and before the village awakened, an attentive listener could hear the approaching footsteps of spring.

We opened the doors of the barn and the oxen moved out like patriarchs, slowly, majestically. They closed their eyes to the sunlight and, with snouts steaming, inhaled the fresh air. The freed goats and sheep chewed longingly on the new tree sprouts. Ice on the nearby river broke into pieces and floated downstream, and when, on one melting and dripping day, the sparrows returned from the south, spring was officially declared in the mountains of Kurdistan.

On a sunny morning after one of his leisurely walks along the river, Ali Bey spoke to his longtime servant: "Musto, take somebody with you and go to Kel Dag tomorrow. Cut down a suitable tree that we can put across the river for a bridge."

"Yes, my bey, consider it done, my bey. Tomorrow I will fulfill your command."

The next day Musto, Guelo, and I went to Kel Dag. We made a fire there and toasted the breads we had stuffed into our sacks. I guarded the four oxen we'd brought to pull the tree—to make sure they would not stray or be attacked by wolves—while the Kurds chose a mighty cedar tree and downed it with their axes. They slashed off the branches, secured the trunk with thick leather strips, and fastened it to the bulls. We started for home, happy and singing.

Soon after, when Musto had planed one side of the trunk, he went to Ali Bey and announced that the tree was ready. We returned to Kel

Dag and the oxen noisily pulled the trunk to the riverbank. The men lowered it into the water and, with ropes from the other side, pulled one end to the opposite bank. The other end of the trunk remained on our side, and so the work was finished. I think no bridge in history was constructed in a shorter time.

"Now that the bridge is ready, take my uncle's calf across tomorrow," said Ali Bey. "We took care of him all winter, it is enough. Take him back."

Early the next day Musto led the black, skinny, one-year-old calf out of the barn. He cleaned and brushed him with quick, expert strokes and combed his hair.

"Let them see that we cared for him well. In a way we were smart to do it. We fed him our hay, but his dung remains with us."

He tied a braided rope of goat hair around the calf's neck and placed the other end in my hands. The bey, watching from the house, leaned out the window and called to me:

"When you see my uncle, tell him to come and visit us."

I rejoiced that they were sending me to Roosku. I confess now that I had fallen in love with the woman who lived there, Lutfiye, the wife of our bey's uncle.

The previous summer, when I'd been sent to deliver a message and had to pass their house, she was sitting out front. She called me to her, asked my name, introduced herself, and started a chain of questions.

"Are all of Ali Bey's three wives at home? Do they quarrel? Does Fetiye take good care of you and the other Armenian boys and girls? Do the wives cover their faces from you? Which hanum do you like the most? Which of us is more beautiful, Fetiye Hanum or me? Does she intend to have any children? Well, even if she does, she has little chance... after all, how many nights a week does Ali Bey sleep with her?"

After answering as well as I could, she led me to the kitchen, prepared some egg toast and set it before me. "Eat as much as you can.

Who knows how they treat you there."

She was a beautiful woman. Her skin was not like that of the Turkish hanums, who were pale from being covered and indoors most of the time; it was a healthy pinkish white, so transparent that you could see bluish veins, especially over the rounds of her protruding bosoms, like violet stems fallen in milk.

Her forehead was not very wide but it was clean and shiny. She spoke always with a smile and smiled with her eyes, too. Her hands were so soft and white that one would think she did not rub them together even to wash, and that somebody had anointed them with fine aromatic oils.

When I stood before her in my coarse, shabby shepherd's clothes, I was ashamed and confused, and lowered my head. I feared that if I looked directly at her, my eyes would betray the turbulence in my soul.

"Why are you afraid to look at me?" she asked softly.

"I am not afraid."

"Then why do you hang your head?

"......."

"Would you like to live in our house?"

"My master is back there."

"Won't he give you to me?"

"I do not know..."

She was so close to me that I could breathe the scent of her enchanting body, and I was nearly shaking.

"Run away from them and come here. Look at your clothes. I will take good care of you."

"......."

"Kiss my hand."

I kissed.

"Again!"

She put her face close to my mouth.

How much time had passed from that day—a month? a year? a

century? I had kept every detail of it in the deepest part of my soul, and from time to time I would take it out, live it again, and put it back like a happy dream.

And now they had put the calf's rope in my hand with instructions to take it to her house.

May the day you were born be blessed, dear calf.

I took the rope and we started our journey. My heart was singing. Spring flooded the land near and far…how suddenly it had come. Tree branches were swollen with new shoots to welcome the joyous birds; barn doors were opened wide and all the animals were now outdoors to drink in the life-giving sun. Small white clouds, like clumps of washed wool, sailed across the sky; the earth groaned and vapor rose from the thawing soil and quickly disappeared.

I walked, nose up, smelling the greenery, the sun pouring over my face and shoulders, and my heart sang like the Kurdish women chanting in the fields. I stopped at a creek by our clover field and washed as well as I could and straightened out my clothes.

Would I be able to see Lutfiye? Would she still be interested in me? If she asked again whether I wanted to stay there and be near her, I would shout, "Yes I do! Yes!"

I continued on. The road curved by the cemetery. The Kurds were afraid to pass it at night, believing that restless souls in the form of domestic animals would rise from their graves and wander about in the dark.

On a cold day last fall, the shepherd Chako got sick and almost died. He stayed all night in the water mill, freezing, because he was afraid to walk along the cemetery road to return home. Why should man be afraid of the place that holds the remains of his forefathers? When I die I would like, if possible, to be buried in earth that is saturated with the dust and bones of my ancestors.

True, this particular cemetery was a gloomy place, yet for some reason it was favored by the sheep. They liked to graze here all day and then settle down among the tombstones and weeds, knees folded, ruminating contentedly.

Finally we were near the famous bridge of ours, which I somewhat helped to construct. The roar of the river could be heard long before it was in sight. Although the water level was well below the bridge, occasionally a big frothy wave would slap the bottom of the tree trunk, leaving it wet and slippery.

Before long the melting snow and spring rains would raise the river enough to carry the bridge away, I thought. I stopped at the river edge, suddenly alert. The ground under my feet was shaking. Even without the calf, it would not be easy to cross that bridge. The churning water had bitten into the banks on both sides and reddened the river; the foam was yellowish and the current was fierce.

Each time a cloud eclipsed the sun, the earth darkened and then brightened again, changing the water back and forth from a dark to lighter color of blood.

I shortened the rope in my hand, recited "Our Father" and stepped toward the bridge. The calf, seeing the water, stopped, terrified. He dug his forefeet into the ground and refused to move, not one inch. I could not blame him; he had no sweetheart across the river, nor could he recite a prayer to muster up courage. Maybe a handful of salt would persuade him. I tied him to a large bush and returned to the village.

The bey was sitting at a window, smoking. "What happened? Did you deliver him already?"

"No, Bey, the river is high and the animal is afraid to go with me. I came back to get some salt. Maybe he'll follow me for the salt."

"Take the salt, and take somebody with you to help. One of you pull from the front, and the other push from behind." His voice was annoyed. "Do whatever has to be done and finish this job!"

"Is anyone available?"

"Take Osman with you. He came into the house a few minutes ago."

Osman was having his meal. I waited until he finished and had taken a twig from the fireplace to light a cigarette.

"Let's go," he said.

We reached the riverbank, untied the calf, and started toward the bridge.

Again the same. The calf would not move even one step. We held the salt under his nose. No help.

"You pull him from the front, I will push from behind," said Osman. We tried. No use.

"Stop. I know what to do. Come here and stand at his right side."

I obeyed.

He moved to the left side, pulled out his six-shooter, and, before I could open my mouth to speak, fired it under the calf's ear. The terrified animal, instead of running across the bridge as Osman had expected, jumped high up and fell into the water. His head came to the surface a couple of times, down, his muzzle was up to take a breath or two, but the current was so strong that his efforts to reach the bank were futile; he went under and disappeared into the muddy waters.

"What did you do, Osman!" I shrieked, and ran downstream, hoping that if he surfaced close to the bank, I could grab a leg or somehow help him out of the water.

After some minutes, when all hope was lost, I went back. Osman was sitting on the rocks at the head of the bridge, serenely having a cigarette, the smoking gun at his side.

"The big noise of this pistol was too much for that little calf," he announced, and slipped the pistol back into its holster.

Despite my distress, I could not help marveling at how easily the problem was solved in the mountains of Kurdistan.

When Abbas saw how enthusiastically we welcomed the early spring, he cautioned: "Beware the fifth of April, it separates the bull from its mate." Then, in stumbling Turkish mixed with Kurdish, he explained that once, on the fifth of April, he had taken his oxen to a distant field for sowing when a severe storm broke. He could not make it back home in time, and one of his bulls choked and died.

We listened with smiles and skepticism. I wanted to tell him that the animal must have died for some other reason but it seemed sense-less to offend him.

Fortunately I said nothing, because, on the morning of April 15, only ten days after his 'foreboding' date, the weather suddenly changed. Dark clouds blackened the sky and erupted into a violent storm. We were barely able to rush the herd home. The hills and valleys whitened and the air was so thick with snow it was hard to breathe.

We all fled indoors and were obliged to listen to Abbas intoning, "Didn't I tell you?" Only the dogs remained outside, unaffected by snow or cold, running to and fro, noses pointed to the incoming wind.

The blizzard did not last long; the wind subsided and although it was late, we took the herd out again to find some greenery under the snow. Doing this was essential, because by early spring no hay was left in the barn and the animals had ravenous appetites. Many of them had two hearts beating within them and ate to sustain two lives.

"We are lucky this year," said Osman, looking over the swollen sheep. "Almost all of them are pregnant and the birthing time is close."

After we brought the herd in, we lit a big fire and sat before the fire-place until I heard Fetiye Hanum calling: "Muselim! The bey wants some water. Go to the fountain and fill this jug."

She handed me a copper jug that was inscribed "In the name of Allah," no doubt engraved by an Armenian artisan.

It was cold. Nobody was outdoors. Only the fountain, twenty paces from the house, gurgled alone in the night. On the way back I heard a strange noise coming from the woods. I stopped and listened; I did not know what it was.

I took the water to the guest room, filled a goblet, and offered it to the bey, who covered his head with his hand and drank (to drink water with head bare is a sin).

When he had thanked God, wiped his mouth, and handed the goblet to me, I said: "Bey, on my way back I heard sounds coming from the forest but I couldn't make anything out. It was not a bird, not a fox or a wolf…it was more like a goat bleating, but the herd is in the barn already."

Fetiye, always alert and half listening, jumped up from the divan: "You must have left a goat behind when you brought the animals in. Go and look for it."

I hesitated, but she pushed me toward the door: "What are you waiting for? Get Osman and some of the other boys and do not come back until you find it!"

Osman, like Fetiye, was upset when he heard. We lit a large pine branch in the fireplace and started out.

"Where did the sound come from?" Osman asked.

"Behind the fountain."

"Let's take the dogs, they can help us. Call Komo."

Osman had barely uttered his name when Komo appeared, poking into my pockets for food. I leaned down, took his head in my hands, and locked my eyes into his: "Look, you fool, everything in its own time. Time to—"

Before I could finish, he tore away and raced into the woods.

"He found it, he found it!" shouted Osman. Holding the burning bough over his head, he rushed after him.

"Wharf, wharf, wharf!"

Running over the soft, wet snow, we came to the bellowing noise. In the yellowish light of the torch was a goat that had given birth to three kids and was hovering over them, yowling.

"I'll be damned! It's Chakur," Osman exclaimed.

Komo, head down and tail wagging, bounded back and forth around them, sniffing the helpless creatures that were totally new to him. With not a moment to lose, we tucked the kids under our coats to warm them. We started back home with the mother goat following us, but in a few moments she turned back to the spot in the woods where she had given birth. We went to her and let her see the kids, pulling them out enough to show that they were not left behind. Her motherly instinct calmed, she circled us and decided to come along.

Our entrance into the guest room was a jubilant parade of conquering heroes. We put the kids on the colorful carpet a few feet from the fire and covered them with a shawl. A few minutes later one of them died. When the other two had revived from their half-frozen state, I turned them on their backs and gingerly settled them on my lap as Osman slowly, very slowly, dripped warm milk over my little finger that I put in their mouths.

One hour later they had already wobbled to their feet and were under their mother, sucking her milk-laden teats.

"Let this be a lesson to you!" scolded Fetiye Hanum. "From now on, when you bring the flock in, make sure to count them." She sent us out.

Ali Bey called me back. "Muselim my son, take good care of these two kids. You found them, you saved them, they are yours. Let them be the yeast of your future flock."

"Thank you, Bey!"

Chakur's giving birth was like a signal to the other animals. One morning we went to the stable and found that the cat in the hayloft, three goats, and four ewes, had given birth overnight. During this period we did not let the animals graze too far away, because several times a day we had to shout for somebody to come and take another newborn home with its mother.

Osman taught me and Khoren how to recognize an animal that

was in labor and how to help it, if needed, on the spot.

"When you see an animal not eating, mouth pressed tight, panting, worried, you can be sure that she has labor pain and the time has come. From that moment, keep your eye on her, and if she lies down, get next to her, be ready. Very soon her water sac will burst open and the kid's two front feet will come out, and squeezed tight over them will be the nose and head. Once the head comes, you take hold of the feet and very slowly and carefully, you pull. With your left hand you catch the baby under its belly, just like I am doing now; with your right hand you wipe the nose and mouth, and then bend over and blow into its nose so that it can take the first breath….Then tie the navel so it won't bleed, pour a little salt over it, and set the kid in front of the mother goat so she can lick it dry and clean, and allow the two of them get acquainted. When the kid's hoofs darken—they are born with soft hooves—it will try to get up on its feet to suckle milk. When it is able to do that, and after it is well fed and the mother goat has had enough time to sniff it and verify that it is hers, you pick it up and tuck it into your big pocket if the weather is cold. If it is warm and sunny, you leave it with the mother."

Within two weeks more than 280 kids and lambs were added to our flock. They thrived in the warmth of the stable, feeding on their mothers' milk, and when spring had softened the outdoors, they were handed to me and Chako to be grazed. Our duty was to feed them and keep them away from the mother goats until the milkers had done their work. Now you will ask, How can the offspring get enough nourishment if their mothers have been milked? First, the newborns learn very fast how to graze and nibble grass. Then the mother goats, while they are being milked—in one of nature's miraculous and wondrous ways—are able to pull up some of the milk and save it for their little ones. When the newborn comes to her, wiggles its tail, and bumps its head to her underside a couple of times, the limp, emptied teats again swell with milk for the hungry offspring.

The sweetest times for me in the mountains were those days, after the milking was over, when we released the animals and mothers and kids would find each other, running to and fro, bleating, sniffing, bumping, pushing. A few moments later, almost instantly, everything would be calm and a great silence would come over the scene, now transformed into an outdoor dining area.

Sheep do not accept lambs that are not theirs and will not feed them. Goats are more tolerant and sometimes allow another's kids to suckle. However, goats are wiser than sheep. Sheep are born stupid and die that way, failing to learn anything from life's experience. They blindly follow anything that moves, even if it leads them to fire or death. During the summer, when the sun is hot, they tuck their heads under each other's bellies and form a circle where they remain, unmoving, until the heat subsides—which is why shepherds take them out at night.

I had started to say that Chako and I were responsible for grazing the newborn animals; actually, the kids were delegated to me and the lambs to Chako, because handling lambs required his greater expertise.

We gave them our best care until they were grown and had forgotten their mothers and their tasty milk. Now it was time for them to join the big herd. Our separate duties were over.

FOR MAKBULE

Some weeks earlier, in February, news had come that the Russian army had occupied Erzurum,[6] the regional headquarters of the Turkish 3rd Army, not very far from us.

Long before the Turks heard of this defeat, a great upheaval had shaken the snow-laden roads leading there and the surrounding

---

6 The Russians marched into Erzurum on February 16, 1916. In World War I Russia fought with the Allies (British Empire, France, Italy, United States) against the Central Powers (Turkey/Ottoman Empire, Germany, the Austro-Hungarian Empire, the Kingdom of Bulgaria) and other countries.

Kurdish-Turkish villages. One such village, Chobanle, with barely one hundred homes, had turned into a military center where vestiges of the Turkish army sought refuge and, after stocking some rations, headed inland to face the awful winter of Anatolia. Their misery was terrifying. Blackened by fumes, dirt, bitter cold and drought, emaciated by famine and privation, pursued by the enemy and frigid winds, tired, tormented, wounded, and dispersed, they came in hopeless lines and passed through, cursing. Whom to curse? What to curse? They did not know. All the blame was put on the "cause," but who or what was the cause? Nobody could explain. Half naked, faltering and bloody, without shelter, they died bleeding in the snow, calling for Allah. Horses and oxen fell, exhausted, and their owners did not stop to skin them. Old men and young boys who had brought animals and rations for the fighting men, expecting to return home safely, were also engulfed in the disaster and swept along with the hopeless fragments of the retreating troops.

The nation's dread of the Russian army rolled over the snow and reached our village, which was barely one hour away from Chobanle. "The infidels are coming!" were the words of the day.

Even during that agony, the government found time to hunt down the remaining Armenians for deportation. Our master Ali Bey and the other beys, unwilling to be deprived of their pretty young wives and unpaid workers, did not hand us over. But hundreds of other unfortunate Armenians were collected on the pretext of deportation and massacred on the frigid plains.

The starving wolves that had once ventured into the Kurdish villages to scavenge for food faced no peril now; their tracks did not appear in the snow near stables or on rooftops; all the roads were littered with corpses, so there was no need to endanger themselves.

Abbas's dog Chomar got rabies and had to be shot because he ran out and ate human flesh. At least, that was what poor Abbas said, weeping bitterly as he held the dog's head on his knees.

Ali Bey roasted all his chickens that died of disease and sold them to the soldiers at the roadside; he ordered a flour soup to be made in the largest pot available and sent a cup of the hot brew to each man. If their fervent gratitude and blessings counted for anything, I am sure that Ali Bey was forgiven for all his sins and even now is lying upon the most exquisite, carpeted lounge in the paradise of Islam.

Among the soldiers was a wounded Turkish officer who sought shelter and was permitted by the bey to stay in our stable. He was a frozen skeleton, a miserable ghost barely able to move and breathe. His blond beard was black with mud, and he moaned endlessly. He kept asking for water and drank insatiably. The bad smell coming from him terrified me.

In the morning the officer was dead.

After that incident, Ali Bey did not allow anyone to stay overnight in our stable. He called me to him and directed: "From now on, absolutely nobody is permitted to stay here. Warm them, feed them, and send them on their way; I want no further complications."

"Yes, *efendim*. Your wish is my duty."

And so we did. During the entire month of March, the plodding lines of wounded came and went, often putting me in a difficult position. They sometimes arrived when the sun was sinking behind the snowy hills and the wind was about to refreeze the barely melted ice. On those occasions, some of the rejected men would refuse to leave.

"Are you not Muslims? Have you no heart? We do not want anything from you! Where can we go on this cold night?...Do not forget that we are the soldiers of the government!"

Once, when I insisted repeatedly that they had to go, one of them reached for his gun.

"Oh, you are a *gavur* [infidel]."

By April 1916, the roads were opening up and the first groups of migrating Turkish villagers started to pass through, trailing the last remnants of the army. They came with huge, golden-colored oxen pulling wagons that were piled high with family members along with female sheep. They came night and day, one by one and in groups, and dispersed into the Turkish interior.

In those days of fear and waiting—who knows what ill luck brought him?—a *hoja* who was expert in circumcision showed up in our village. Our masters were delighted, and for the moment forgot the dangers surrounding them. Ali Bey sent messengers to his father and brothers.

Nine Armenian boys were collected from four villages to be circumcised. To this day I have not been able to figure out why the haste. Whatever the reason, there was no escaping our fate. Khoren wanted to flee, and Krikor hid behind the barley storage—I had to use all my ingenuity to get him out.

A curtain was hung at the top of the stairs on the upper floor of the house so the hanums could stand behind it and watch the ceremony. Most of us did not wear underclothing, but for this occasion underwear was distributed to those who had none. Heavy cloths were brought and spread on a dark and damp section of the ground floor, and after circumcising us without medication or any other balm, we were thrown into that cold, windowless corner.

Shepherd Osman was our "godfather" and advisor. He stood above us and recited a litany on the superiority of the Islamic religion, praising its paradise, the houris, and above all exalting the enjoyments promised after death to Muslims while we lay on the floor in pain, disconsolate and bleeding.

After some two or three weeks, we managed to stumble out into the sunshine where the fields and trees had already started to bloom. Thin shoots of wheat had pushed up through coffee-colored patches of earth, day by day growing taller and greener.

Our patrons found themselves facing a serious dilemma: to stay and hope for the mercy of the Russians, or leave?

One day Ali Bey called me in: "Muselim, what do you think? Shall we stay or pack up our things and get going?"

"Bey, that is for you to know."

"I want to know what *you* think."

"What can I say, Bey? If we stay, the enemy might come and kill us, and if we go they might not come at all and we could end up somewhere in misery."

"If they do come, do you think they will show mercy?"

"I do not know, I have never seen a Russian. I do not know about them."

"But as a Christian, would you talk to them in favor of us," his wife intervened, "or would you have them kill us?"

The treachery was obvious. Many suspected that the Armenians would side with the Russians against the Turks. "Bey," I said, ignoring her and addressing him: "Let us go. If I were in your place, I would not trust the enemy. Because of your graciousness we are true Muslims, and besides, nobody would pay attention to anything we had to say. Let's go. I have seen only kindness from you, and I will stay with you always. If you stay, I will remain with you here. If you decide to go, I will lead the family."

"Very good, my son," the bey replied, moved. "I was always sure of your loyalty. Go and pray that this heavy burden is lifted from our nation."

I bowed and left the room.

Weeks passed, weeks of uncertainty and anxiety. The deportees were arriving from districts closer and closer to us, and with them came the terror of Russian bayonets.

The deafening thunder of cannons reached our village. Several families took all their belongings and headed out to Dersim, abandoning their huts, leaving doors ajar.

On most mornings Khoren and I left in separate directions with the herd or flock assigned to us, and later circled so that we could join up and spend the day together. We needed to share our thoughts in safety. We agreed that, although tempting, it would not be wise for us to cross to the Russian side. That would mean leaving the girls and all the younger children behind, and the vengeful Turks would surely fall upon them after our escape. We agreed to stay together and await the outcome.

"Do you speak any Russian?" Khoren asked.

"No, you?"

"I don't either."

"When they come, how will we make them understand?"

"We'll say, 'Armeni, Armeni,' and cross ourselves. Surely in that huge Russian army, there must be a few Armenians. They'll take us to them and we'll explain everything—how they slaughtered all the Armenians in Turkey."

"Which one should we have them kill first?"

"There is no first or last. All of them."

"All of them?"

"All of them."

We were sitting at the riverbank, dreaming and planning, when a young Turk approached. He was alone. His belongings were in a dirty handkerchief tied to his walking stick, which he carried over his shoulder.

"*Merhaba*, hello," he said.

"*Merhaba*, where do you come from and where are you going?"

"Do you ask the bird in the sky where he comes from and where he goes?" And he started his history. He was a peasant from the out-skirts of Basen, about twenty-two. His face was dirty and vacant. He said he had already killed enough infidels in the Armenian massacre to assure his entry into paradise. Now he was bound for Ak-Dagh-Maden, where he had an aunt.

"Don't you have family, relatives? Where are they?" asked Khoren.

"My father died when I was four, and my mother is on the road behind me. I didn't wait for her. We passed a deserted Armenian village and slept in the ruins of a house one night. But in the morning, my mother could not continue. 'My son, my feet are gone,' she said. She wanted to rest there for a couple of days.

"What could I do? 'Yes, let us rest,' I said. I pretended to get some food and did not go back. As it is, I have a grudge against her."

He continued: "Since last summer, I had an Armenian girl named Makbule in the house. Ah, she was such a beautiful piece, a true houri. I was never able to control her or make her love me. But for six months I had the pleasure of her. She had a body as hot as fire and flesh as soft as a dove....Ah, what a sacred houri she was, what a promised houri of paradise."

"Where is she now?" I asked.

"Only Allah knows," he said dreamily. "She escaped. I suspect my mother helped her to get out. She was jealous. When I left the house, I locked the door behind me. When I returned that night, she was not there. I pulled out a knife and ran after my mother, but Allah held me back and gave me the heart not to spill Islamic blood....I have known many women, Kurd, Turkish, Circassian, Chechen...but that Armenian girl—oh, nothing like that Armenian girl. What a warm body she had. Give me a cigarette."

"If we had any cigarettes, we'd smoke them ourselves," Khoren answered, and started to undress.

We had no underwear; whatever we once owned had long since been worn to shreds. Now we were in clumsy overalls that Abbas's wife had fashioned for us from wheat sacks. Khoren unhesitatingly pulled off his garment, exposing to the June sunshine the fresh, slightly plump body of a boy of sixteen. I stared at him, trying to guess what he was up to. No luck. But he did not let me wait long.

"Aren't you coming in to swim, Muselim?"

"Sure I am." I started to undress.

"Both of you have such white skin," observed the Turk. "If you were not circumcised, I would take you for *gavurs*."

"You fool!" snapped Khoren. "Do you think that only the infidels have light skin? You should see the hanums!"

"Are they beautiful?"

"Beautiful is nothing," said Khoren, rolling his eyes rapturously. "When they take a bath in the hayloft, Muselim and I watch from a small hole on the wall…how they scrub their arms, how they soap themselves in the tub. We see their nakedness, white and soft…"

Cutting off his words at the most exciting point, he started to walk toward the river, to a deep spot where we'd built a makeshift pool with a circle of stones and branches. Once in the water, Khoren jokingly fell on me and pretended to push me under.

"Pray that the Turk comes in to swim with us."

"Why? What for?"

"We're going to choke him."

"Are you crazy?"

"Did you forget Makbule?"

"What if somebody shows up?"

"Who's to come? Almost nobody is left in the village and anyone there is busy."

"What if we are not strong enough? Besides, that scoundrel is lying, he's making things up," I tried to dissuade him.

"We are two and he is alone. Listen to me or I'll not speak to you again," and with a heave he dunked me under.

When I rose up to take a breath, the Turk was already in the water, examining us with lewd eyes and touching our bodies in pretended play, his mouth watery.

"You didn't finish telling me about the hanums," he reminded us.

"What do you want me to do? Hold you by the hand and take you to the hole in the wall?" snapped Khoren.

Then he proposed a contest to see who could stay under water the longest. First the Turk and me, then the Turk and Khoren, again the Turk and me. Amid the noise and splashing, Khoren told me to be ready, and plunged below. A second later the Turk let out a terrible scream and fell over on his back; instantly I threw myself on him, shaking, and with all my strength forced his head under the water. The Turk struggled, scratched, grabbed hold of our arms, gasped to say something, but in vain; Khoren and I managed to keep his head under the water as large, thick air bubbles started coming to the surface.

"One minute more!" yelled Khoren, heaving. "One minute more and we will send this dog to…another…world!"

In truth the Turk was weakening; he was barely struggling now, the air bubbles were diminishing, getting smaller, and soon they were tiny, almost none to be seen, and then they were gone.

Khoren and I climbed out of the water, hurried into our clothes, guided the animals along, and left the valley behind us.

That afternoon, when we were comfortable and safe, having our bread under the pines, I noticed that Khoren was eating with his left hand.

"Did you hurt your right hand?" I was concerned.

"No, it's nothing…it's dirty."

"So wash it!"

"I have to wash it at home with soap." Seeing that I was puzzled, he added: "Remember when the Turk let out that awful scream?"

"Yes."

"It was I who made him cry like that. I was afraid we wouldn't be able to overcome him so I squeezed his testicles with all the strength I had, with my right hand."

His words were barely uttered. We could not eat. It was getting dark anyway. We took the herd and headed home.

⌐➤❀➤⌐

I was to take a packet to Ali Bey's brother, Kiazum, and one of the villagers was assigned to accompany me so I "would not get lost." En route we passed the ruins of a small Armenian village, and although it had not been torched, the houses were shells—the windows, doors, lumber, everything of conceivable use had been taken. Judging from the rubble of mud bricks, it had not been a prosperous community, yet not one stone was left unbroken.

It was Komushdoon—literally, "House of the Water Buffalo"— and according to my Kurdish guide, it was famous for one thing. "They made yogurt from water buffalo milk that was so thick, you could roll the jug down a hill with the lid open and nothing spilled out."

He told me that our water buffalo and her calf were part of Ali Bey's share of booty from that village. It was an aging animal, languid, and with little milk. But everybody liked her because she was a mild, congenial beast from an exotic, distant land, and so she was looked upon as something otherworldly.

There were no other water buffaloes in our area, probably because the dry climate and rough terrain were not favorable; they needed wet, marshy grounds to thrive. Our buffalo's former home was barely twenty yards away from the river, with murky, soothing pools where these huge, strong animals could wallow on hot days, burying their bodies in muddy clay to protect their skins from cracking.

Now, during a very hot summer, our animal's hide, which was almost hairless, started to dry. The bey ordered a large hole dug near the fountain in hopes that the spilling waters would collect and form a mud lake.

"Let the water buffalo cool off in there, and use any excess water for our clover field," he ordered.

But the thirsty soil sucked up the water, and the shallow crater did not become a pool. The poor animal tried to sink into the wet pit a few times but the water was not deep enough to cover her huge back, her most vulnerable area, and it remained totally exposed. Khoren and I poured buckets of water over her but eventually we gave up. When she lay in the pool, the water moved up and down rhythmically with her breathing.

Uncle Hussein marked her suffering and announced that her back had to be periodically smeared with bear fat.

Where to find bear fat?

Ali Bey sent emissaries everywhere, to the villages of his father, brothers, and friends. All of them returned empty-handed.

The animal's back remained dry, burned by the sun and stung by insects.

Light and hope came from a totally unexpected source. Zindi, who guarded the high plateau, came to report that a bear had stolen one of the hives from Ali Bey's bee house.

"How do you know it was a bear and not thieves?" we asked.

"At first I suspected it was some two-footed animal," he said, scratching his thick neck. "I loaded my rifle and waited."

"Did anybody show up?"

"Yes, but it wasn't a man, it was a black bear as big as a water buffalo."

"Did you shoot?"

"Shoot! Am I crazy? You can't kill a bear with a light rifle."

"Fool! Coward! You missed the opportunity…"

"*You* are the fool! Would you dare to fire?"

"Sure I would!"

"Yes, but you'd leave your mother weeping and your children orphans."

The argument was cut short when the bey appeared. He was about to send a team of hunters to the plateau, but just then Guelo came running in, breathless, saying that a bear had broken into the millet field. He had trampled all around, eaten a lot of grain, and dunged all over. Then, with a dramatic flourish: "He had dunged a mountain high!"

"Is there heavy damage?"

"He flattened half the field!"

Despite hearing this, the bey was pleased, visualizing a twofold benefit: he would address the problem of the stolen beehive and ruined crops, and the bear would also provide needed fat for the water buffalo's back.

A meeting was held. That night, four armed men were to take positions at each corner of the millet field and wait for the bear. When it showed up, they would call upon Allah's protection and fire all together, so that at least one shot would hit the animal.

When darkness fell, everyone gathered in the village center, weapons in hand. Musto suggested taking one of the dogs along but the bey forbade it.

"Suppose," he said, "the dog catches the bear scent and runs ahead of you and attacks him. What happens then? Either the bear escapes or he fights the dog, so you won't be able to shoot for fear of hitting the dog. And if, God forbid, anything happens to my dog, you will not escape my wrath."

Nobody answered. Each man took some food in his belt and they left. A little later the bey and his wife retired to their room as the lights of the house went out.

We, who had the least interest in the bear, could not sleep. We sat in front of our tent, enjoying the cool breeze from the valley and the faint call of an owl coming from the thick foliage. We were not the only ones among the village inhabitants who were sleepless; two Kurdish women came over to join us.

"Muselim," said Khoren, "let's leave and see what's happening at the millet field."

"Are you crazy?" I said. "If they fail they'll blame us, claiming we went and frightened the bear."

The women smiled weakly at each other, not having understood us.

Just then we heard two shots and voices shouting.

"They must have found the bear and killed him," said one of the women.

"I doubt it," I said. "Even if it was dead, the Kurds would not stop until each man had his turn firing into the animal. We heard only two shots. They haven't killed anything."

Minutes later the men returned and explained that they had fired at a dark shadow. They could not tell what they hit because there was no carcass at the site where they had fired. They'd gone over and looked to make sure.

The bey was awakened by the noise and stood at the window: "What happened?"

"We don't know yet," said Musto. "We saw something and shot at it, but…"

"Aren't you ashamed? Four of you can't kill one bear! Damn!"

Early the next morning Shepherd Osman brought the herd in from grazing and let them rest in the shade. The sun was newly up. Although I had not slept, I was not tired. I told Osman about the night before. He listened very closely and came up with an inspiration.

"Get the dogs and let's go look for him."

"The bey does not want us to take the dogs along."

"We will take only one, and we won't tell him."

"What if something happens to it?"

"What can happen? Nothing will happen."

"The bey thinks that if the bear is wounded he'll be crazed and might harm the dog."

"If he is wounded and bleeding all night, he is either weak or dead. And if he is not wounded, we won't find him anyway. Let's take Komo and have some breakfast before we go."

We gulped our food and Osman left. Fetiye Hanum was at the window, calling out the daily instructions. I stepped forward: "Hanum, please let me go to the millet field with Osman, we think that the bear last night—"

Ali Bey, standing behind his wife, broke in. "Go, my son, go, but be careful."

Osman had shoved a big pistol into his belt, and an axe with a long handle hung from his shoulder. We set out.

When we were close to the millet field, he spurred the dog: "On you go, my lion, and find that bear!"

It was not hard for Komo. He turned, zigzagging a couple of times and hurtled into the thick bushes. We ran after him. He stood rigid, barking at a pool of dried blood. The blood trail led us into the woods where, apparently, the bear had stopped for a while and continued toward the valley. Looking down from the valley rim we saw the river flowing like a stream of molten silver, and on the pebbles bordering the water was a huge shape, black as coal, as large as a bull, lying motionless. We whooped a cry of surprise and ran down. The dog was far ahead of us. He circled it, sniffed, growled, determined it was dead, and stood aside. I called him to my side and ruffled his head: "Komo, you are a one and only! There's no other like you!"

"All wounded beings, human or animal, crave water when they are wounded," Osman said. "And when they drink, they die. That is why this troublemaker tried so hard to reach the water."

"What are we going to do now?" I asked.

"I will wait here. You go home and tell them."

"I'll take Komo so the bey will not know we brought him here."

"Take him, I do not need him anymore. I will start skinning the bear—it's a huge beast, it will take a long time. Tell them it is the size of a water buffalo. Let them bring some horses and mules to carry the meat and the fat. What we really need is a wagon, but there is no road to pull a wagon."

I reached home before noon and spread the news. Everyone was excited. Messengers were sent to the fields and hills to inform the heroes of the night of their victory. Shevku hurried to the edge of the cemetery and bellowed to his father who lived on the opposite hill. A Kurdish boy ran to one village, others flew off in different directions, and soon the whole world knew.

When I returned to the river site, people from all around had come to get some bear fat. They complained of rheumatism, back pain, chronic itchiness, and the bear fat was balm for all such ailments.

Our servants helped Osman finish the skinning and then attacked the meat and the fat, using heavy swords, hatchets, and axes to whack, cut, and distribute the pieces. Sulo, exhilarated, lit a fire with the brush and twigs we gathered from the ground and started to cook.

When the bear's stomach was slashed and opened up, the men found a doughy mass of beeswax as large as the head of a lamb. We took it home to show to the bey and the hanum—evidence of the theft from their bee house.

"Don't the bees sting the bear when he eats their honey?" I asked Osman.

"The bear submerges the hive in water and kills the bees before opening it," he said.

The men put the bear's head and skin together, loaded it on a mule, and brought it home. It was salted. Eight days later they stretched the black form under the sun so it would dry without shrinking.

When it dried, the servants nailed it to the wall of the bey's guest room so that when he entertained his visitors and related the story, he could sweep his arm toward the wall, saying: "And here is the hide of that beast."

The water buffalo and the calf, plundered from Armenians, now had their backs generously greased with bear fat. The next day Sulo and his ten-year-old son were severely ill from eating too much bear meat. The son died before nightfall.

I returned from the grazing hills one day to find that Ali Bey was sick in bed. A doctor had been summoned.

"Doctor!" I burst out. "Are there doctors in these mountains?"

"There is an infidel living near Mad Shero who knows about medicine. We sent for him."

Mad Shero was the most bloodthirsty, ferocious, heartless, Turk

I had ever known. I knew that the "infidel" who was called had to be younger than twenty, otherwise he would have been killed. Ali Bey was Shero's friend and if the Armenian was not able to cure the bey, I worried for him; he could suffer Shero's wrath.

I was buried in my thoughts when the reputed doctor arrived. He was a boy named Murad, barely eighteen, who had worked in a pharmacy for six months in his hometown, running errands back and forth, and was now a "doctor."

I understood why he had assumed that title. In those days, many of us grasped at any thin opportunity to stay alive. Some had presented themselves as shoemakers, some as seamstresses, tailors, blacksmiths, carpenters, and some as doctors. The Kurds had no artisans or professionals. All the skilled crafts had been performed by Armenians, so taking on such identities was readily believed and a way to survive.

He was a light-faced young man, well mannered, still wearing the European clothes of his home. He asked the bey to open his mouth. With the confidence of a veteran physician, he used a spoon handle to press down his tongue. He examined his throat and placed slender fingers on his wrist to check the pulse. His expression was serious.

They were impressed. He played the role of doctor very well.

He had no medicines. He recommended rest, primarily, and a dressing to reduce the fever. Hearing the word "dressing," the women looked at each other, puzzled.

"What is dressing?" asked the bey's wife.

"Ah, forgive me," he said, and explained. Again, they were impressed.

During the night, however, the bey worsened and started hallucinating.

The doctor was called out of bed and taken to his side.

"I know of a medicine, but how could I put my hands on it?" he said, soberly.

No one spoke.

He meditated. He asked if they had any lemon citron.

No. "Nothing like that here."

"Maybe the elder bey has it," someone suggested.

Probably yes; a man would be sent for it.

The elder bey lived in Huni, and the Kurdish servants, as before, refused to go there at night because the road led past two cemeteries. In the darkness, the restless and sometimes vengeful souls of the dead rose out of the ground in the form of animals and went after passersby. Wasn't it last winter that a little dog followed the Kurd named Sedat and transformed him into a rotting corpse? They shuddered, recalling the incident.

Fetiye Hanum, the bey's senior wife, threatened to inform the government so that the servants of military age would be sent to the battlefield; the others, she would personally throw out of the house to die of hunger.

No use.

She promised to give them anything they wanted.

Nobody moved.

"Tomorrow in the daylight, even if you send us to hell we will go… but at this time of night…" said Musto, looking down at his feet.

"Tomorrow, the next day, the day after, and every day in creation, you all go to hell!" Fetiye cursed and returned to the sickroom, crying.

The door was ajar, and when I looked in she was still crying. I went to her.

"Hanum."

"What is it? What do you want?" she said, her voice shaky and annoyed.

"Hanum, I will go."

"You? At night? Alone?"

"Yes."

"Aren't you afraid?"

"I am not afraid of cemeteries and evil spirits; I am only afraid of humans. Even so, I believe that if I explain that I am on my way to get medicine for Ali Bey, I will not be harmed."

"Then go, and may God protect you. We will never forget this."

"What shall I tell the elder bey when I see him?"

"Tell him his son is ill, he has a high fever. The doctor recommends citron, lemon sour. If he has any, we need a little. When the bey recovers, he'll buy some and return it."

I was tying up my moccasins when she added: "Don't forget to stress that the medicine is for his son, Ali; otherwise even if he has it, he will not give it to you."

I started out. It was a moonlit night with not a soul around. As I said, I feared men more than ghosts. Although I had nothing but my moccasins and the ragged clothes on my back, a robber could easily kill me and throw my body into a ditch. Who would ask questions?

One less Armenian. Who would care?

I passed our village cemetery without incident and came to the water mill. No sign of anybody and no sound from the millstone. I crossed the bridge and saw the lights of Rooskn, and could make out the villa where Lutfiye Hanum lived.

What was she doing at that moment? I tried to guess. Probably in bed, swathed in a sea of silk and muslin and dreaming of flaming loves, I said to myself. If she asks me again to be one of her servants, I will accept.

I walked fast, lost in fantasy. The road wound through the hills and the moon shone brightly on the bare rocks, turning them almost white. The valleys were dark with no greenery, black and mysterious.

I started to sing. It was a melancholy tune with a simple story of broken love. All the songs I knew—Armenian, Turkish, or Kurdish—were sad, inspired by homesickness, or lost love, or the unfortunate. I figured that when people were lucky, they were so busy being happy that they didn't have time to create songs.

I arrived at Huni, shepherd's staff in hand. It was a beautiful summer resort with about fifty houses, known for its mulberry trees and a small lake, where the elder bey's pigeons congregated all day.

Opposite was Ibrahim Bey's house, with a light in a window. I was hoping to finish my errand quickly and return home when the village dogs attacked me, and if not for my heavy stick, they would have chewed me up on the spot.

Someone came out to investigate the racket.

"Hey, who are you?" he shouted.

"I am Muselim, Ali Bey's servant. Call off these dogs!"

"What are you doing here so late? Can't you wait until morning?"

"No. I need to see Ibrahim Bey about his son."

"I'll be damned. The bey is awake. He is in his nightclothes, sitting at the window."

I went to the window and greeted the bey with a deep, reverent bow: "I am Muselim, Ali Bey's servant."

"What do you want? Why are you here at night?"

"Fetiye Hanum sent me. Ali Bey is ill. We called a doctor who recommended lemon sour. I came to borrow some if you have any. I bring respectful greetings, the hanum kisses your hands."

"What is wrong with Ali? What the hell does he have?"

"He has high fever; when I left home he was hallucinating…"

"Let him croak!" he erupted. "Let him perish, do you understand, let him die! Keeper of three women! Huh! Husband of three wives… Who does he think he is? He dares to compete with his father? Just because his father has three wives, does he also need to have three wives? Well, now, everyone can see the result!"

He paused, took a deep breath, collected himself, and continued:

"One Chechen, one from Laz, and one Armenian! What is that? Is it a collection or a public display? One was not enough, two were not enough, and so he took a third. Who is he to sleep with three wives?"

I listened silently to his outrage. The man was deeply offended, viewing his son's three wives as a brazenly competitive attempt to match him. Venom had collected in his heart, and here was an opportunity to spit it out, hoping perhaps that I would carry it back to his ailing son.

"Were you afraid of the dogs?" he suddenly said, changing the subject.

"Yes, Bey, I was."

"With that faint heart, how did you manage to climb up the mountain? You and your countrymen (he knew I was from Shabin Karahisar)... didn't you know that the State would squash you with one finger, like a bedbug?"

Silence.

"Speak! Give an answer!"

"What can I say, Bey? My family, my brothers, and, as you say, my countrymen did not consult me when they climbed up to the fort."

"Huh, you managed well to get out." He paused, coughed, and reflected.

"Go to sleep now. Tomorrow we will go together to see Ali."

"Forgive me, Bey, I cannot wait until tomorrow. I promised the hanum to return tonight."

"In that case, go! Get lost!"

I bid him goodnight and moved away, but he stopped me.

"Come to think of it, why did they send you here? They have plenty of Kurds around, what's wrong with them?"

"They are afraid to pass the cemeteries."

"Aren't you afraid?"

"I am not afraid of dead people, Bey."

"Even if they turn into ghosts?"

"Even if they *are* ghosts."

"I ought to go over there and take you away from Ali and keep you for myself," he said, half to me and half muttering to himself.

I rushed home and told Fetiye Hanum, who was waiting anxiously, that the bey had no lemon citron.

The Turkish hanum, who knew her father-in-law well, asked me to tell her exactly what had happened and to leave nothing out.

"Nothing important. When I got to Huni he was sitting at the window; I spoke to him from the street and conveyed your greetings, and—"

"Forget that. What happened next?"

I related everything, word for word, but I did not repeat his oath to "let him die."

Fetiye listened and cried.

"He said he would be here in the morning."

"It does not matter now," she said, heartbroken.

I left to get some sleep.

The next day, just after sunrise, a boy rushed in and announced that the elder bey was on his way. "I saw him passing the river on his big red horse and with two of his dogs," he said in a single breath.

We were upset. We were afraid of him. He was like an Old Testament Jehovah, a stern and bearded old man with his own rules and philosophy.

When his horse stopped at our door, we ran to lead him and his dogs to the guest room. Almost immediately he went to see his son. He shut the bedroom door. We remained outside. We could not hear what passed within.

By afternoon Ibrahim Bey was on his horse, ready to leave. Fetiye Hanum came out to bid him farewell, her eyes swollen from crying.

The bey had advised his son, at bedside, to leave the village and escape the path of the enemy. He declared that his son's illness was caused by having three wives. I recalled his words: "One Chechen, one Laz, and one Armenian girl!...Huh!"

Three days later, like a candle extinguished, Ali Bey was gone. Loud sounds of mourning came from his bedroom. The dogs in the hallway started howling. The sad news spread everywhere. Grieving friends and relatives streamed into the village and our home. Every time a newcomer arrived, the laments rose to a crescendo and then diminished until another came to pour oil on the fires of sorrow.

By noon, Mehmet Bey arrived from Roosku with his charming wife, Lutfiye Hanum. Fetiye fell upon her, sobbing: "My Lutfiye, your brother-in-law died, what am I to do? I am alone; who will protect me now?"

Gesturing toward us, the negligible Armenians, she moaned: "They also got sick, we left them in cold, dark corners, but they recovered. I cared for your brother-in-law day and night, I hovered over him, I did everything possible. Couldn't fate have taken one of these boys instead?" And she started beating her knees.

"Don't cry. This is how your destiny was written. No one can understand the will of Allah," said Lutfiye, trying to console her.

This hanum did not pretend sorrow like some of the others who dabbed handkerchiefs to their faces at every turn. She wore a purple coat of fine velvet and was ready for every need. She took over the memorial dinner, had the oven fired, and helped the girls bake bread.

After the burial, she stayed on for several days. When she met me in the hall, she said: "I will talk to Fetiye and ask her to give you to me. Do you want to come?"

I did not answer.

The one who mourned Ali Bey in an extreme, most heartbreaking way was his young Armenian wife, Kamile. She wept day and night, had fainting spells, and visited his grave twice daily.

True, we more or less liked Ali Bey—we owed our lives to him—but her excessive grief troubled us. After all, he *was* a Turk. The other girls, especially Mariam, were hostile toward her, and I had to stop them from spitting at her.

How to explain Kamile's behavior? Maybe she feared her uncertain future—being married off to a common shepherd or a foul-smelling Turk, or handed to a random Kurd as a gift. Perhaps she truly loved the Bey; it was not the first time that had happened.

Like the servant girls, Fetiye was upset and did not hide her feelings: "Well, that's enough, everything has a limit," she berated Kamile. "You could not have loved my husband more than I..."

Mariam witnessed the scolding and almost jumped for joy; she left her work to run and tell the others.

On a cold morning the following week, we found our dog, Bogar, dead in the courtyard. Somebody passing there during the night, perhaps a fugitive soldier, must have fired a bullet into the animal. The roads were thick with the remnants of war. Day and night, the escapees and wounded continued to come, human misery and wretchedness, begging for a cup of soup or a night's shelter.

With Ali Bey gone, the Kurds, who formerly had robbed the Turks on the pretense of selling or trade, became more aggressive. They left their homes and fields, took up arms, and went "hunting," alone or in groups, hiding along the road from Erzinjan, attacking, robbing, killing. As the defeated Ottoman forces fled, they were joined by hordes of Turkish civilians swarming along the roads, flanked by yellow oxen and herds of black sheep.

Amid all this, Ali Bey's youngest brother, Nazum, arrived unexpectedly, announcing: "I came to help and protect you."

Fetiye was touched and grateful. She started looking after her appearance and even courted her brother-in-law. But he paid no attention. He would disappear for hours and, upon returning, ask the servants to prepare hot water for his bath.

The news spread throughout the village, where only one question mattered: "Where does he go and whom does he sleep with?"

The villagers spied on him and found that he went to Roosku and had been staying at his uncle's house.

"Ah, Lutfiye is there," cried Fetiye. "I did not expect this of her!"

Still, she had hopes of marrying Nazum, but he was not interested.

Emboldened, she faced him: "What does Lutfiye have that I don't have?" she demanded.

"Lutfiye has grown daughters, you have none."

Fetiye's jaw dropped. She was astonished.

"This week I will marry her daughter, Merouze," he continued.

"What will your wife say when she hears about it?"

"She is not here. She will find a closed book. She will be upset and cry a little, and then accept it. What did you do when your husband married two other women after you?"

"He had reason. We had no children, we could not have any."

"Our case is similar. My wife gave me two daughters, but I want a son," Nazum told her.

Fetiye was consoled enough to make up with him. "And I blamed Lutfiye!" she confessed.

In truth, I was happy to hear the explanation; the thought of Lutfiye in Nazum Bey's bed had wounded me. But how was I to know that he was after her daughter?

Soon after, the elder bey, Ibrahim, everything forgiven and forgotten, arrived at our village. Whether he was motivated by fatherly feeling or the prospect of a feast, I do not know, but he braved the frigid winter and snow to celebrate his youngest son's second marriage.

Ibrahim Bey had seen much of life; he had traveled to many places, even to Constantinople to have dentures made. He was not a radical Muslim. He had divided his wealth—four villages—among his children while he was alive to prevent arguments at his burial; he had given our village, Aghullar, to Ali Bey.

He enjoyed life and lived it to the fullest. Happy with women and raki, he did not await the rewards of an afterlife. He would down the raki with one gulp, sit with his feet tucked under him, and order the servants to bring his saz.

He knew a single monotonous tune. To help at the bey's drinking feast was torture because he expected everybody to listen to him, serve him appetizers, and care for his dogs, Moris and Jibo. This chore was given to me on a freezing day with icy winds so strong that I could hardly breathe. I took the dogs to the stable and waited a while, and after striking them lightly a couple of times to make them obey, took them back to the bey. They both immediately started to bark at me.

"You bastard, you beat my dogs!" the bey shouted angrily.

"No Bey, I did not."

"Am I to believe you or my dogs? My dogs never lie!" And he unleashed his sack of curses at me, my religion, beliefs, parents, race, leaving nothing untouched.

Later that day, when the winds had calmed, I went to the river to fish with a few of the Kurdish boys. The current was steady but calm. Close to the bank, where the current was very slow, a school of fish stood almost motionless. I moved silently, aimed my pistol to the center of the group, and fired. A tower of water erupted and showered down. When the turbulence settled, the fish floated to the surface, white bellies up.

"Boys, collect them fast, before they regain consciousness!"

We used long, leafy branches to catch them and pull them ashore.

"This for me…this for you…this for Bado…"

We separated, each happy with his bounty, and headed home.

"What are those?" asked Sehel, who was frying dumplings in the kitchen.

"They're fish. I just caught them."

"What are you going to do?"

"What do you mean? What do we do with fish? I'll clean them and grill them. The bey will have them for his appetizer."

"The bey does not like fish."

"He does! I know. I have seen him having fish and enjoying it."

"I told you, the bey does not eat fish, he does not like it. We do not eat fish either."

"Then I'll grill them on the fire and eat them myself."

"The fish from that river are not for eating. Take them out, take them out of this house, out of this kitchen! Give them to the dogs!

No, don't give them to the dogs either, throw them out, throw them back into the river! Do whatever you want! Who asked you for fish! Take them out of this kitchen, do you hear? Take them out now! Fast!"

"But why?"

"Why? Why do you ask? I tried not to say anything, but you force me. You are to blame, it's your fault that I am forced to speak! Are you going to eat the fish that fed on the flesh of your mother? Last summer, this river was filled with Armenian corpses. How do you know that your mother's body was not with them? You yourself told us that the soldiers threw her from the cliffs to drown with your other relatives! How can you offer us the fish that came from that water! And then you want to eat them yourself? What a stomach, what an appetite, *Allahum*, my God!"

I ran out with the fish and fell into the snow, weeping uncontrollably, calling for my mother.

CHAPTER 4

A New Home, 1916

The weak sun and melting snows brought longer lines of soldiers, with many more wounded and sick, straggling past our village, warning: "Escape if you can. The infidels are coming!"

We prepared to leave.

It was not easy. Family belongings were organized for days with little sleep for anyone. We bought several horses for the hanums to ride. After all, they were the wives of beys, accustomed to feathered pillows and soft rugs; they moved only between the kitchen and the guest room and had almost forgotten how to walk; and they debated endlessly whether to travel singly or all together.

Finally the bags were tied, loaded on wagons, and the wheels greased when Ibrahim Bey arrived to bid us farewell and dispense his instructions.

I saw Musto outside looking bewildered and anxious.

"What is it, Musto? You seem lost."

"It's that…"

"You don't know what to do after the bey leaves?"

"I think I'll go back to Dersim."

"Are you sure Dersim is safe from the Russians?"

"*Wallahi,* I swear, I don't know. If they come as friends, we will greet them with salt and bread. If they are the enemy, we will face them with rifles."

He lowered his head and walked to the stable.

Knowing the outlook ahead was bleak, we left together in one large group. After a long and burdensome journey we arrived at our temporary quarters in Bogaz Veran and settled into an almost palatial house set aside for us by the well-known Alishan and Haidar beys.

Everyone had come along with us except for Ali Bey's brother, Rufet, who preferred to stay home and confront the Russian army, if need be, rather than suffer the hardships of winter on icy roads.

Events proved that he chose well. The Russians did not come. And although the remnants of the Turkish army occupied our former village—and set fire to the entire oak forest before moving out—Rufet was spared a miserable trip, and his financial loss was minimal.

Within days of our arrival Fetiye was at the window, peering at the mountain peaks, weeping and lamenting her lost home and husband.

Ali Bey's youngest brother, Nazum, had managed to acquire one of the vacant positions of mudur, the district administrator, in the region of Zara. His happiness knew no bounds. His first and second wives quarreled endlessly because they were forced to share a single room, and even refused to sit together at table. Nazum Bey escaped from the hell of his family on the pretext of heavy responsibilities in his new position: "I'll get settled and prepare accommodations for you," he promised, and left.

Barely one month later, he returned with two Kurdish servants to help the family pack up to join him: his two wives and two daughters, his brother's widow, Fetiye, and three servants to attend her.

But before we were able to leave, Nazum Bey decided to send the grieving widow back to her father. Her eccentric behavior ("She wanted me to steal a goose from a town official") and her inappropriate efforts to find a husband threatened his honor and the security of his new post. He allowed us, the Armenian servants, to decide whether we wanted to go back with Fetiye Hanum or remain with him.

Mendoohi and I preferred to stay.

We did not know when we might ever see her again; as she was about to leave, we went to kiss her hand. She was moved and blessed Mendoohi, promising to call her back some day. I waited for her to extend her hand to me to kiss, but she unexpectedly erupted: "May the bread I fed you be damned!" barely suppressing her tears.

I was startled and upset, not for the curse, since I had worked more than enough to earn my keep, but because she had been kind to me in the past. Sehel, who knew her well, once told me that if I were older, she would have married me. After that, I noticed that Fetiye Hanum seemed pleased when I was near and found reason to expose her naked upper body, saying, "Muselim is like my son, there is no harm."

After she left, I did not see her again and heard no news about the boys and girls who served her in our old village. I learned only that Ali Bey's Armenian wife, Kamile, was married off to a foul-smelling Turkish *hoja*. She must have feared something like that, I thought. No wonder she was so inconsolable at Ali Bey's grave.

THE PERILS OF INTEGRITY

My new master was not a bad man. Nazum Bey was sensible, modest, and godly, although he did not pray five times a day, or deny himself raki, or fast during Ramazan. Given his way, he would have removed the lines of the Koran that prohibited alcoholic drinks. He had no part in the Armenian massacres and lootings; he could not kill a chicken or watch a sheep being slaughtered. Knowing this, I bore no grudge and had no vengeful feelings toward him or his family. After all, he was Ali Bey's brother. I served him obediently.

His first wife, Naileh, was a true hanum, educated, beautiful, slender, intelligent, pale, and intensely religious.

The second, Merouze, was his cousin and the opposite of the other—she was healthy, plump, red-cheeked, and had no interest in religion.

His daughters were from his first wife. Kadriye, the elder, was about my age and really beautiful; her sister, barely ten years old, was a dark-skinned, spoiled brat.

I loved Kadriye at first sight. She was like an angel, with transparent pink skin, blond hair, fine eyebrows, and sweeping eyelashes. Nothing about her could be improved...how could anyone help but love her?

We were now settled in Karaja Veran, where Nazum Bey was the official mudur in charge of the village. Everything was new to us—the surroundings, the Kurdish villagers, their habits, attitudes, and the village itself. It was a beautiful area with houses spread over the valley slopes, and rich with water springs. We lived in the house of a widow, Zeineb. She took no rent from us because Nazum Bey, as mudur, had saved her youngest son from being drafted by assigning him to a crew that transported goods to the front.

Our village was impressive. Official business was conducted in a government building with a telephone and telegraph room, although without instruments, and space for a jail on the ground floor.

Two rooms were allocated to the mudur, who sat as judge to hear complaints and resolve conflicts. We were pleased with the villagers and they were happy with us. Regrettably, though, many escapees from the army passed through here, and the Turkish military patrols, in fierce pursuit, made life hell for the Kurds, all in the name of duty.

On one occasion a *Cherkes* (Circassian) major came through with a brigade of one hundred guards and, on the pretext of searching for deserters, tortured many of the Kurdish villagers. More and more of them appealed to Nazum, tearfully begging for his help.

"Mudur Bey, you are our father and protector, please save us..."

"Mudur Bey, they set my house on fire with my son in it."

"Mudur Bey, they torched my field…they fed their horses first…"

"Mudur Bey, we sacrifice our souls to you, they treat us as though we were Armenian infidels…"

Nazum was deeply affected. He ordered me to saddle the horses. "Let us go to see this heartless dog," he said. "Does he think we have no authority here?"

We reached the Cherkes village in about forty-five minutes and were directed to the officers' quarters. Polite talk was exchanged until the mudur explained his mission and requested an end to the scourge.

"Are you joking?" said the major.

"No, I am serious. This village is under my protection."

"Do you have any idea what you are saying?"

"I know what I say, and what I hear."

"Do you understand that our country is in danger and you are trying to interfere with my military duties?"

"Is it your duty to terrorize our peaceful countrymen?"

"This man has lost his mind!" shouted the major, and turned to his guards: "Throw him out, throw this bastard out!"

The mudur paled and started to shake. He was powerless. He was facing Cherkes guards ready to give their lives for their commander, along with an army outside.

We mounted our horses and rushed home, defeated and humiliated.

Although disputes between Turkish civil and military authorities were ongoing, the military always prevailed in time of war.

The mudur wrote a long report and sent it by special courier to the county seat. Within weeks he was called to the military court in Sou Sheri. High Commander Vehip Pasha wanted to see him.

He was charged with "jeopardizing the nation's military objectives" and "conspiring" against his country.

One morning soon after, the mudur mounted his horse and rode away. Days and weeks passed with no news from him, not one line. We were left alone. There was famine. We had no cash reserve. Naileh Hanum sold a few pieces of jewelry to buy wheat. Our days were hard. We had nothing to eat. The only cow we'd brought with us when we moved was pregnant and had no milk. We lived on boiled vegetables.

On a black day, the village elder came to the house, looking sheepish and somewhat apologetic. He told the hanum that a successor mudur had arrived, and had sent him to fetch the official keys from us.

We were frightened. Obviously, our Nazum Bey had been removed from duty. What happened to him? Where was he? Was he in prison, or hurt? Was he executed, or hanged, or set free? Why hadn't we heard from him?

Later that week a policeman appeared, saying that the new mudur wanted to see me and Mendoohi.

"Why do you want the children?" asked the hanum from the half-open window.

"I am not sure, Hanum *efendi*, but I think we have orders to deport them."

Naileh Hanum's already pale face turned white. Her thin hands trembled and she touched her heart. "Water, bring me some water," she said.

We ran with the water pitcher. She was shaking so I held the cup to her colorless lips. After a few gulps she paused, took a deep breath, rose from the divan at the window, and before our astonished, gaping eyes, walked to the door and opened it.

"Come in," she said to the policeman.

The policeman obliged.

"Go and tell the official who sent you here that until I get written instructions from my husband, or have news of his sentence or death, this boy and this girl will remain with me, in this house, in this room. And woe to anybody who approaches this door. Now go!"

Turning to me she said: "Load your pistol and show me where to put my finger to shoot!"

"Mother!" screeched Kadriye. "Mother, you are not going to kill anybody!"

"No my girl, I won't kill anybody. May God keep that from this house. I will not kill anybody."

Mother and daughter sat side by side, crying.

She was grieving and overwhelmed with uncertainty. Her brave and noble husband, a fine Turkish bey, had left his family on behalf of the Kurdish villagers.

"He threw himself into the fire to save these worthless people," she sobbed.

Just then Zeineb came in, saying that the new mudur was waiting to speak to the hanum. She went to the divan, covered her face, and turned to the window.

"Hanum *efendi*," said the Turkish mudur from outside, "I assure you, taking away the children that you protect was not my doing. New orders came to collect the Armenians again. But if you need them, I will be pleased to wait until Nazum Bey returns. I hope he is back with his family soon. I am praying for it."

The hanum, soothed that he would not touch us before her husband was back, thanked him wholeheartedly. He bowed deeply and departed.

"Don't trust him! Don't go outside!" Kadriye cried out to me.

"There is nothing to fear; I believe him," said Naileh Hanum.

Oh God, I thought, here is a Turkish family protecting an Armenian boy, an orphan. What a world!

That night Zeineb, always aware of what was going on, pulled me aside in the street. "Don't be afraid," she whispered into my ear in broken Turkish. "My daughter-in-law's father and my son Izzet are in the mountains. If those dirty Turks come to take you, run straight to my house. I will hide you until nightfall and then take you to them."

"But you said your Izzet was lost, and you cried every time you thought of him!"

"Izzet is in the mountains. I was crying to mislead the Turks."

I put my arms around her and kissed her creased, sunburned cheek.

She was delighted. As she turned the corner to her house, she put her finger to her lips: "Do not tell anybody!"

Soon after, I was in the forest gathering wood when a bulky figure emerged through the trees. Holding a long-barreled Mauser rifle, with two cartridge belts of ammunition crosswise over his shoulders and chest, two rows of ammunition around his waist, a silver-handled knife in his belt, this moving armory came up beside me and asked if I knew him.

"Izzet, is it you?" I asked, smiling, and put out my hand.

"How do you know that I am Izzet?"

"You look like your mother."

He was a boy of twenty or twenty-one, with a kind face.

"When I get home, do you want me to say hello to your mother?" I asked.

"Sure."

We sat on the ground side by side and talked about unimportant things. When we got up, he warned me not to tell anyone, except his mother, that I had seen him.

"Am I crazy? Would I do such a thing—especially when I know you'd find me and cut my throat with that dagger of yours?" And I don't know why, both of us, standing and looking at each other, laughed.

What I had said was not impossible, but we laughed anyway.

Only the evergreens in the forest showed some color, but the tree buds had started to form and the grasses had awakened. The sky was deep blue. In the distance, women in multicolored dresses were gathering dry wood, and we could hear the faint melodies of their songs.

"Is it your job now to go out for the firewood?" asked Izzet.

"Yes, the village people used to do it for us, but we have a new mudur and we've lost our privileges. I don't mind because it's a good excuse for me to get away from the sad atmosphere at home...and I like collecting the wood."

"Do you want me to help you?"

"No thanks, I already have plenty."

We parted. When I got home, I put down my load and ran to Zeineb.

"I saw Izzet in the mountains."

"Oooh."

"He was armed, I was afraid."

"Oooh."

"I was really frightened."

"Oooh...why be afraid of your brother!"

"I should not have been, I know, but he was so big and heavily armed that..."

Zeineb's face was happy, bright and shining.

When I think of the people who were good to me during those days in Kurdistan, there are more than I can count on ten fingers.

One of them was the Turk with a round face and light beard, who baked the daily ration of bread for the military. He was a very good man, and the one who gave me a loaf of bread for helping him in the mornings, a huge advantage for me. By seeing how much dough was kneaded, I was able to guess the size of the military force to expect. Sixty loaves was the usual ration for the existing village personnel; every two loaves above that counted for one man; one hundred extra loaves meant that fifty soldiers would arrive the next day to search for escapees. I would give the exact number to Zeineb, who in turn passed it on to her son and the others in the mountains. The escapees either ran off and hid, or, if the situation warranted, ambushed the patrol.

The Turks probably suspected that somebody was warning the

fugitives but nobody guessed that I was the informer, and they were never able to figure out how the information was acquired. Even Zeineb did not know my source.

One spring morning she asked me to stay at her house for a few days to protect her daughter-in-law while she went to Divrig to collect some money owed to her.

"The girl has no sense and the boys are always after her. I do not think leaving her alone is a good idea....I will repay you when I return."

"Don't mention repayment, and do not worry. I will take care of her like a brother."

When she left I was not sure why, exactly, but I trembled with anticipation. One thing was obvious—Almas was foolish and carefree.

What was it I yearned for? I did not know how to explain my feelings.

⤙⟶ ❀ ⟵⤚

The house where I would spend the night was a large open square with an earthen floor and high roof, and no partition but a storeroom. The fireplace, in a far corner, smoked continuously. Light came from a skylight, leaving the corners in shadows.

When I arrived, Almas was at the door with a tune on her lips and bracelets jingling on her arms.

"I am supposed to sleep with you until your mother-in-law returns from Divrig."

"With me? In my bosom?"

"I meant in the same house with you!"

"Oh..."

"Didn't your mother-in-law tell you?"

"She did."

I left, my head spinning. What did Almas mean by asking if I would sleep in her bosom? Hadn't Zeineb told her I would stay there to guard her and keep her from ill doings?

Why did my heart beat fast when I thought of her? Every time Almas passed by in a hurry—and she was always in a hurry—some part of her shook. Her eyes were small but expressive. Her mouth was beautiful, with fine red lips, a small chin, and a beautiful bosom. Oh, her bosom…

Months before, when I had seen her crying, I pitied her and asked why.

"He beat me," she said.

"What did you do? Was it your fault?" I asked.

"I did nothing…I do not love him. I would rather carry stones on my back all day than sleep with him."

Her confession had not surprised me. Her husband, Dibo, who came home for a short leave every month or so, was unsympathetic, lumbering, ugly, with dark skin and a sagging lower lip. He always walked with his face down. How she was pushed into marrying him, I do not know. Were there no other youths in the village she could have eloped with? In these mountains, it was quite common for lovers to elope overnight. Surely it was better to flee with a loved one rather than staying home to yearn for what might have been.

Several hours after Zeineb left, the weather changed unexpectedly. The sky darkened and thick snow abruptly whitened the surroundings. I was concerned about Zeineb on the road.

"Don't worry, nothing will happen to her," Almas said.

I hoped the storm would keep Zeineb trapped away from home.

It lasted four days.

Their servant Ali, a lanky, thin boy, came early each morning to clean the stable and feed and water the animals. He would stack enough wood to burn all day, scrape the snow off the roof, and then try to coax Almas to sleep with him.

"Get lost, you naughty dog!" she would say, wriggling out of his arms.

The tempest hit with full force, unyielding, sweeping the mountaintops bare and burying our village in the valley. Zeineb's house was completely blanketed with snow, leaving it almost dark indoors.

When I entered, Almas was standing just below the skylight, look-ing up, her head back. Her white neck was so beautiful in the firelight, I felt a great desire to kiss it.

"Everything is covered. If anybody tries to look in, it is impossible to see us," she said.

We sat down at the fireplace. The oak logs were burning, blue, orange, and sometimes gold, changing the color of Almas's skin. She sat to the right of the fireplace, I on the left. We were silent, like two strangers. When she looked down, her eyelashes fell in shadows on her face. She started to sing a mild, sweet tune.

I tried to figure out what she wanted. Stupid, I thought...even if she tells you, what can you do? Why should she like you when there are many experienced Kurdish boys around?

She coughed. "I seem to have a chill," she said. "I need to warm my chest to stop the cough," and with her eyes fixed on me she started to unbutton the upper three mother-of-pearl buttons of her blouse, absently, indifferently. Then with the same calm, she folded back her collar and put her hands, warmed by the fire, on her bare bosom, caressing, and again looking into my eyes said: "Don't look."

Too late. I had already seen the rounds of her breasts cupped in her hands, and the nipple of one.

"Don't look!"

"I am not looking. Do you want me to close my eyes or leave?"

"No, stay here, but don't look."

Her warm palms stroked the mysterious roundness of her breasts as she uttered sounds of joy and satisfaction.

"I am going to ask you a question," she said.

"Ask!" I said in a small voice that did not belong to me.

"How come the nipples of my breasts stick out when they are cold and they melt away and disappear when they are warm?"

"How do I know? I am not a doctor."

"You are not a doctor, but you are a *flah* (converted Armenian), they know everything."

"Maybe they do, but I do not. I am ignorant."

I started to shake. My teeth were chattering.

"What happened to you?" she asked, her eyes open wide.

"I don't know. I am cold."

"Come closer to the fire."

"It won't help," I said.

"Then get up and go to bed."

"What about you?"

"I will cover up the fire for tomorrow, and I will come too."

Soon the house was in total darkness. My reasoning was gone. I heard her light footsteps and my heart jumped almost out of its cage. Oh my God, Oh my God...

The footsteps stopped. She did not come.

I felt relieved, and disheartened.

I folded my arms under my head and rested on my back. A sliver from the skylight was barely visible, or maybe it seemed so to me. The only sound was the wind slapping the mud bricks on the roof. I strained my ears to hear her breathing; no, she was not close enough. Then I wondered what position she was in. I imagined myself in her bed, close to her under the warm covers. My heart started to pound again. *Are you crazy? I asked myself. What are you doing in her bed? What did you promise Zeineb? To look after her as a brother...Are these brotherly feelings? What was the color of Almas's breast in the light of the fire? Rose or orange...? Why can't I remember? "She is ignorant, many are after her," Zeineb said before leaving. Who could know that her absence would have such an important role in my life? What role? After all, what has happened?*

You crazy girl, how do I know why your nipples disappear when they're warm and stick out when they're cold? Am I a doctor or an expert? I haven't even touched one of them yet, though I have wanted to close my palm over one or the other. *Am I the person to be asked such questions? Am I...? What if I get up and go into her bed? Will she throw me out? What if she complains to her father or brother-in-law? Then they will come straight here and finish me. Nobody would ask questions...If I get up now and tiptoe to her bedside and raise the edge of the coverlet...how would she react? Let's stop and think sensibly. We know that she does not love her husband. Besides, I am younger and better looking. She told me she would rather carry a load of stones on her back than go to bed with him. Why did she say that? Was it an invitation? When she was caressing her breasts by the fire, she made little sounds....Years ago, when I was still a child, the women would feed their babies in front of me. In those days I saw it as a sign of affection, but now other feelings come into my head.*

At noontime when the snow started to cover the skylight, she said, "People looking in can't see us." Did she actually mean: "We can do whatever we wish without fear of being seen?"

Let me get up and go beside her. Isn't there a safer way? Too bad I have no experience. How can I have, when I am barely seventeen years old? When we were put on the road to exile two years ago, I thought babies were brought by storks or something like that.

The roosters are crowing again. It must be close to sunrise, and I am wishing impossible things. What is so impossible...? I am dreaming about pleasant things, is that bad? Oh, Almas! Almas, what have you done to my soul...?

"Almas?" I said, in a voice barely audible.

"......"

"Almas."

"What is it, what do you want?"

"I am cold."

"Do you want me to get up and put another carpet over you?"

"No, I don't need it," I replied in a small voice, very small, and tucked my head under the cover.

Why didn't she say, "If you are cold, come to me, my bosom is warm."

If only she had...but she did not.

Why didn't I say, "Let me come to your bed so you can warm me." But when a man is stupid, as they say, "God first takes away the mind, then the soul." It should be the other way around...first the soul. I started to talk nonsense. Why didn't I say, "Let me come to you so you can warm me up." Why didn't I say...

I am stupid. I do not know how to take advantage of opportunity. Had she objected I could have said that we are like brother and sister, and it is permitted. What a lie! Some brother and sister. I want to take her in my arms, kiss her small red mouth, and press her body against mine the way their servant Ali does. After finishing his house chores, Ali squeezes and pinches her body, laughing and teasing.

Do I need to tell Zeineb when she returns from Divrig? I would be crazy to do that. It would mean misery for Zeineb to hear about her daughter-in-law's casual ways. And if Ali were dismissed and held a grudge against me, he would have good reason.

Two days passed. The sky still pressed low on our village. Almas was chirping like a bird, running about as though she did not know how to walk. The third day, toward noon, she took my hand and led me into the house. When she closed the door behind us, I thought that she would fall into my arms. How lucky that I was not the one to make the first move. She sat me by the fireside, went into the storeroom, and emerged with a portion of excellent moldy cheese and lavash bread, saying, "Eat!"

Again that night I was sleepless for a long time. What was she up to? What did she want? Was she trying to reward me or was it her simple way of saying something more? Which was it...? Which?

By morning the weather had cleared. The sun shone, the doors of the stables were opened and the animals brought out for watering.

Zeineb returned.

Her face had darkened from the piercing bitter winds en route. She pulled me aside and looked at me questioningly.

"Zeineb, elder sister," I said. "Everything went well, nothing unusual happened."

The next day she made a rich, pastry-like bread and set it before me.

"I could not have trusted a Kurdish boy half your age, but you are Armenian and I trust you."

The pastry thickened in my mouth. I could not get it down.

We had lost all hope when, one afternoon, without a word beforehand, the mudur appeared at our front door. We cried, we laughed, we were overjoyed, we cried again.

He had been demoted by the war tribunal and, in an act of mercy, been appointed to a small district in the mountains. Although this new position meant exile to a remote, backward corner of Kurdistan, he was grateful that his life had been spared. He told of seeing cellmates sent to the gallows, of prisoners ripped apart by inept firing squads and thrown on snowy banks for hours to bleed to death.

"In Sou Sheri, where I was imprisoned, a man's life is not worth that of a chicken. Thanks to Allah, I am saved." And he vowed upon the Koran that henceforth he would "shut one eye and one ear" to the complaints of others, and would never again intercede on their behalf. "Allah is Witness, I repent...I have had my lesson!"

For several days we prepared for our journey and sought information about the roads ahead. If the towns and roads here, under government control, were unsafe and swarming with escapees and peasants, what would await us in the far mountains? We knew that venturing out anywhere was too dangerous for ordinary travelers, but we hoped that having a "government official" with us would help to ensure our safety.

The village head loaned us three horses and assigned three Kurds to accompany us as guards and guides. Zeineb's youngest son and another lad, Gazin, also volunteered to join us. The latter hated me utterly and I felt the same about him, but he was known as the best marksman in the village.

Two days before we left, the mudur told Gazin to take me out and teach me how to shoot—"it might be needed on the road."

We borrowed rifles from the military armory and walked well beyond the village.

Spread before us were the open fields, the vegetable gardens, and a line of tall poplars bordering the creek. High above, on a thin branch, was a blue jay. Gazin, who not only hated me personally but despised me as "a worthless Armenian," raised his rifle:

"Do you see that jay perched on the branch?"

"I see it."

"I will take it down. But first, the branch."

Before his words were out he fired his rifle, breaking the branch, and as it fell, a second bullet hit the jay.

Gazin turned to me with a scornful grin. "Now it's your turn."

"What do you want me to try for?"

"That horse grazing at the other side of the field. You can't even hit his shadow."

His voice and stance were so venomous that I could hardly keep from putting a bullet in his head. My throat was thick with rage as I said: "At the side of the hill ahead, do you see the white stone?"

"Which, the one as big as an ox?"

"No, the other one to the left, about the size of a tobacco box."

"Yes, I see it."

"You won't see it anymore." I stepped away, rested my rifle on a hedge, took a deep breath, aimed and fired.

The stone disappeared.

"You didn't get the stone," he said, taken aback. "You hit the ground and the dirt covered it up."

"Go and look for yourself. I am going home."

After we had returned, the mudur asked Gazin, "What happened? How did he do?"

"Not bad," Gazin admitted, grudgingly. "Better than expected for an infidel."

"Bravo, my friend! It is not in vain that you climbed to the fortress!" (The mudur knew that I was on the mountain with my people when they fought.)

"Thank you, Bey."

He turned and went into the house.

Two days later we bid goodbye to Karaja Veran and set out on the road. All our good friends came to see us off, bringing gifts and accompanying us part of the way.

The guide provided for us was Hamza, a wise and experienced mountaineer. He was a giant. His heavy beard rested on his open chest, and his eyes, deep-set in a stern, smallpox-scarred face, were wary and always moving. But occasionally, when he smiled and revealed his white teeth, his face grew remarkably benign and kind. Now he was leading our small caravan, Mauser rifle on his shoulder, walking straight and tall, giving us hope and confidence.

The spring weather had warmed this part of Kurdistan. The roads, though rugged, were dry and edged with thick greenery. We moved along hoping to reach our destination without mishap. The silence was broken only by the clopping horses and the chant of crickets.

I, rifle on my shoulder, was walking beside Farieh, the youngest daughter, who sat on a pile of bedding; sometimes I shifted to the other side of the wagon near Kadriye. We spoke occasionally. Secretly I wished for some danger, an incident that would allow me to protect her and shed some blood...not all my blood, but a little.

Several hours had passed when we entered a forest, moving through ground cover that was thicker, smelling musty, lush, and wet.

It seemed as though the sun had not penetrated these evergreens for so long that the trees had to reach their thin branches higher and higher to the light.

We stopped to rest and water the horses.

"See how the noble horse drinks," said Hamza. "They drink almost as humans do, they draw it up and gulp it down. They do not lap up water like the dogs. Only animals that eat meat lap up the water...like dogs, lions, wolves."

I looked at him, surprised. "I did not know."

"Our ancestors knew that, and their ancestors before them."

I believed him, as I was always learning about nature and animals from living with these nomadic people.

We had a light breakfast and continued on our way. The forest was so beautiful that we forgot our fear of thievery or a possible ambush. We proceeded slowly, enveloped in the pleasant, cool atmosphere. The flora was changing; the emerald grass was replaced by soft ferns with wide leaves. Except for the occasional trickle of a creek or the rustle of leaves, there was no sound, not the chirp of a bird, not the buzz of an insect.

I do not know how long it took to cross the forest, but light was streaming through the branches and brightening our path. Warm air passed over us, and the ground was hard. Now we could see the blue sky and distant hills, bare, volcanic. I quickened my pace and caught up to our guide.

"Hamza, where are we?"

"If we continue at this pace, Allah willing, we will reach a caravan-serai [roadside shelter] before sunset...and Yelijeh by noon tomorrow."

Encouraged after a peaceful journey of so many hours, we moved along, talking, when we spotted two riders at the foothills to our left, obviously following us. If they had been on the road in front of us, or behind, they might be travelers, but they were moving parallel to us, and at the same pace.

"They are bandits," Hamza stated, watching them with hawk-like eyes. "They are armed and have accomplices; sometimes they signal them with signs. Everybody in these mountains is armed. We will move on cautiously until we know what they want or until we get to a safe place. We have women with us…we cannot fire a single bullet."

The mudur looked worried. The women wrapped their *charshafs* [long black overgarments] around them.

I hurried to Kadriye. Walking beside her horse, I started to dream. I saw myself performing acts of heroism to protect her, and when we were safe, her admiring and grateful father would kiss my forehead and cry: "My son in law!" "How did you know?" I would ask. "My son, nothing escapes the eyes of a parent."

I awakened when my foot hit a stone. We continued on.

Finally Hamza decided to end the uncertainty. He put his palms up to his face, framing his mouth, and shouted: "Ho! Ho! Are you Kurds?"

The reply was shouted back: "We are Kurds, we are Kurds. What do you want?"

"We are government officials, and we are going to Yelijeh. We are thirsty. Is there any water near here?"

Turning to us, he explained. "Better for them to know that we are not ordinary travelers. Being government officials might fend them off if they have any bad ideas."

They replied that they had no water and there was no water nearby. They would send somebody from their group to talk to us.

We pulled up our horses and waited.

A good-looking mountaineer came skipping over the rocks and greeted Hamza, who had stepped off the road with a couple of our men. They talked, but we could not understand them since they spoke in Kurdish and we spoke Turkish. Finally Hamza returned, looking concerned, and went to the mudur:

"They do not know what to do with us—rob us or let us go on," he said, watching them steadily. "Either way, they are afraid of doing the wrong thing. If they let us go, they might be punished for losing their prey…if they rob us, they could be punished for robbing a bey, and a government official at that. They want to hold us until one of them gets to Izzet Bey for his orders, or…"

"Or what? Who?"

"They say that if you truly are Nazum Bey, why wouldn't you and your family be Izzet Bey's guests for the night?"

Nazum Bey paused, then nodded very deliberately. "Let them lead, we will follow," he said. "And once I set eyes on Izzet Bey, I will ask him how he dares send his dogs to rob his godfather's son."

Hamza's face brightened.

"You mean to say that your father is Izzet Bey's godfather?"

"Yes, of course. My father Kujorzade Ibrahim Bey is godfather to both Izzet and Mahmoud Bey."

"What are we waiting for? Thanks to Allah we have nothing to fear," Hamza exclaimed, his voice rising.

"Ask," said the mudur, "if they are sure the bey is in his summer place."

"I asked. He is there."

"Ask again. We don't want that dog to run out on us from shame."

⁓⊷⊛⊶⁓

We started out again, happy to be spared a possible bloody encounter. We walked, one behind the other, along a narrow pass winding through a shady valley until we came to a hill.

"We climb here," said the bandit guide, stopping us at a spring. "We can rest a little and have some of this fresh water. There is no water up there; we use melted snow for drinking."

We sated our thirst and prepared to follow him. The trail was rocky and steep, and the sun was hot, causing the horses to pant and sweat as they climbed. We cursed Izzet Bey and his hospitality…why couldn't we go our way in peace and comfort?

Toward evening, tired and beaten, we reached the top of the hill where we saw several stone houses, the bey's summer place. Izzet Bey, who long since had been informed of our arrival, ran out to meet us and embraced the mudur with "one thousand apologies" for causing any trouble: "How could you pass so close to my summer cottage without stopping to share my bread and salt? How is it possible?"

Hand on his chest, he smiled, bowed, and issued orders to his servants.

Half-naked children and fretful dogs surrounded us as we were led into the guest room with separate sections for men and women. It was an expansive square space, laden with carpets. The ceiling was high and a little shadowy. The walls were bare except for different types of firearms hanging from pegs. A large black bearskin was set before the fireplace.

Sitting cross-legged on carpets and cushions puffed with the softest wool, the beys asked for news:

"How is Ahmed Bey?"

"He is well, thank you."

"How is Mahmoud Bey? What is Ibrahim Bey doing? Is he still hunting? Does he have any falcons? How many dogs does he have? How many wives? Has he any children from his latest wife? A son?"

I moved to the women's side of the room. Kadriye was sitting by her mother, smiling and happy because new excitement had come into the routine of her everyday life.

Our hostess, Izzet Bey's wife, a beautiful young Kurdish woman, sat with her guests, the hanums. She had red lips and long black eyelashes. Her black hair covered her shoulders, back and bosom. Over her long, wide pants she wore a triple-layered dress and an embroidered violet shirt. She was aware of her beauty and drifted to and fro slowly, knowing that everyone's eyes were upon her. When she moved, tinkling sounds came from gold coins in her hair and on her arms.

It was time for dinner, and dark-skinned servants were holding up large serving platters piled with the wonderful bounty of fields and mountains.

The mudur's daughters held back, displaying no hint of hunger, a sign of etiquette for young ladies. They waited to be coaxed. They nibbled small pieces, fit for a bird. They were accustomed to being surrounded by servants and were happy with the attention in this new setting.

"My little hanum, please taste this cream."

"Please have a piece of partridge, my hanum."

"Take some honey."

"My hanum…"

The men's section was blatantly opposite. There was music, raki, singers, appetizers, tobacco fumes, and flaming faces. The rules of civility were abandoned. They were eating, drinking, singing, shouting.

Izzet Bey, throwing his head back and downing a glass of raki, bellowed, "Call Kiraz! Tell her to come!"

"Where did you get this good raki?" hastened the mudur, his mouth full.

"From Malatya."

"To your health."

A young man was playing the saz and singing a love song. When it was over, he started playing a dance. Kiraz, summoned by the bey, stood by looking embarrassed.

"Come, my girl, dance for us," he urged.

She blushed and bit her lips. Finally she thrust herself to the center of the room and started to dance, her eyes half closed. With every move her long hair flipped on her back and over her young breasts; her skirts whirled. The music got faster and she was almost flying. Her red apron enfolded her like a curtain, and when her thighs were exposed, she slapped them with her hands.

A plump patriarch, sitting cross-legged on a cushion by the door, looked on disapprovingly. The boys and girls carrying trays of food slowed their steps to linger and watch.

The dance ended and Kiraz ran out, breathless. The mudur told me to follow her and give her a gold coin. I had a hard time persuading the girl to take the money. When I got back, the men were all drunk, shouting, paying no attention to the music. Still, when the music stopped, they urged it to continue.

The mudur's head dropped and his mouth fell open. We let him sleep there and covered him with a felt cloak.

WHEN THE MOON IS NEW

It was late night when I left the gathering and, after checking on the horses, went to bid the ladies good night.

"What is the bey doing?" asked Naileh Hanum.

"He is fine. He is already asleep."

"Was he drunk?"

"A little."

"Did he do anything to shame us?"

"No Hanum, he was tired, he simply fell asleep."

"Now go and rest. But keep an eye on the bey."

"I will sleep in the same room."

Everyone was ready for bed. I was tired but did not want to sleep. Seeing the beys all together in those surroundings and Kadriye there too, my head was clouded with crazy thoughts. Could an Armenian boy be forgiven for loving a Turkish girl? How was it possible to cross the deep and bloody chasm that separated the two enemies? Besides, I was a guest in the bey's house, a servant. I owed my life to them. Was it fair now to desire that family's most beautiful flower? I had no answer.

I must have walked about fifty paces outside when I found myself surrounded by a strange silence. It was different from anything I had ever known…it was whiter, deeper, more divine. In the starry sky, a crescent moon shone like a blade, its milkish glow covering the fields and the tops of distant hills. The valleys seemed darker, bottomless, with gorges hiding mysteries. Although the forest greens and fields were black and obscure, the barren slopes of the hills were visible in the moonlight. Everything was so calm and peaceful that it seemed inconceivable that evil or injustice existed in this world, or that human beings would ever spill each other's blood. It was as though God had secretly descended and was walking in slippers through the soft starlight.

Awed and overcome, I prayed: "Our Father, who art in heaven, hallowed be Thy name..."

I looked around at the distant fields and again my heart was flooded. After all, I thought, the earth here was not like the earth of my fatherland. In our own fields, wherever we dug, we would find the shattered bones of Armenians, crushed skulls, severed arms. Our soil would reveal pieces of broken plows, crosses and gravestones, or church bells and stones from monasteries. And if one looked well, one might find silver coins engraved with the heads of helmeted kings.

I envied these people and their peaceful mountains. The mountains of my ancestors, like the domes of our churches and monasteries, had felt more scorching by fire than by moonlight, and our people had seen more tears than smiles.

Who knew? Perhaps I was standing now on land that was once part of Armenia. If so, there must have been a church down there, people working on farms, choirboys, students studying the alphabet...a water mill under the shade trees...water buffaloes tumbling in the muddy waters of the fountain, and nests of sparrows.

And prayers. Armenian prayers.

"Make our labors bountiful and good..."

Wasn't this the theme of Armenian prayers?

And I thought, if my ancestors had changed the words of their prayer just a little, to "Make the blades of our swords sharp," our fate would have been totally different and the country below, swimming in misty valleys, would be ours.

Oh, if only by some miracle in the morning, to see the sun rise above these mountain peaks, over the land of my forefathers.

After enjoying Izzet Bey's hospitality, we started out again for the mudur's temporary post in Kabak Chevlik, where a house awaited us. Although the mudur had been assigned to a town some distance away, this was the regional transportation hub; goods and equipment en route to the war front passed through here, and so it became an official control point with our mudur in charge.

From the first day, despite my name, Muselim, the local Kurds guessed that I was not a Turk. I was not unhappy about this, because the Kurds looked upon their Turkish rulers as a source of unspeakable evil and malice, so it pleased me that they realized I was not a Turk. Who knew when I might need their help?

I took advantage of the bond forged by our mutual enemy and was soon accepted by the Kurds as a friend and ally. Several officials, including the *muhtar*, the village head, whose name was Deylem, began to share confidences with me. And one day a beautiful young woman stopped me to say that I was one of them; she knew that I honored their religious beliefs and superstitions, and was not a "dirty Turk."

Some weeks later I was walking near the fields, whistling a Kurdish tune, when I met the muhtar.

"*Merhaba!* Hello," he said.

"*Merhaba*, Muhtar!"

"Would you roll a cigarette for me?" he asked.

"Why not?"

I knew he had something to say. He took the cigarette, drew in slowly, puffed, and sighed deeply:

"I am worried about Shero's sons," he said. "The two older ones are in the mountains with their firearms and comrades. But the two younger ones are not made for hardship. They evaded recruitment and are at home with traces of milk still on their lips. If Mudur Bey could think of a way for them to work for him, something official, they could live openly instead of having to hide in fear. And it would very much help that impoverished family."

We had walked to the edge of the cemetery. Below us the white roofs of the village shone like white sheets under the bright sun, and a creek of melted snow curved under our feet.

"You know," I said to him, "you ask for a difficult thing. The mudur is not the only government officer here…all kinds of officials come and go every day. But I think he might want to do something to legalize their status. Ask the boys' mother to come and speak to the hanum; I will talk to the Mudur Bey and we will see."

We parted on the muhtar's "May Allah give you many long days" and a handshake. He returned to the village and I went home. Trying to shake off misgivings, I headed for the mudur's office to keep my word.

That afternoon an old Kurdish woman with sickly eyes appeared at the door and announced that she was the grandmother of Shero's sons, Ako and Zeki.

She handed me a packet: "An insignificant gift, a small prayer rug for the hanum." It was a rug with beautiful patterns, smelling of wool and fresh dye; obviously the weaver had just tied the last knot.

I took the old woman and the rug to the hanum. The woman paused, took a breath, lit a cigarette, and explained the reason for her visit.

"These children, my grandsons, are no longer mine, they are yours, my Hanum," she beseeched. "Let them be your slaves and your guard dogs during the day, but at night let them sit at my table and sleep in peace under my roof. I know that this is impossible for the older ones, but if it is your will, if you are able to take the young ones...I entrust you to God and the fate of my grandsons to you. May you live long, live well, and have no cares, no pain, and no days of sorrow. I am an uneducated, simple woman. If I speak more words than necessary, please blame it on my ignorance and lack of knowledge. My Hanum, may Allah give to you, your children, and the bey many long years. May white hairs grow on the bey's chest [hoping he would live to a ripe old age]. May you both live long and well so that we, too, can live in the shadow of your graciousness."

She bent to kiss Naileh Hanum's fragile white hand.

"No, you are as my mother," said the hanum, moved, pulling her hand back. Pleased to have the chance to do a good deed, she touched the old woman's shoulder: "I will speak to my husband and we will try to do the best for your grandchildren."

"Stay alive and well. May Allah bring you joy. May the stone you touch turn into gold."

Coffee and cigarettes were offered; the old woman was thanked for the rug and sent on her way.

The sun was about to sink behind the mountains when the grandchildren showed up—two young Kurds without mustaches or beards. One was tall and slim, with a stern-looking, oval face; the other was medium height, with flashing eyes and wet lips, a boy who looked as though he dreamed of girls and frivolity.

They stood erect, facing me. Frightened, smiling weakly, they shuffled their feet, folded their arms, swallowed several times, reddened, and looked at each other. Finally the shorter one spoke.

"I am Shero's son Zeki, and this is my brother Ako."

"I am Mudur Bey's servant and secretary."

"We know."

They followed me, each trying to stay behind the other, until they reached the guest room and rushed forward to kiss the mudur's hand. Then stepping back, and back, hands on their bellies as a sign of respectful greeting, they stood erect and silent.

"How old are you?" asked the mudur.

"I think I am eighteen," Zeki answered, "and my brother is seventeen."

"Proper age to be drafted," said the mudur, glaring into their eyes.

"Yes, last year the recruiting officer said the same thing, but my grandmother did not think so and we became runaways instead."

"You mean to say that your grandmother is a better judge than the government?"

"......."

The silence went on. I knew that the boys regretted a thousand times that they had come.

"Well, we will try to arrange something for you," said the mudur. "Now go home, and on your way stop to see the muhtar and tell him to come here."

Bowing deeply, they left.

"You frightened them," I said to the mudur, "especially Ako; he was so scared..."

"Even if those boys were drafted, what could they do?" The mudur sighed: "Alas to the country that depends on them for protection."

"Why? Zeki could be useful," I said. "He was watchful; he looked clever."

"That one is a scoundrel," said the mudur. He meditated for a moment and told me to inform the hanum that he would "save the boys."

Before long the muhtar arrived, swinging his long arms like a windmill. We stepped into the mudur's office together. After the usual greetings the mudur asked him the ages of Shero's youngest sons.

"I do not know for certain, my Bey. They must be sixteen or seventeen, there are no records."

"Can you prepare two official records and have them verified by the imam?"

"Yes, my Bey, of course."

Son of a bitch, I thought. *He takes the credit for a good deed and lays the responsibility on somebody else's shoulders.*

The next day the brothers showed up, smiling broadly. Zeki handed me a basket. "My mother sent these eggs to the hanum."

"This cream is for the bey's breakfast," Ako said.

I went to the hanum and presented the gifts, mimicking the boys' accents and gestures. She smiled, saying, "Poor things…"

What "poor things?" I thought. They were lucky; others would have to pay at least forty gold pieces to buy favors like this.

Toward evening, when it was time for me to clean the stable and groom the horses, I saw the two brothers rolling up their sleeves to start on the horses.

I was very happy.

CHAPTER 5

Crime and Punishment

Torrential rains swept away the bridge that connected our village to the Kangal road, and when the last angry storms subsided, our world slowly emerged, shaking itself out like a drenched dog.

The mudur decided to write to the authorities in Kangal and ask for assistance to build a new and sturdier bridge.

"Do you think they will pay attention to us?" I asked.

"The military convoys pass over this road—they can't ignore us. When you write, be sure to stress that the waters are so high that the pack animals crossing the river with their heavy loads are submerged; the equipment is soaked, ruined before it gets to the front. Make it sound tragic, exaggerate a little."

I wrote at length to the mayor, magnifying everything. The mudur read it, liked it, and signed it. Along with the letter, we did not neglect to include ten fish, in a nicely woven basket covered with fresh green leaves, for the mayor's wife, with the personal greetings of our hanum. We sent the basket by special courier.

That afternoon I left for the village. The air smelled of wet soil and rain. Field boundaries had been wiped away, embankments were flattened, debris and disarray were everywhere, and many crops were totally destroyed. Along the riverbank, trees were uprooted and dead birds and feathers protruded from the branches.

The villagers, mainly elderly men and women, were repairing roof-tops and trying to clear the wreckage left by the torrent. Many looked forlorn, unable to decide where to start and what to do next. The streets, gashed with holes and trenches, were filled with muddy water, fish swimming in some of them.

I passed the house of our office janitor, Hekar. His daughter Besy was trying to fix something on the roof. She waved, her arm clinking with trinkets, and called out: "The hanum sent for my mother but she is not here!"

"Where is your father?"

"At the government office."

She was on the roof, above my head. I was below and we were bantering with sweet things in mind.

"Did you get much water in the house?" I asked.

"A little; we were lucky. This morning my mother and I cleaned up most of it."

"It was unbelievable!" I said.

We looked at each other and smiled.

"I need to bake bread but I am out of firewood," she said. "My dough has risen and I'm afraid it will turn sour."

"Why did you knead the dough if you had no firewood?"

"I have wood, but it's an oak log, and I'm not strong enough to chop it."

"Do you want me to do it?"

She untied the house key from her belt and leaned over to hand it to me.

My eyes dropped to her breasts almost hanging out of her shirt, and to savor the moment I grabbed her thumb and said, "You don't have to go over to the stable to climb down; jump now and I will catch you."

"It is high."

"I can catch you."

"You can't."

"I can! You're scared!"

She jumped down, parachuting her skirt as I circled her waist in midair.

"Now do you see I am not scared?"

"Yes."

"Take back what you said!"

"I do."

She turned, pressing against me, her breasts touching and burning my arm. I opened the door with the key and we rushed inside.

She was already in my arms.

When I freed myself and took a breath, I teased her: "I'm going to tell your father."

"Then I will tell my mother!"

She came close to me again.

Besy was the first girl I ever kissed, and the taste of that kiss was a new discovery for me.

I never imagined that Armenians would be involved in constructing the new bridge, but they were. I was sure that any remaining men in our region had been forced into the so-called workers troops and killed. Fortunately I was mistaken; some were still alive!

Not long after we applied to the authorities for help to construct a new bridge, a convoy came through looking for the government building to use as its headquarters—a signal that the bridge construction had been approved. A commanding captain and his secretary, staff, families, children, and servants were in the arriving wagons.

As the newcomers stepped down, I was amazed to hear everyone but the captain and his family addressing each other with Armenian names like Vart, Siran, Kevork, Antranik, Grandmother, and Mariam.

It was the first time since the summer of 1915 that I had seen an entire

Armenian family. Oh my God, oh my God. There were parents and elders, adult men, women, and children. There was even a breast-feeding baby and a boy about my age. Happiness flooded over me.

They waited to be directed to a place where they would pass the night. The mudur was perplexed. "Where can I put them?"

Kadriye, who liked to be involved in everything, was excited: "Muselim, Muselim, go and ask them where they're from."

"I already asked. They are from Ordu; they are Armenians converted to Islam."

She said to the hanum, "Mother, let's call them in and talk. They are from Ordu and they look respectable; I am lonely and fed up with these illiterate peasants."

The hanum sent me to invite them over for coffee.

The newcomer women, pleased with the hanum's invitation, brushed away the road dust, beautified themselves, came to the house, settled into the cushions, made the introductions, and began answering endless questions.

I stood nearby.

"Do you know that our Muselim is also a convert? A little while ago I told him that when he feels like it, he can speak with you in Armenian [this was totally forbidden] and sometimes he can even complain about us," Kadriye said mischievously.

"My little hanum," answered the woman called Mariam, "our presence under this roof already reflects your goodness and your nobility. Please do not tease the poor thing, we know you are joking." Her Turkish was perfect.

"Can't he speak for himself?" said Kadriye, turning toward me.

I did not answer.

Outside, the rest of the group waited in the sun. The the head man of the village, the muhtar, knowing all the facilities in his area, found shelter for all of them, including three workers, I learned later, who were Armenians.

As the visitors bid their hostess good-bye, uttering "one thousand thank yous" and other elaborate courtesies, Mariam whispered to me in Armenian: "My dear boy, that girl is a scourge."

What a misjudgment! Kadriye a scourge…my God, what a mistaken thought. Her negative remark churned in my mind for hours and days. How wrong people can be. Could she not differentiate between mischief and malevolence? How could Kadriye be a scourge? It did not take much intelligence to know that God had created her in one of his happiest moments, when he was not tired. If Mariam had been as clever as she seemed, she would have said, "My son, anyone living under the same roof with her is indeed fortunate."

Of course, for that woman it was inconceivable for an Armenian boy to love a Turkish girl, or for a Turkish girl to love an infidel Armenian.

True, there were the Kurdish girls, Elif and Besy, and I cared for their friendship, but my feelings toward them had nothing to do with love. It was my body that wanted them, whereas Kadriye lived in my soul. I was ready to do anything to please her. I served her happily with utmost attention, and when I was in bed at night, I thought of her and endlessly relived the moments between us.

I went out the next morning to find that she was up and talkative. "My father praised you yesterday. He is very pleased with you, son-of-an-infidel."

I knew that when she flirted with me, she would call me *gavur* or son-of-a-*gavur*, and that expression, so offensive on other occasions, turned into sweetness on her lips. She could not attach an affectionate word to my name—after all, she, too, knew the chasm between our people.

I said, "I am at your service, what do you wish, little hanum?"

"Little hanum? I am not young enough to be called 'little.' I will be eighteen in May."

"You are right," I said.

As she turned, I moved close and opened the garden door for her. No one was around. She reached out and touched my arm, "thank you," and went in.

There were more escapees in the mountains than anyone realized, and they were no longer scattered and disorganized. They had formed bandit groups that raided and plundered villages near and far; we heard of looting and killing even in distant places. Special gendarmes were sent after them, only to disappear without leaving a trace. We were lucky not to have been attacked, because we could not have protected ourselves.

Hearing these conversations among the Kurds, I was able to pick out names like Hasan, Kunjul *Oghlu* (Kunjul's son), or Sher *Oghlu* (Sher's son), and I suspected they were leaders of the top bandit groups.

Our field workers were evasive when I questioned them, as was the muhtar. But Elif—the woman who had said to me, "You are one of us, you are not a dirty Turk"—and I had become close, and she swore me to secrecy before speaking: "Hasan is the leader of our boys in the mountains. He commands two hundred to three hundred horsemen, but he usually moves around in smaller groups so as not to burden his people," she explained.

"How old is he? What does he look like?"

"I have never seen him, but he is the most courageous one in our mountains."

She sighed.

"What is it?"

"Do you have to know everything? I thought about my husband."

She stood at the center of the big room, dabbing her eyes with her red apron. I knew that her husband was in the army, and I envied the man who had somebody to weep for him.

"Don't cry," I said, going to her. "The war is not over yet. Any day now your husband might be coming back."

"You don't know him. If he were alive he would have been here long ago! Do you think the others hiding in the mountains are smarter than my husband?"

She started to cry again.

Taking her by the arms, I turned her to me: "You cry hopelessly for something you are not sure of. What about me, who has lost all my loved ones and parents, what should I do? Should I stick a knife in my belly or throw myself into the river?"

"I know!" she said, through her tears. But you are a man..."

"You mean that men should not cry?"

She nodded.

"And who ordained that?"

"I don't know."

She wiped her eyes and we looked at each other and smiled. We felt closer than before.

"I consider you as a brother," she said.

Many images flew through my head, but I said nothing and left.

Once home, I went to the hayloft where I had hidden a bottle of raki and took it to the mudur.

His eyes sparkled. "Where did you find it?"

"Eat the grape, but ask not about the vineyard," I said quoting a popular Turkish saying.

I went to the kitchen to find some appetizers, not expecting to find Naileh Hanum there.

"Did he find some raki again? Where did he get it? Who brought it?"

"I don't know, I didn't see," I lied.

I took the tray to the mudur, planning to visit Elif after he was drowsy with drink, but as they say, Saturday came before Friday. It was barely dark, and the mudur was only half drunk when the terrified cowherds rushed in, bellowing: "Hasan! Hasan has raided the village!"

⌁⬥⌁

The villagers, administrators, servants, police, and government officials all were panicked. The farm boys reported that the forest was teeming with horses and horsemen. We could hear the distant sounds of hooves and neighing.

"My house is ruined," lamented the mudur, fearing for his two wives and his beloved daughters.

The young brothers Zeki and Ako disappeared as if whisked off by a wand. One of the other servants fled to a nearby village, and Bozo and I were left to protect the house. Even the caretaker, Hekar, was not around.

I took two hundred bullets and gave another two hundred to Bozo as we positioned ourselves behind a wall, feeling tense and anxious. The mudur stayed indoors with his family, poking his head out every few minutes to ask what was happening.

In a while Hekar appeared, offering to fight with us and "shed blood" if we could give him arms.

"Go back and take care of your wife and daughter Besy. If you hear anything, let us know."

Another quarter hour passed. An awesome silence descended over the village. No movement. We were as still as partridges that had seen the shadow of a hawk. The mudur put his head out again.

"One of you, go and see what's happening."

Pistol in hand, I proceeded to the main village square, where only a few dogs were about. The Sher *Oghlus* would know what was going on, so I headed to their house.

"Sit down," said the old lady. "My grandson Zeki is out asking around; he will be here soon."

"In truth, we did not expect to see anything like this from your

Kurdish compatriots," I said.

"Expect what? What did they do?"

"What more could they do? Everyone is terrified! The whole village!"

"Don't believe everything you hear," she said. "If they planned to attack the village, you would never know they were coming. They would strike as lightning, take what they wanted, and disappear."

I left her and ran home to tell the mudur. "The old woman is right," he said. "Dogs do not eat dog meat. If something bad is about to happen, it will happen to us [being Turks and representing the government]. The villagers themselves have nothing to fear."

He had just uttered those words when I saw a shadow moving at the street corner.

"It's me," came Zeki's familiar voice.

"What's happening?"

"It is Hasan," he said casually, as though it was an everyday happening. "He has a hundred horsemen with him."

"Is he crazy?" I yelled, without waiting for the mudur's reaction. "He can turn our village upside down, but the government won't forgive that! It will track him and destroy him and all his followers!"

"My father and uncle are with Hasan, I just came from there. He is not going to raid the village."

"We are saved."

"That's not all," said the Kurdish boy, scratching his neck. "They want to see the Mudur Bey."

Were these people idiots? Did they think we were foolish enough to believe that if we went to them, they would let us return home? It was an impossible request. I waited for the mudur. Without hesitating, he said firmly: "Wait until I get dressed," and went into the house. We remained outside. After a few minutes that seemed like a century, I followed him.

Everyone was gathered in the guest room. They were crying, some openly, some hiding their tears, trying to persuade him not to go.

"Heaven save us, if something happens to you, we will be left alone and without protection. Who will take care of us? What are we to do amidst these low peasant Kurds?"

"The only way to avoid robbery is to befriend the thief," replied the mudur. He had selected the suit he wore for formal receptions. He reached for his necktie.

"Let me do it," said Naileh Hanum, tying it with trembling hands.

The mudur gulped, trying to remain calm, but his mouth was dry and his lips moved continuously; he seemed to be reciting prayers from the Koran.

I spotted a bottle of raki on the table at the side of the room. I filled a cup to the brim and went to the mudur. He swallowed it in one shot.

"That was a good idea. Another."

I gave him another.

"Make sure that nobody fires a gun while I am with them," he said. "No one is to know where I am, otherwise we will be court-martialed."

"Husband, say good things," his wife begged.

The mudur was magically restored. He stood erect, ran his finger-tips over his mustaches, and had an air of confidence as we stepped outside.

"Inform them that we are coming!" he directed Zeki, who bowed and disappeared like the wind.

We did not speak as we walked past the village and to the trees at the edge of the woods, where Zeki was waiting.

We followed him, single file in the dark, I behind the mudur, rifle on my shoulder. At a certain point Zeki stopped and whistled. A huge Kurd, armed from head to toe, appeared from nowhere and waved us on. Every five or six paces, a mountaineer came out of the darkness and joined us. I knew the forest well, and I realized that they were leading us on a twisting path. That way we would see the full force of men and arms—rifles stacked in pyramids and ammunition belts dangling from tree branches—to say nothing of the magnificent horses. Here and there, men were clustered around glowing fires.

Finally we came to a glade and a flowing spring. A large group of Kurds sat around the blazing fire. They rose at once and stood as statues. One of them approached the mudur with his hand outstretched, saying in perfect Turkish, "Welcome, Mudur Bey. My name is Hasan."

He was a good-looking young man in a military uniform that was molded to his sturdy body.

"I have heard about you. I am pleased that we meet in a friendly atmosphere," said the mudur, dabbing his sweaty forehead with his handkerchief.

Hasan gestured him to the white animal skins spread out for them. They sat side by side and exchanged the numerous polite expressions that are customary in Turkish encounters. Cigarettes and raki were offered. Hasan swallowed the first cup of raki to show that it was not poisoned. The mudur responded by grasping the cup firmly and swallowing the contents in one shot.

"Take another one!" said Hasan. "I ordered it from Malatya. When we are on duty we do not drink, but we made an exception today, knowing that you like good raki."

"What else do you know about me?" asked the mudur, smiling.

"We know that you generally treat our people well and do your job conscientiously, which is why we felt free to arrange this meeting."

"Thank you. I promise not to disappoint you."

I was standing a proper distance away, motionless, with the muzzle of my rifle pointing down.

The men stacked fresh branches on the fire, lighting the mudur's face. He had reddish hair, nice features and a pleasant expression. The raki had bolstered his confidence.

"I hear that the Sher sons are with you," he said.

"They are over there, by the tree," Hasan nodded.

The men bowed deeply, palms on their chests.

"That one," said Hasan, pointing to another, "is Kunjul *Oghlu*. His reputation must have reached you by now."

Kunjul *Oghlu* bowed respectfully, hand on his chest.

"Next to him, the three beardless boys are my guards," continued Hasan.

The three youngsters bowed similarly.

"That one is my sergeant, Khalil, and this one without a beard is my brother, Khudur."

Khudur bowed and bit his lips to hide his laugh.

"Gentlemen," said the mudur, "I am pleased to meet you all, very pleased that we have been friends thus far and will continue to be friends."

He took a cup of raki and raised it over the group. "To your health."

Again silence. We heard many footsteps and horses neighing. A moment later the music of a saz filled the air.

"That is Farhad," said Hasan. "His playing is unrivaled. Would you like me to call him?"

"Another time," the mudur replied. "I cannot stay, but on another occasion I promise to hear him." Then he told me to have two of the biggest, fattest sheep from our flock delivered to Hasan's men for a barbecue.

"There is no need, thank you," said Hasan.

"Do as I ordered," the mudur said to me. "Send Kamal to choose them and bring the sheep here."

"As you wish," said Hasan.

"And now I ask permission to leave," said the mudur, extending his hand.

Hasan turned to his men: "Ahmet, Suleyman, lead the Mudur Bey."

"If a time comes when you need anything, do not hesitate to let me know," the mudur said, looking back. "I will do everything within my power..."

"Thank you. I am sure of that."

We set out as we had come.

"My friend," the mudur confided to me when we were alone, "if word of this visit ever gets out, we are lost."

"That won't happen," I said. "In a few hours, right after they've chewed up the last bones of the barbecue, they will disappear and our village will return to normal, saved from disaster."

"Pray God that it is as you say," he said.

By now we were nearing our house: "We are back. Open the door, we are back!"

Kissing, laughing, crying, thanking God, the household was reunited with vows that a sheep would be sacrificed and the meat distributed to the poor.

Outside, Bozo was waiting for me impatiently. I explained everything to him and, suddenly very tired, threw myself on my bed with my clothes on.

The next morning, after Zeki and I finished our work in the stable and were washing up, he said that his mother had saved some thickened cream for us.

When we were at her table, I told one of the brides serving us that I had seen her fugitive husband the night before.

"We saw them too," she said, beaming .

"Them? Did they come here or did you go there?"

"They came here." Then she whispered that they were "still here."

"In broad daylight?"

"Yes. What is there to fear? Isn't the Mudur Bey our friend?"

"But Mudur is not all-powerful!" I roared, surprised at her ignorance. "Yes, he promised to protect you, but that is if he hears about the movements of the security police, so that your people can take precautions! You don't expect him to say to the authorities, 'The Sher Oghlus are our friends, do not search their house and do not trouble their runaways.' Can we do that? No, of course we cannot! You must be cautious always!"

They looked disappointed.

"Do you want to tell the boys yourself?" asked the mother. "They do not pay attention to what we women say."

"Call them."

The front door, which had been left ajar, was pushed closed. The fugitive Kurds were called from their hiding place.

Happy and smiling, the brothers emerged. They were rough, clumsy, unlearned people. I sat with them and calmly explained that we were not almighty, and not to expect miracles from us.

They listened attentively and nodded their heads to show they understood. That over, I asked about the town of Dersim: were there any Armenian fugitives there, and what was their condition?

"We don't know how many or anything about them...we don't know."

They were quiet for a time. Finally the elder said: "You are our friend and brother. We have shared bread and salt together, and we will not forget what you have done for us. If some day you need help or you want to escape to Dersim, just let us know. We will take you there safely on the wings of a bird."

I thanked them for their promise and for their trust, and headed home.

The mudur greeted me with a wide smile.

"I was at the village—Hasan sent someone."

"What does he want?"

"Nothing. He brought two baskets of grapes for the hanums and two kerosene tins filled with raki for you."

"Two kerosene pails?"

"Uh-huh!"

Hasan could not have sent anything more valuable to the proverbial drunk.

That night the mudur got drunk on the Malatya raki, plopped down on the sofa, and slept. Taking advantage of it, I went to see Elif and recounted everything from the day before.

We sat side by side on the threshing floor in the moonlight. Stacks of wheat husks, waiting to be threshed, were lined up near us. On one side the mounds looked golden in the light, while our side was dark. The field murmured with singing crickets, and fireflies blinked everywhere, giving a mystic air to the starlit night.

"Do you know what?" I said, looking into Elif's sleepy eyes. "If the Turks come to collect us again, I am going to find a way to get to Dersim. I will become a Kurd and live with them in peace. And someday, maybe I will…"

"You will what?"

"What would you expect? I'll marry a Kurdish girl. I am old enough, I am seventeen."

We looked at each other in the dark and, without another word, rose to our feet. She went to her home and I to mine.

Some days later, a captain with a black mustache and beard, with the harsh glare of a Turk, pulled up his horse at our house, stepped down, and announced politely: "Please inform the mudur that Captain Ahmed Bey wishes to see him."

"Who is he? What does he look like?" asked the mudur.

"I do not know. I've never seen him. A young redheaded corporal is with him."

We waited for Naileh Hanum to gather up her sewing and leave the room, and invited the two newcomers in.

They had been sent to oversee the construction of the bridge. One was the supervisor and the other an engineer. They ate with the mudur, relishing their meal, and after expressing "one thousand thanks," left for the quarters that the village elder had arranged for them. Once gone, the mudur started cursing both of them, from their primeval ancestors all the way up to their Prophet.

"Isn't their Prophet also yours?" I asked, barely able to suppress my laughter.

"Shut up, idiot, or I will tear your mouth!"

I believed him as my eyes fell on his large, thick hands, and I kept still.

The next morning the two officers visited again with papers for the mudur's signature, to "help them perform their official duties of bridge supervision." The mudur complied.

I wrote a letter to all the village heads in the mudur's jurisdiction, which he signed, asking them to assist the captain and his aide, with no opposition, and to help in carrying the construction materials to the designated site. Those who did not cooperate would be punished.

"What, specifically, are these materials of construction?" the mudur asked.

"Trees and lumber."

"How will you pay for them? Do you have the money?"

"We will give the people government bonds, payable after the war."

Now it was clear. This would likely cause some trouble, the mudur warned, because instead of sending soldiers to take trees from the forest, they would be confiscating "private" trees from the villagers.

"You must know how hard it is for a farmer to strike an axe to a tree that he has planted with his own hand," the mudur explained. "For him, trees and animals are members of his family. I am saying these things so you will be cautious. Do not take all the trees you need from one village or from a single owner. Distribute the burden so you will minimize problems and protests. Remember that your headaches are mine as well."

They promised to follow his advice, thanked him and left, after which the mudur cursed them again. We prepared a list of villages to be surveyed for lumber and sent Bozo, our young Kurdish servant, to deliver it to the captain. When he returned, Bozo reluctantly told me that the captain's Turkish aide tried to make a pass at him. I couldn't help laughing. Bozo was too ashamed to tell the mudur.

Preparations for the bridge were already under way. Wet, heavy logs arrived every day from nearby villages, but the captain and his aide were not to be seen.

"The honey and butter from our Kurdish homes tastes good to them," the mudur declared, ending his sentence with a juicy curse.

We three servants—Bozo the Kurd, Niazi the Armenian, and I, had become close friends and spent all of our leisure time together. We spoke in Turkish most of the time, although Bozo learned a few Armenian words. We kept no secrets from each other. Although the three of us were about the same age, they followed my lead. We always planned our work so there would be enough time at the end of each day to swim in the river. Unfortunately, the authorities decided to construct the bridge at our favorite spot for swimming, where the water was quite deep. With that gone, Niazi thought that if the three of us worked together for half a day or so, we could construct a dam with stones and branches and make our own pool for swimming.

He was the best swimmer among us. He had lived at the seashore all his life before the deportation, and when he talked of the sea, of Ordu and his old friends, his eyes grew misty.

"They massacred everybody and deported those who were left," he said. "We saw so much cruelty and torture, death and illness, on top of starvation....Dogs did not suffer what we went through, yet God was with us. We lost two uncles but most of my family stayed alive. You know, my grandfather is an exceptional man of strong character, a man of iron."

"Is he? You wouldn't think to see him, he looks like an ordinary old man."

"He seems so, but with all this horror and tragedy, he does not cry. Since leaving Ordu, we've all cried for one reason or another. My mother misses her possessions, somebody else recalls her wedding or other happy times, we have all cried over our lost home…only my grandfather has not wept, except on one day. During the forced march, we reached a point of land, the last spot where we could still see the ocean. He stood and stared at the water shining in the distance.

"We won't see the ocean again," he said, wiping his old eyes.

"Is the sea worth crying over?" I asked, having no idea because I had never seen an ocean.

Niazi grew sad with his recollections. To pull him out of it, Bozo started to describe, in colorful detail, how the engineer tried to make a pass at him.

"How did you manage to get rid of him?"

"I hit him in the chest with my fist, spit in his face, and ran out. Fortunately he is not strong; one blow and you can flatten him to the wall. I am telling you so the two of you will be careful when dealing with Turks. They are dirty, they are homos." Bozo spat with anger.

"Oops," said Niazi, "so that is why he asked me to teach him Armenian…"

We laughed and, holding our noses, jumped into the water.

⇤ ⊛ ⇥

The pile of logs on the riverbank spread wider each day as tree trunks arrived from nearby villages. The three Armenian workers lifted, shaped, and classified the heavy logs while the other men basked in the warm sun or slept under the shade trees. The Armenians dared not complain because the others, all Turks, would band together and beat or kill them. Both sides were aware of this, and so the prevailing side enjoyed its advantage. But each day the Armenians became more and more exhausted from the heavy work and meager rations.

One of them, Hagop of Malatya, told me that he was going to raise high his axe and "cut their heads off, one after the other," as they slept.

"What then?" I asked. "Have you thought about that?"

"Damn it! I don't care. What happens, happens."

"No, Hagop," I said, "it's not like that. You will jeopardize yourself, and many Armenians who have nothing to do with the bridge would be punished mercilessly. News of your deed will be magnified and spread everywhere. Another government decree to "Collect and Deport," meaning "annihilate and exterminate," would be issued. I know, because we receive those notices every few months, and I hide them from the mudur.

"And don't forget, the captain is away now, but when he returns every man will have to work whether he likes it or not. Things will change."

"They won't change! This is not the first time we work for him! Once before we protested and he said: 'Who do you think you are, you infidels, to complain about the soldiers of the government?' and he came on us with his whip and beat us so viciously that to this day, we bear the scars."

Confused and depressed, I listened silently, when suddenly Hasan came into my head. Hasan!

"Hagop, my countryman," I blubbered, "I have just one request."

"Speak, my brother, say it."

"Promise to be patient for a few more days, please."

"What can I do anyway? My heart is pained, I am exhausted and I have said foolish things. Forgive me."

"There is nothing to forgive, my brother, nothing."

HASAN

Towards evening, news circulated that Hasan had been involved in a fight with Turkish gendarmes and that some of his men were wounded. I tried to find out where he was, but nobody knew. However, Elif would probably know because her brother was with him.

That night while the mudur was in a drunken sleep, I left the house. The moon hung above the darkened forest, spreading a dull yellow light over the fields. The fragrance of autumn was everywhere; the crickets were calmer than in the summer and the stars seemed to melt into the damp night as I walked to Elif's house.

I climbed up to the roof to see if she was asleep. A faint yellow light came through the square opening at the center of the roof. In a far corner of the house, standing before the almost-spent fire, she was undressing. Slowly.

In those days, boys my age had flexible concepts of morals and ethics. Lying at full length on the roof, I watched with great pleasure as she undressed. I did not see anything improper in it. I felt no shame or pangs of conscience. And when Elif bent down to cover the embers for the next day, leaving the house in darkness, I climbed down quietly and knocked at the door.

"Who is it?" she asked.

"It's me, Elif. Open the door."

"I am in bed."

"I have something to tell you!"

She opened the door: "Well, come in and say what you have to say."

I took her warm body in my arms and covered her protesting mouth with kisses.

"If the mudur wakes up now and doesn't find you, where will you say you were?"

"That is not for you to know."

We both laughed long and hard, and stayed close together for a while. Finally I got to the subject of her brother and Hasan, and told her I needed a big favor.

"What favor?" she asked, her eyes widening.

I sat at her knees and talked about the torments that Hagop and his mason friends had endured from the Turks at the bridge. I explained that after losing their homes and families, now three of them were forced to do the work of twelve men—and this while being left hungry with less than half the daily rations. "The other day," I added, "one of them was almost ready to cut their throats with his axe, but I persuaded him not to do it. I promised to help them and punish their torturers."

"But how?"

"Hasan can do it."

"Woo! How did you think of that?"

"Listen to me, and I leave the rest to you. Go to the forest and find your brother; then the two of you explain it all to Hasan. Tell him what I promised the bridge workers. I leave the type of punishment to Hasan, but please make sure that nobody—aside from yourselves—knows that we are asking this to settle a score for the Armenians. Otherwise we are doomed; they will crush us to pieces, leaving nothing bigger than our ears, and throw us to the dogs."

"If Hasan asks who wants this favor, what shall I say?"

"Tell him it is an abandoned Armenian orphan who is a friend to all Kurds and to Hasan. Assure him that someday, somehow, some way, I will repay my debt to him."

"All right. You can trust me to do it."

"Elif, you are unsurpassed. Good night." She slowly closed the door behind me.

"Good night."

It was high noon, four or five days after Elif had carried my message to Hasan, when Captain Ahmed Bey and the engineer rode into the village, tired and dusty, and dismounted at our door. The captain, looking bitter, said he wanted to see Mudur Bey.

I told the mudur that he was waiting.

"What's his headache now?"

"He did not say."

"Well, invite him in."

The captain hurried up the stairs, hand on his sword, vowing that he was en route to the county seat to personally protest the harm wrought by the Kurdish hoodlums in this region.

"What hoodlums, what harm?" the mudur asked, surprised.

"Your county is ruled by bandits!" the captain shouted, "and you are aware of nothing!"

The mudur, sitting cross-legged on a large pillow, was pale and shaky, whether from fear or anger I could not tell. He lit a cigarette and looked up, saying:

"Captain, sir, do not forget that you are talking to a government official, and if you represent the Turkish army in this war, I represent the civil authority of this area. I hope that mutual respect will prevail."

"In that case why don't you stop the hoodlums that are obstructing our work!" the captain bellowed. "I am talking about the Kurd bandit chief, Hasan!"

"All that is new to me," said the mudur. "We have seen no unlawful incidents here. If there are culprits, as you say, it is up to the army to find, arrest, hang or shoot them, according to military law—the troops in Kangal are precisely trained for that. What do you expect me to do with two horses and one and a half gendarmes? Can I go after them?"

The captain softened and lowered his voice, but said nothing about having encountered Hasan. I realized that something had happened after my appeal to Elif, and was happy but also worried.

The captain mumbled apologies and left.

The mudur sent me to the engineer to learn what had occurred, but he refused to say anything except that their last stop was in Tekke.

When the mudur heard, he ordered me to send for the muhtar [head man] of Tekke and "bring him here." Fortunately, he was visiting our own muhtar, and I was able to rush him to our house.

The mudur rejoiced. "Sit down and tell me," he said.

"Tell you what?"

"Anything that happened the past few days."

"Nothing happened in the past few days; everything happened this morning."

"Then tell me what happened this morning."

"My pasha," the Kurdish muhtar began, "we were having breakfast when my son came in to say that Hasan and his men had entered the village. I was terrified. I ran out to warn them that the gendarmes were here with their commander captain. 'Turn your horses away and leave,' I said. Hasan did not listen. He dismounted and asked where they were. I told him they were up in my guest room, eating. He pulled out his whip, went upstairs, and marched in. Everybody jumped up from the table and moved to a corner of the room.

"'Captain *efendi*,' Hasan said, 'when our people cut down their trees for your bridge, do you record the names of the owners of the trees?'

"'No, we do not pay attention to details. It does not matter, the government is going to pay them later.'

"'When?' Hasan asked.

"'After the war,' said the captain.

"Hasan asked him if he believed there would still be a government after the war, and if he knew how far the Russians had advanced. Then he told him that the Ottoman army was retreating from the battlegrounds, beaten. He said 'beaten.'"

"Continue," urged the mudur, annoyed.

"'They are retreating like beaten dogs,' Hasan said. Naturally the captain did not respond. At that point Hasan moved very close to the captain, almost leaning on him, and said: 'Never mind that, but can you tell me why you have stayed in our region for over ten days? Is it laziness, or do you especially like our butter and honey, or is it that you cannot part from our beautiful young girls and Kurdish brides? You can be sure they don't even look at your kind.'

"'My son,' I said, going to Hasan, 'forgive him, let him go for my sake. He and the others have learned their lesson, let them go. They are the government…some time later they might return and cause our mothers to weep over us.'

" 'Do you want me to cut out their tongues so they can't speak?'
Hasan replied. " 'Hasan, my son, if you respect my beard, let them go.'

"They went out. We brought their horses and gave them their
weapons, but just as they were off, Hasan held them. 'Before you leave,
chop some wood for this man's fire. You have been living here for eight
days, eating, drinking, paying nothing.'

" 'I do not need them to cut wood for me; let them go as quickly as
possible,' I begged, but Hasan did not listen. He ordered our men to
bring two axes, threw one of them to the captain and the other to the
engineer, taunting: 'Come on, let's see how good you are with an axe!'

"The Captain started to weep.

"Hasan jeered: 'Aren't you ashamed? What have we done to you?
Aren't you a soldier? Do you not honor the sword hanging at your
side? Have you no pride?'

" 'My dear Pasha Hasan, please, I beg you,' I pleaded.

"He pushed me away. And standing in front of the captain, told
him to pray that he would not be skinned. He said he would let him go
to hell, but he wanted first to present the members of his team. Then
Hasan lined up his men and introduced them, one by one, *by name!*

"There is nothing much left to say, my Bey. After that, the captain asked for permission to go, promising Hasan not to return to this
region again. As they were leaving, Hasan said: 'I have a word of advice
for you. Go, and try to forget what has happened today. Forget especially the name of this village and the names of its people, because they
have a habit of skinning anybody who remembers or speaks about
them—a bad but worthwhile habit.' "

***

Late afternoon brought lengthening shadows and the sounds of field
workers and animals returning home. The mudur was deep in thought,
his eyes fixed on a pattern in the floor carpet. He had forgotten that

we were there, so I motioned to the muhtar from Tekke to leave, and walked him out.

When I returned to the room, the mudur was still absorbed. He had not moved. I thought he must have been debating whether to be happy, or whether to regret his relationship with Hasan. I decided that as long as it remained hidden, he was the winner.

CHAPTER 6

A Hero Falls, 1917

Strong winds howled through the hills and valleys, and the air thrashed with yellowing leaves. Along with the last of the field beetles, we prepared for uncertain and awful days.

Flocks of birds crossed the gray sky in triangular patterns, their beaks pointing south. A few days before, when the sky was filled with impossible colors at twilight and the sun tipped only the highest mountain peaks, my heart almost stopped as they passed, blackening the sky. Of course one could not count how many, but I think there were fifty or sixty thousand.

Where was their compass? What calendar? Who advised them and where were they heading? What nests had they left behind on distant shores? Where would they build their new nests to raise the next generation?

Sometimes when they passed low enough, I could hear the leader's rallying calls or a weak one's pleas, "Slow down! Wait for me," and my heart filled with pity.

During our deportation, the weaklings were inevitably shot to death, and many who managed to continue on would utter, "He is saved," almost envious.

My God, what black days they were.

Remembering, I could not help asking: "God, can you tell me when our flight will come and who will lead us? How many springs and winters must we endure, waiting?"

Winter was not yet here but its cold breath was on our necks. I helped Elif carry in the hay and straw and spread the washed wheat grain on her roof to dry, and I coated her house and barn roof with clay to prevent the heavy rains and snow from seeping in.

All the birds had migrated. The forest was silent except when the wind passed through the evergreens, leaving behind eerie whispers and murmurs, and as tree boughs leaned to and fro, each falling leaf had something to say. The vegetable garden had a ruined look, with vines of cucumber and squash uprooted and stacked in the center of the field, waiting to be covered at night with white frost.

After winter had come and gone, thin sprouts would push out from pockets of soil and in time become golden husks of wheat. The seeds sown by the farmer are called "light and blessing," like the flour and fragrant bread rising in the oven. In my mind, bread signified the joy of eating and the torture of hunger. My people and I were left starving for bread during a black summer that lasted for centuries. Since then, bread had become sacred for me, and my love of it was close to worship.

When I passed by abandoned villages, I knew why smoke did not rise from rooftops and fresh bread come from the ovens.

I knew that the shattered skull and bleached bones at the side of a road belonged to an Armenian farmer returning home from his field.

I knew that the prior of that ancient monastery had been conducting Mass when he was slaughtered.

I knew that if I entered one of the forsaken houses, I would find words of despair scratched on the walls in blood.

I knew that if by some magic I found a notebook on the floor, it would contain a child's homework, $4 + 6 + 2 = 12$.

I wondered if God did not see, or had not seen, the evil that befell us. Would not even a simple peasant's soul wither to see his own hand-iwork destroyed if drought ruined his vineyard or locusts swept his fields bare?

Were we not the dwellers of His vineyard? Had He not created us? Why did He get angry and abandon us?

And what of the people from Ordu, especially the elders? At noon, when the sun was high, the old man and his wife would sit by a wall to warm their bones. They knew that before summer came, they would be buried in damp soil, far from their birthplace and their beloved sea.

They were not concerned with the present. They preferred to live in the past. It was as though they wanted to prove that they did not belong to this part of the world where they had fallen by chance.

The old man did not come out of the house without his frayed tie and riding coat, once black, now discolored to a greenish hue. He did not care. His wife's clothes were also worn; she did not care either. She was always well groomed. Her white hair was rounded at the back of her head and held with a comb studded with colored stones. They emerged from the house hand in hand.

Silk necktie and rounded hair in the remote mountains.

The old legends say that fallen Armenian kings lived proudly, befit-ting their royalty, even after being taken captive.

The old couple from Ordu, like fallen rulers.

If I were not so young, and death and old age thousands of miles distant, I would wish for a life's companion like the lady from Ordu.

But I was still here, far from old age…

Why then worry about autumn?

News came that the Cherkes commander chief, Kamil Bey, was again en route to our region to pursue escapee soldiers.

I knew that if the mudur was sure that Kamil Bey could capture the fugitives, he would happily betray Hasan and his men without a second thought. He rued the day that he had met with the deserters, and he worried about the consequences if it were revealed.

On the other hand, he could not forget that Hasan had insulted and punished the man known as the Black Captain, and he was happy not to have been the beneficiary of that honor.

Worried more each day, he said to me: "My friend, both ends of my stick are dirty, and I don't know where we are headed. May God show us the right path."

"*Inshallah*" [God willing], I replied.

"I think, and ponder, and I can't find a solution," he moaned.

The question remained unsolved, because Kamil Bey was almost upon us. Just after our man had left to warn Hasan that the troops were chasing him, the village was crowded with tall, handsome Cherkes soldiers moving through on horseback.

At the same time, the Sher *Oghlu's* mother and daughter-in-law appeared before the mudur, confessing that their boys were in the house. The two women started to cry and pound their knees. "Black ashes have fallen on our heads. What a black day. If my boys are caught, they are lost…it is the end. For shame, my boys will perish…"

"Shut up for a moment. Go inside to the hanum and leave me alone to figure something out," said the mudur, annoyed.

The two women kissed his hand, leaving it wet with tears, and left.

Once again the mudur regretted his pact with Hasan. He mumbled to himself, despondent.

"Maybe the situation is not hopeless," I spoke up. "I think they have a secret hiding place in the house. We need to encourage the women to go home and look busy with their usual chores. If the boys are not discovered by nightfall, they might be able to slip away in the darkness."

The mudur agreed to send the Kurdish women home, and I would accompany them.

The soldiers had taken over the village, but, luckily some of the houses were not yet guarded. The women and I entered the Sher *Oghlu* house and closed the door behind us.

"Where are they?"

"There, under the hay."

Knowing that the soldiers would suspect the highest stack of hay, I carefully leveled the area without raising any dust so the piles all around were almost even, barely two feet high.

"What if they come to get hay for their horses?" asked the mother.

"They won't take hay because we'll put a big sack of barley in front. The Cherkes adores his horse and when he sees both, he will surely fill his horse's bag with the barley."

We did so. Then we swept up the house, brushed the dust off ourselves, and left the front door ajar. "Let them see that we have nothing to fear and nothing to hide. I will return. Do not be afraid…stay calm," I told them.

After leaving, I ran into Kamil Bey's brother, Muhiddin. He was checking a list of names before positioning a guard at the door of each family known to have deserters. The muhtar was with him, pointing out specific houses.

Back home, I reported what was going on to the mudur.

"Meantime, I have decided to invite Kamil Bey for dinner," he said.

I hurriedly put the guest room in order and left to find the commander. He was in the muhtar's office, drinking tea, sitting cross-legged on the divan. He was a handsome young man with reddish hair and very blue eyes. He had an effeminate air about him.

"What time does he expect me?" he asked.

"The sooner the better, whenever you wish."

Apparently he was bored, because he rose, ready to go.

We walked in silence; he led and I followed at a respectful distance. When we arrived home, the mudur was waiting.

"Welcome, my Commander Bey, welcome!"

"Happy to meet you, Mudur Bey, my brother."

They exchanged flatteries back and forth, asked about each other's health, and offered cigarettes as the enticing whiffs of grilled meat came from the kitchen.

"Something smells good, bring us some appetizers," the mudur ordered.

I brought a tray with a bottle of raki that Hasan had sent, along with small kebabs of roasted meat.

They touched cups and drank.

When the alcohol started to warm them, the mudur instructed me to make sure that Kamil Bey's soldiers were being well cared for, as well as their horses.

"Have two or three lambs slaughtered so the men will have a tasty meal," he shouted after me.

"My brother, my dear brother," urged the Cherkes commander, "why do you trouble yourself? Our soldiers are used to hardships."

"Hardship elsewhere…this is my region, and they must not want for anything. After all, they have risked their lives to come here, searching the dangerous mountains and valleys to protect us from the deserters."

"Thank you. Many, many thanks," said the commander, touched by the speech.

"Why do you wait? Go and see that everything is done!" the mudur scolded me.

"While you are out, find my brother, Muhiddin, and bring him here. Tell him I want to see him," Kamil Bey added.

"With pleasure," I answered, and sped out.

In the village, soldier guards now stood in front of every house that was known to have deserters, including Sher *Oghlu*'s, and their inhabitants and animals had been put out on the street. If the fugitives did not surrender soon, the animals would be confiscated and the houses burned.

Some of the panicked women ran to me.

"A fire has befallen us!"

"Can't the mudur do something?"

"The cows need milking, and the oxen are hungry!"

Of course their first concern was neither the cows nor the oxen—their sons were in the houses, hiding. I tried to calm them with assurances that everything would be resolved. I had no reason to be optimistic, but at that moment I believed what I said.

Sher *Oghlu*'s old mother sneered at my words; she was wild.

"What kind of mishap is this? What ill fate is this? What scorching?" she wailed over and over, pounding her knees.

The guard at her doorway was fed up with her laments and curses. "If you don't want your house in flames," he shouted, "with you standing on top of the ruins like a raven, see that your sons and grandsons surrender!"

"My sons are not here, how can they surrender? The government came two years ago and took them away as soldiers!"

"Maybe two years ago they were drafted, but two hours later they escaped, and since then they've been at home sleeping with their wives."

"How do you know they are sleeping with their wives? Are you standing over their heads watching, shameless dog?"

"Don't curse, old woman. I'll stick the muzzle of my rifle in your mouth and break your teeth so you can't bite anymore!"

"You expect us to say nothing?"

"If your sons and grandsons don't show up before dawn, we will torch your house and throw you in the flames so you will shut up."

"Did you hear? Did you hear that, Muslims?" shouted the old woman, totally agitated. "Where on earth does a Muslim burn the house of another Muslim?"

"You call yourself a Muslim?" the guard bellowed.

"What am I? An infidel?"

"Worse, you are trash!"

The old woman was crazed, and since she did not have the strength to fight him physically, she continued cursing. "May fire scorch your belly! May your house burn so you die in flames! May a hundred bullets tear you to shreds, the hell with you..."

"Don't bark, bitch!" shouted the guard, raising his rifle to her. "Now!"

The old woman did not budge. "And now he calls us dog!" she cried, her pained eyes blinking rapidly. "Now he calls us dog!"

I was glad this was taking place in the street where the fugitives hiding inside could not hear, otherwise they'd have rushed out with drawn rifles and daggers. I approached the old woman and whispered comforting words to calm her. Not possible. I gave up. And since I had been there too long, I hurried off to find Muhiddin.

I led him home to join his brother, the commander, in our guest room.

The brothers spoke in their native Circassian language, which we did not understand, but when they paused and Muhiddin seemed ready to leave, I said in Turkish, which everyone understood: "Some of the families have been thrown into the streets, their houses are locked, and guards are stationed at doorways threatening to burn down their homes. The din of bellowing animals reaches the sky, and the entire scene takes me back to the days of the Armenian deportations."

The raki had made the mudur sensitive; his voice quavered and his eyes were moist. "Kamil Bey, my commander, do not make my people suffer for a couple of bandits. I am their master, their judge and protector. Do not disgrace me before them."

Muhiddin was still in the room. Kamil Bey turned to him and ordered him to lift the blockade, saying: "Mudur Bey is justified. We don't need to frighten the women and children for a couple of escapees. We can capture them in the mountains and deal with them."

The mudur was almost in tears as he thanked them. "My brother," he said, embracing Kamil.

"My dear mudur..."

"Muselim, why do you stand like a piece of wood! Fill the glasses with raki."

I did. They drank. I filled the glasses again. They drank again.

As the commander's brother was leaving to carry out the order to lift the blockade, he kicked me at the front door. "You bastard infidel, I will teach you not to stick your nose in matters that do not concern you!"

The drinking cycle and a lavish dinner followed. It was toward morning when Kamil Bey was ready to depart, bidding lengthy farewells. The mudur ordered me to accompany him. Luckily for me, we met Bozo at the front door. I grabbed his arm and told him to go with Kamil Bey in my place. I was afraid of this business. Why be a fool and risk martyrdom?

I need not add that after the blockade was lifted, the Sher *Oghlu* boys slipped out of their mother's house and escaped into the forest. The following day their happy grandmother came to us with a ram as a gift.

The sad news burst like a bomb over the village. At first we did not believe it; we did not want to believe it. But when the details reached us, there was no doubt. We were heartbroken, but the mudur was happy. He thanked Allah and ordered a bottle of raki to be cooled in spring water.

A couple of days later, we heard the story of how Hasan was killed and the details of his funeral in his birthplace of Khavak.

He was fishing with two of his men when Kamil Bey's soldiers surrounded them. They fought. Kunjul *Oghlu* managed to escape on his fleeing horse. Hasan remained with his aide, fighting together and helping each other until they almost managed to break through the siege. But unfortunately, the aide was wounded. Hasan refused to leave his faithful servant in the hands of the enemy. He continued to fight until he was out of ammunition. When the Cherkes soldiers realized this, they rose up together and charged, riddling his body with bullets.

"They could not lift his body from the ground; it had to be rolled into a carpet and carried home like that," the muhtar reported, weeping.

He had every right to cry. "In our world, men cry only over the graves of their heroes," Hasan had once said. The muhtar was crying because a hero had fallen. And Hasan, who had befriended his people, who was revered by all Kurds, who symbolized their opposition to the tyranny of the Turkish government, a much adored hero who defended them courageously, was unexpectedly taken from their unrealized dreams for the future.

Soon all the Kurdish poets and singers dedicated verses and songs of praise to Hasan and to his valiant deeds.

Doesn't every nation worship its heroes? I wonder if, since the beginning of time, a nation exists with no heroes. If so, it does not love freedom, or has not shed blood for it.

HAGOP OF MALATYA

The work to replace the bridge was finished. Most of the labor crew left except those who were needed for maintenance, and Hagop of Malatya was assigned as supervisor.

Soon the convoys carrying supplies started to cross the bridge, slowly, wheels creaking and scattering the fish below.

Bozo, Niazi, and I had piled up a barrier to form a deep pond under the bridge. When the weather was good, we would go swimming there and relax under the shade trees, eating our catch of barbecued fish that were much too bony but so tasty we ate them without adding salt.

We had no net or fishing rod, and using a gun each time was not practical, so Hagop had shown us a way to make a catch. He would put a handful of flour on a rock and wet it with the milky sap of an herb-like weed. Then he'd shape the dough into pill-size, tiny balls and cast them into the water as he walked upstream. The fish eating these balls were poisoned; some jumped out of the water, but most of them floated to the surface, belly up. We snatched them instantly, threw them on the fire, and ate right there on the spot.

Sometimes the mudur's youngest daughter, Farieh, came with me to the bridge, and Hagop would join us, serving her eagerly.

"My little hanum," he'd say, "I apologize for having nothing but these simple things to offer you," and place the fattest and the best-grilled fish before her.

"Yakoob, you are a good man," she'd say, smiling, and Hagop would hastily blink tears from his eyes.

When we were alone, I asked him why he was so taken with that girl.

"I have a daughter her age," he said.

I did not want to poke at his wound, so I kept quiet.

It was Hagop who broke the silence. "Damn it, when will this cursed war end?"

"Let us say it ends. What will you do? What can you do?"

"You ask me that? I will look for my family!" he almost shouted.

Silence again.

"How did it happen?" I asked, but instantly regretted it.

"They took them. I was not home...they'd put me into the army." He wiped his eyes with his thick fingers and his shoulders shook as he started to sob.

I reprimanded myself. Stupid! Why did you cast a stone into his ocean of sorrow? Don't you know that every Armenian's story is the same? What matter how it started?

I let him be. After all, what could I say or do to console him? Did I not have the same pain? Wasn't I eaten up with loss?

God, being a God, could not bear the death of His son, so He thought of the Resurrection to bring him back to His side. Yet we? How are we to endure it?

Does the word "happy" exist in our language anymore?

We have forgotten how to be happy because ghastly images are engraved in the depths of our eyes. The only way to be rid of them is to poke out our eyes. And we do not have the courage for that.

The sun slipped behind the hills, leaving the valley and most of the village in pale shadows. Dust settled over the colors on the western horizon like ashes on a burning log.

Hagop and I got up and parted without further talk. He headed to his army quarters and I went home.

The V shape of migrating birds on gray skies was gone. The sleet roared everywhere, freezing the river and icing the thick white snow that blanketed the hills, leaving only the twigs of evergreens and junipers to mar the vast panorama.

During the silence of night, when the wind stopped for a moment, one could hear the crackling of the earth by listening carefully in the darkness. Men, animals, even dogs were all indoors under the cover of sheds and rooftops that threatened to collapse under the weight of snow. All the chimneys smoked, and when a stable door was opened for some reason, the warm air rushed forth, heavy with the smell of dung and hay. Horizons and sky pressed low upon the fields and sometimes disappeared into an icy mist. And so, days and weeks reluctantly followed each other and became months as we awaited a hint of spring.

It was still very cold when an exhausted boy hobbled into the village. Icicles hung from his headgear, and his nose was half frozen.

"The convoy!" he gasped, breathless. "They got stranded on the road. If you don't want them to freeze to death, you have to move fast."

The village came to life. Doors were flung open, and the outlines of men and dogs appeared on rooftops in the snow.

"Hozan, hey Hozan, Guelo, Musto, Ibo, Ahmet, Osman. Come quick! Let's get going, the people are stranded."

The village elder urged everybody to run fast. "We can't lose any time! The gendarmes, the secretary, the baker, the bridge workers, call all of them. We must save the convoy!"

The mudur echoed the call.

They all started out on the road along with the dogs.

Strong gusts had piled the snow into high banks between the hills. On and off behind a curtain of snow, we could see a black line moving along the valley. A little while later the line grew thinner and thinner until it became invisible, engulfed by the unbroken whiteness of the storm.

Half an hour passed, one hour, an hour and a half, and still no sign or news from the searchers. Finally, two hours later, I thought I saw the black line moving in the distance and fired my gun in the air three times.

The shots resounded over the snow. "They're coming!" I shouted, running. "They're coming!"

Everyone was excited. The villagers stood near the road, trying to see the dark spot, hands over their brows, voicing words of hope and encouragement.

Finally the moving line was clearly visible, changing shape, proceeding slowly but steadily. Oh, they were already on the new bridge, shaking the snow off and stamping their feet, shouting to each other in rapid bursts. The dogs barked excitedly, nonstop, running back and forth, filling the air with happy anticipation.

The procession entered the village. Old women and men, who were spectators up to now, stepped forward to pull the wagons and their frozen occupants and to help with the animals. Muhtar Deylem, silent and motionless, stood at the edge of the village, surveying the scene.

The convoy was at the village center: donkeys and oxen, two skinny horses and twenty porters carrying supplies for the fighting army. They had started out from Kangal the day before on a clear morning and got caught in a storm that they had battled for more than sixteen hours. Everyone wondered how they had managed to survive. The oxen's hooves were torn and bleeding. The horses were snorting puffs of steam, and the men could barely stay upright.

Guiding the march down the street was our servant Bozo, balancing a bag of wheat on his shoulders. Niazi, the Armenian from Ordu, was behind him, also carrying a bag. Others followed—Turks, Kurds, dogs, and guards, and finally came Hagop of Malatya, struggling with a large heavy bag, sweat dripping from his forehead.

"What is this, Hagop?" I said, pitying him. "Couldn't you find a lighter load?"

"My brother," he said, his breath steaming, "this is Dohan's load."

"Who is Dohan?"

"Dohan is the ox, the brave one," he said, nodding at the huge, exhausted yellowish ox beside him. Then, lowering his voice: "My ox."

"Your ox?"

"Yes. Do you think I suffered with this heavy load for two hours in the snow for an ox belonging to a Turk? No. Your brother is not a fool. When we found them and I saw the ox, my heart started to pound. It looked very much like my ox. I went over to him, balanced his load, and started to help him. The more I looked at him the more I was convinced that he was mine. But he is so very thin, I could not be sure.

"I went to the owner and exchanged a few words, and asked him where he got the ox. He bought it from a Kurd in Malatya. I asked how old he was, and he said, 'He is getting old; he was four when I bought him, now he is close to seven, but he is still stronger than two four-year-olds. Don't judge by his looks now. I have yet to see him tire or give up on any load.' That left no doubt. No question. It was my Dohan.

"I stood in the snow in front of him, kissed his muzzle, his eyes, his eyelashes, I scratched his head and neck, but I still felt uneasy. So I untied his load and hoisted it onto my shoulders. You know the rest."

The villagers and precinct officials had already put away all of the cargo and most of the animals. Dohan and couple of oxen were outside, being herded into a stable. Hagop protested. What! Put his Dohan under the same roof with those inferior animals? In a common stable? It was unheard of. Had they no conscience?

"What do you expect?" I asked. "Does the ox belong in a palace or in the guest room?"

"If they do not understand," he replied, offended, "they are Turks, they are Kurds, they are dogs…I realize they cannot comprehend. But you? You who are Armenian and my brother, and have shared your bread and salt with me, you—if you do not understand, that stabs through my spleen. Don't you understand, my dear brother, that this one animal is the only thing left from my home and hearth? Wife, parents, children, field, vineyard, land, everything…I have lost it all. Do you understand? Everything. I am alone in the entire world, exiled and alone. And God pities me and sends me Dohan. Now you come forward and tell me not to care for him, my gaunt, worn animal…to allow him to stay in an ordinary stable with the flea-bitten animals of strangers, in a common barn where he won't be able to find a decent corner to rest his weary bones all night. How is it possible? You have to feel that…How is it possible? He has served me long…he…"

"It is not in our hands, Hagop, it is not our fault that your ox, like you, was taken by force into the army and had to work in this godless Kurdish desert. If it were up to me, I would save not one, but a thousand young Dohans for you."

He sank down and started to sob like a small child. He was exhausted.

After consulting with the muhtar, I told Hagop to stop crying, that we were going to move Dohan to a place where he could care for him and spend his leisure hours with the animal.

Persuading Dohan's Turkish owner to allow this was difficult. Threats and arguments ensued, which were unexpectedly resolved when the mudur's youngest daughter, Farieh, who had been standing nearby throughout, said in her high, innocent voice, "If they let anything happen to your ox, I will tell my father. Do you know him? I am Mudur Bey's daughter."

All the objections melted away. My friend Elif happily offered her stable, which had ample hay and barley and was warm and comfortable. Dohan and Hagop moved into it, and the heavy wooden door closed behind them.

The short winter day ended and enfolded the village. Although there were no stars or moon, a mystical and opaque whiteness radiated from the snow covering the village. A starving wolf howled from the distant valley; the village huts slept peacefully, eyes closed. Lying in my bed, I thought for a long time about Hagop. Later that night, Naileh Hanum brought a large bowl of yogurt soup, fragrant with mountain mint, to take to him.

"A man who loves his ox that much cannot be bad," she said as she handed me the steaming bowl.

When I went to the stable, Hagop had made the ox comfortable and was watching him chew on hay, admiring his moist nose and mouth. His face was bright and he looked pleased. He smiled when he saw me. He started talking about his animal, his cart with a cherrywood shaft that made a creaking sound, his wheat crop, how his thresher was filled, and his welcoming house. He was living the past and had forgotten that he was in a Kurdish stable. He talked as though his village had not been destroyed and flames had not engulfed his barns. It was as though nothing had been captured, plundered, despoiled. In his eyes, his Armenian village was at peace, sleeping blissfully after a long working day, and his explaining that "my shaft was made of cherrywood," meant "my throne was embedded with diamonds."

The morning was clear and cold, but as the sun rose above the horizon, the melting snow started to trickle from sheds and rooftops and formed narrow creeks in the streets. Villagers and dogs poured out. The elderly sat in rows along the stone walls, enjoying the sunshine.

The sky was cloudless, and the chirping of partridges came from the valley.

It was time for the convoy to set to the road. The heavy door of Elif's barn opened slowly and Dohan emerged in a thick cloud of steam, imposing, magnificent, moving with majestic calm. He was clean and combed, his belly was as full as a drum, and his back was straight enough to put a row of eggs on it. His muzzle was dotted with golden pieces of hay. His ears hung loose and his eyes shone.

A load was placed on him and he was attached to a wagon.

The muhtar, Farieh, and I joined Hagop to follow the caravan to the edge of the village. There, Hagop stopped. He went to the Turkish boy in charge of Dohan, pressed a silver coin into his palm and said: "Take this silver, and in the name of Allah and the Prophet, take good care of this ox. Last night, I coated his hooves with tar so they won't get lacerated on the icy road."

He bent, wrapped his arms around the animal's head, put his cheek against his muzzle, and closed his eyes. He stood motionless for long seconds, then stepped back and said: "Go, and may God be with you."

The convoy moved forward, drawing a wavering line across the level white plain, and slowly disappeared into the horizon.

Hagop of Malatya returned home. After that, nobody ever saw him smile. He lived like Lazarus of the Bible. The Bible says that Lazarus lived for twenty years after being restored to life, but he never, ever smiled.

⟶◈⟵

January 1918. Famine, terrible famine…and winter. Anyone who has not witnessed the long winters of the mountains of Kurdistan has not seen a winter.

In those difficult days, the Ottoman Empire was still at war, making life even worse for its already starving population. The government call for supplies was ongoing and endless; equipment, leather, wool, and animals were needed, the latter to be eaten as well as for transport.

The troops stole from the rations they hauled to the front because they were hungry, having found no food at the designated stops. Before any wheat reached the fighting military, it was contaminated with all sorts of foreign material, dirt or hay that had been added to replace the stolen allotment. Animals were reduced to skeletons while the starving horses chewed on each other's tails.

Unimaginable famine. The horrific snow and blizzards of the Kurdish mountains, and it was not yet February. Everyone knew this was the time when hungry wolves brazenly descended into the villages, ready to attack anything alive.

The house we lived in was situated at the rim of the village, apart from the other houses. It overlooked the bridge and the sweeping valleys and hills beyond. I would go outdoors late at night, rifle in hand, as the wolves scattered in all directions, frightened by the crunching of my steps on the icy ground. Not one of the numerous bullets I fired seemed to find its target. If it did, the other hungry wolves probably devoured the carcass...who knows?

Aside from the fear of wolves was the threat of bandits. Our mountain ally, Hasan, was dead, leaving us more vulnerable to marauders. With this in mind we stayed ready, but we knew that if we were attacked, we could not last more than a half hour.

Fortunately, the women felt secure. To bolster their confidence and to impress the workers, we stayed alert day and night, constantly checking the weapons and ammunition hanging on the wall.

I fixed a cot in the stable, which was attached to the house, and slept there next to the mudur's horse, pistol under my head. Bozo slept at the door, and another servant was in the barn. If danger came, our strategy was planned, and we had schedule of round-the-clock watches.

One night, when everyone was asleep and the house was quiet except for the howling wind, we heard a terrible scream. I jumped out of bed—I had my clothes on— grabbed my gun, and ran out.

In the falling snow was a woman, barely clothed, calling, crying, blubbering something. The others came.

"What is it? What happened?"

"He stole it, he took it…he stole the food for my children…he stole it. Mudur Bey, do something, catch him! He took it and ran."

""Who took it?"

"My brother-in-law."

"Which way did he go?"

"I don't know. I was half awake, I heard a noise. When I opened my eyes the door was open and snow was blowing in. The little flour I had, my brother-in-law stole it and ran away!"

There was no need to hear the rest. I rushed toward the bridge looking for signs of movement.

The mudur called me back, exploding, "You fool! Are you crazy? Can't you see this is a plot to leave the house unprotected, to drop our guard? Isn't it obvious? Have you no brains?"

We all went in. But we could not sleep. We restarted the fire.

The mudur told us to go to bed, took his wife's hand, and retired. We were left in the room—Minireh, Merouze (the mudur's second wife), Kadriye, and I.

"The whore…bitch…shameless," Merouze began. "Half naked, she comes and calls for the mudur."

"Have you ever starved?" I said.

"What do you mean?"

"I am saying that a small handful of flour meant survival for her and her children. She could not think about dressing or anything else."

"You are naïve. She came in the middle of the night to show herself to the mudur…right up to his door."

I went to see the woman in the afternoon. A corner of her house had collapsed and the snow was blowing indoors. Her children, thin and hungry, were playing with a kitten in the corner. After hearing

her story and calming her fears—she thought she was being taken
to prison for disturbing the hanums—I went to see the head of the
village, the muhtar. Despite his protests ("What difference does one
Kurd more or less make to you?"), I arranged to have a little food taken
to the woman and for a couple of men to repair the collapsed section
of her house.

As I was leaving, he called me back: "Do you sleep with her?"

"What are you saying?"

"Tell me, do you sleep with that woman?"

"No! What do you want me to swear on?"

Voices were coming from the guest room when I returned home.
The Armenian women from Ordu had been invited to visit, and were
arranged on the colorful settees with the hanums, talking over the previous night's incident.

"She came in the middle of the night, half naked, screaming,
'Mudur Bey, Mudur Bey,' right in front of his door."

"The whore."

"Bitch!"

"Shameless…"

It was not until early spring that the mudur told the family more about
his court-martial and imprisonment.

"Human life had no value—every day, eight to ten people were executed by the firing squad. I was lucky, so very lucky to get off cheaply.
One day I was taken to an investigation room for questioning. A secretary read the accusation against me. It said that I had hindered the
government and its war effort. Could there be a more serious crime?
But apparently my time had not yet come, or perhaps somebody's
blessing helped me. The major at a desk told me to sit and offered me
a cigarette.

" 'Nazum,' he said, 'it is because I do not believe all these charges that, instead of hanging you, we are sending you to a new location. When you get to your new headquarters, I advise you to conduct yourself differently. We are at war. Our military sword is sharp enough to cut from the left, the right, from behind, in front, all directions. Do not try to oppose it, else you are doomed. Do not take notice of everything, close one of your eyes and an ear and tie up your tongue. Who are *you* to think you can straighten out this world? Do not forget that our country is at war and in danger, and everybody has a duty to perform. Everybody must sacrifice until this is over.

"'Now tell me the truth. Were you taking any bribes?' he asked.

"'In the name of Allah, I was not!' I said.

"'Then how could you manage on government pay?'

"'My father is rich, a big landowner. He helped me.'

"'Who is your father?'

"'I am the fourth son of Kujorzade Ibrahim Bey.'

"'I know. He wrote a letter to Vehip Pasha asking him to forgive his youngest son because of his age.'

"'My father wrote that?'

"'Yes.'

"Woman," the mudur said to his wife, "do you see? The old man has his faults and caprices, he can be too domineering, but he is a good man. When the need came, he swallowed his pride and wrote to the Pasha. Who knows how much sleep he lost before signing that letter?

"A captain was sharing my prison cell. He had ordered the massacre of an entire brigade of Armenians serving in the Labor Force. Later, when those workers were needed, the Pasha asked for them. It was *he himself* who had given the order to kill them, by telephone, and now he sent a written order asking for them back, as though he knew nothing about what happened….So he accused the captain of killing them on his own.

"The captain tried hard, saying over and over that the Pasha ordered him to do it, verbally. But having no proof, he was sent before the war tribunal and condemned to death. The day before the execution, his wife was permitted to visit him in his cell…his last wish. Their meeting and separation was heartrending; they cried in each other's arms and embraced for a long time. I could not get them out of my head for a week. I could not sleep either. The day after the wife's visit, they took him out in the early morning to the firing squad. The shooters did a bad job, and he was left on the snow to bleed to death.

"Woman, I was lucky, very lucky. Somebody's blessing helped me and I was saved. I got off very cheaply. Otherwise…"

Hearing these details, the elder hanum paled and her lips moved steadily in soundless prayer.

After that experience, the mudur was totally a new man. Not for one moment did he forget the advice he had received. He responded only to written orders; he took no action whatsoever without a written order and without a bribe.

Riches poured into our house. Naileh Hanum's bridal case chimed with new gold pieces that were dropped in one after another.

Every so often the mudur mounted his horse and went to visit the district governor, bribing him to assure that any complaints he might hear about his swelling profits would be overlooked.

Sometimes the governor, making his rounds, was invited over for a sumptuous meal. He was short and fat and loved to eat. After dinner he could not bend over to wash his hands, so two servants were called to assist him, one to pour water over his hands, and the other to hold him from behind to keep his balance.

And at regular intervals, the mudur would send me with another servant to Kangal, the county seat, to deliver gifts of food like butter, honey, lentils, chickpeas, yogurt, and fish, to the governor's most favored wife.

The mudur also found a new friend in Kangal—the tax collector.

He was a big, good-natured man, fond of raki and festivities, and he became a permanent member of his drinking parties, joining the precinct commander and several officers. Weather permitting, they would go to the riverbank with a basket of appetizer meats, fish, a few bottles of raki, and a carpet to sit on. They would eat, drink, and sing, lifting their cups in fervent toasts and sharing stories, true or fabricated. A time would come when they were no longer aware of their surroundings; the more durable ones would mock their drowsy companions and fire their revolvers into the sky to rouse them; another would claim that he shot a star and made it fall. Again they would chant fragments of whatever songs their blurred memories would permit, and after shouting, "I want a woman now!" and calling for "Allah, Allah!" would slowly sink down, mouths open, snoring.

The mudur had been away on business for a few days in early June when a young Kurd came to the front door with word that he would return home that evening with other officials, and we were to prepare for eight people.

"Who are those eight people, do you know?"

"The district governor, Sheik Mustafa and others, guards and servants."

We had to rush. I cut wood to fire the oven. The women prepared some dough. Mendoohi tidied and dusted the guest room and opened the doors and windows to let in the cool air. The hanum told me to get four chickens, "skin them, and put a large kettle of water on the fire to boil."

With the help of two neighboring boys, we chased the chickens and managed to shoo them into the barn.

I went to the kitchen for a sharp knife.

"Who is going to kill the chickens?"

"I, who else?"

"Say *Bismillah* [in the name of Allah] before you kill them."

"Yes, I know. The meat will be inedible if I do not say *Bismillah*."

Kadriye followed me. I took the first chicken from the Kurdish boy, put it on the ground, pulled back its wings, stepped on it, said "*Bismillah*," and grabbing its head I pulled the knife across its neck. Blood squirted out as the bird shivered and tried to escape. I twisted its head and threw it aside.

"What did you do? You pulled the head off and threw it away!" Kadriye burst out.

"Did you want me to keep it? Is there any other way to kill it?"

"You are not supposed to separate the head until it is dead!"

"I didn't know. I will do the others that way."

"You should have let a Muslim kill the chickens!"

"Am I not a Muslim?"

"You are an infidel, converted after; you do not know the ways of Islam."

I took great care with the second and third chickens and did not disengage their heads until they were motionless. The disaster, however, happened with the fourth one: my knife must have struck a bone, and the chicken's windpipe was not completely severed—after all, I was neither a butcher nor a Turk. When I took my foot off the chicken, it started running around, zigzagging desperately, blood flowing from its neck.

Kadriye was white; she leaned against the wall, barely able to stand. Should I run to help her or go after the chicken to finish the job? I ran toward her just as her knees folded and she fell into my arms.

I carried her inside. Sweat was pouring from my forehead into my eyes.

"Bring a glass of water, fast!"

"What! What happened?" gasped her mother.

"When I was killing the chicken..."

Kadriye, coming to her senses, said: "I felt dizzy seeing the blood, that's all."

I looked tenderly at her sweet face and felt my heart pounding.

She was not guilty of the crimes that her race had inflicted upon my people. The blood of those vicious barbarians was not the same blood that flowed through her veins. She could not even stand to see a chicken killed, yet I had blamed myself over and over for loving her. How stupid I am...

When the mudur came home that evening, the official orders for his transfer to new headquarters in Bey Punar were in his pocket.

Early in the morning we began our preparations, and by the next week we were in Bey Punar.

CHAPTER 7

To Bey Punar, 1918

After traveling for days through and over mountains, we reached our new and third official headquarters in Bey Punar. We were barely settled when I heard that an Armenian girl, whose name was changed to Asia, lived with the Abbass family.

"How old is she? Is she married?" I asked the village head, Muhtar Ibrahim, who had told me about her.

"No, she is still a child, about thirteen or fourteen."

"Muhtar, what about the Abbasses? What are they like?"

"Abbass himself is okay, but his wife," he shook his head, "she's a witch. She can knock a rider off his horse. And her son, Veli, God save my enemy from having a son like him. His mother must have been with a Turk. Allah is witness, I'll bet that bastard has Turkish blood; no Kurd, no matter how bad, could be so tyrannical."

"I am going to visit them."

"*Efendim*, my dear sir, if I were you, I would not. Everyone in the village knows that you are a converted Armenian. If you go to the Abasses' house, they will know you are there to see Asia. And you cannot remain there forever!"

"You mean she will have trouble after I leave?"

"*Efendim*, you are clever and I am stupid; you know how to read and write, I know up to A and B. But I have a beard, which you do not. I know the people and the dogs of this village, and you do not. Come, listen to me and forget about going to the Abbasses'. Someday, if you wish, I will arrange for Asia to be at our house and you will visit, too. That way you can meet her and get acquainted."

"Muhtar, you are a good man."

"Thank you. I have business now. May God be with you."

He left. I followed him with my eyes until he turned a corner and disappeared. I sat on a broad tree stump that had been cut down as a seat and, I don't know why, tried to picture the life of a young Armenian orphan with a Kurdish family. Wasn't it true that anytime they were a little annoyed with us or dissatisfied with our services, the words "brat of an unbeliever," or *gavur*—infidel—were hurled at us?

That insult was always hard for me to bear; it was spit out so contemptuously I felt it reached all the way back to my ancestors and their beliefs. Was Asia as sensitive as I was? How much did those barbarous people torment the girl so that even the muhtar warned me against going? Was it right to heed his advice and not pay a visit? After all, if I did go, it would show the Kurds that a person close to the mudur, and somewhat influential—no matter that he was Armenian—was interested in Asia's fate, that she was not abandoned.

She probably has big dark eyes and cheeks like a newly ripened peach, I thought.

"You are mistaken. She is already withered," came a voice from nowhere, and it was so real that I stood up and looked around.

Nothing. I thanked God that I was born a boy. Life for boys, no matter how bad, was a thousand times better than for girls. When knife reached bone and we could withstand no more, at the least we might escape and look for another shelter. But girls—what could they do? At the first opportunity, their owners took them to their beds or married them off to a hateful Turk or a loutish Kurd five times their age, in exchange for a couple of cows or an ox, and then…I am thankful to God, yes merciful God, that I was born a male.

As it turned out, I never had a chance to see Asia. I heard from the Armenian carpenter's wife—theirs was the sole Armenian family in the village—that Asia's real name was Kohar. She did not remember what winds had blown her to Kurdistan, but she knew that her family name was Oumedian.

Kohar Oumedian, thirteen years old, brown hair, tall, and quite mature for her age. She was probably from a wealthy or prominent family because she was "intelligent and very polite." That is all she could tell me about her.

A TRAITOR AND A HORSE

Even before we arrived, our reputation as respectable and conscientious officials of the government had reached the Kurdish inhabitants of Yelijeh.

The former administrator, the mudur, had found a mistress among the village women and confined himself to the four rooms assigned to him, dividing his time between the banquet table and his bed of sin. The villagers deeply resented such behavior. True, they themselves were far from being saints. Adultery was commonplace and even customary among Kurdish men and women. But to commit open adultery with a Turk was contemptible and an unforgivable insult to the entire village.[7]

Our mudur, on the other hand, fulfilled all the qualifications of an honorable Turkish official, bringing with him four hanums (two wives and two daughters), an attendant, a servant and a maidservant, and he was met with unrestrained joy and great hopes.

The hanums were looked upon as fascinating and delightful creatures. From the first hour of the first day, many villagers brought gifts—items from their simple lives and earnest hearts: ten eggs, a

---

7 Government officials in charge of the Kurdish villages were Turkish, and although both Kurds and Turks were Muslims, centuries of dislike, fear, and distrust existed between them.

lamb, a head of cheese, a chicken that had stopped laying eggs, a portion of cracked wheat, some fresh homemade butter—everyday commodities that reflected the bearer's class or social standing. Yes, there were class hierarchies even in the mountains of Kurdistan. How else was it possible to regard an agha, who brought a milking cow, in the same class as the widow who came with six eggs tied in a handkerchief?

I do not know what the mudur thought about them, but I was sure that each of the gift bearers had expectations: a future favor to solicit, pardon for an old offense, or insurance for a rainy day. Evidence came scarcely two months after we had settled, when a Kurd with a jet-black beard and small eyes asked to see the mudur. He was wearing white baggy pants, and his hands were shoved deep into the thick coils of his sash.

The mudur was in his office, sitting with his wife, looking bored.

"A Kurd is here saying that he is the *kizir* [assistant to village head] of Chamluja and wishes to see you. His name is Ismail."

"Does he look civilized?"

"He is dressed in new clothes. He has a dagger and purse in his waistband."

"How do you know?"

"Because he keeps his hand on his waist. If you ask me, he looks like a Satan."

The mudur smiled faintly and told me to usher him in.

Following one polite exchange after another, the mudur grew restless. The kizir had something to say but was afraid to come to the point. He sat fidgeting and moving his feet. He pulled out a large red handkerchief and wiped his sweaty face. He shifted his eyes from the mudur to me, and with a swift jerk of his thumb, beckoned the mudur to dismiss me.

"Muselim, my son, go fix us some coffee."

I went into the kitchen, took out the roasted barley and chickpeas, and put the brass pot into the hot ashes to make the coffee. Moments later when I returned with the tray, the kizir was speaking excitedly and gesticulating. He stopped.

Certain that I would eventually hear about it, I left the room and went to see the mudur's wife, Naileh Hanum. Half an hour later, when he had departed with the usual ceremonial bows, the hanum and I rushed to the mudur's office and stood expectantly.

"Our work is going well," he said. "Do you know why the scoundrel came to see me? He brought me a list of offenders."

"Offenders?"

"Yes, a list of wrongdoers of all types. The best news is that most of them are well-to-do; he thinks a mere notice from me will send them rushing to my door with open money purses."

"Then I was right to call him a Satan."

"What is that to us, as long as he spreads butter on our bread? But I haven't told you the most important thing. He says that a woman from his village, named Katijeh, has an incomparable horse, about two years old. He swears that the likes of this horse is not to be found anywhere—not in our district, not in the entire province, not in the stables of the governor or all the sheiks and aghas."

"If he insists, he must know. But how are we to get hold of the horse? Is the owner on the lawbreakers' list?"

"Her name is not on the list, and the horse cannot be bought with money. The kizir says she is crazy about the animal and even denies its existence."

"Then what are we to do? First we have to confirm that the horse exists, then we have to find a way to get it."

"It may not be hard to find a way," the mudur said confidently. "Her brother is an army deserter, and he lives in the mountains."

"Good enough." I followed his thought. "The next time Kamil Bey comes hunting for deserters, we'll send him after the brother, or to their village."

"Impossible! That would be insane! When he hears about the

horse or if he sees it, God forbid, that is the end. You don't know these Cherkesy (Circassians). They give their souls for a beautiful horse, a beautiful woman, or a fine rifle."

We fell into deep thought.

"Tomorrow morning, leave for her village in Chamluja. Stop at her house and keep your eyes open. Say that you need to tend to your animal and make sure you look around her stable. See what you can find. If you fail in this I will have you skinned alive."

"If the horse really exists, I don't see how it can be kept a secret."

"The kizir swears it exists and is a thoroughbred, but he does not know where it is kept."

"Since he knows everything else, he must know where it is hidden. That rascal is lying."

The mudur, being Turkish, always mistrusted the Kurds and did not argue. Before sunrise the next morning, I set out on my mission.

It was a cool, beautiful summer morning, and the birds were trying to rouse the sun. A blue mist rose from the valley and clumps of white clouds moved lazily across the sky. Heavy dew shimmered like diamonds on upturned blossoms and leaves. As we rode on, tulip buds burst open right before my eyes in the shining sun.

My horse hop-skipped lightly over the path, his small, sharp ears alert to rabbits and other creatures hiding in the bushes. I inhaled deep breaths of fresh mountain air and bent over and stroked my horse's arched neck.

I was almost happy.

A little before midday I arrived at Chamluja, asked where Katijeh lived, and went there to stop for the night. Katijeh was not taken aback to see me. In the villages of Turkey and Anatolia, where hotels and motels did not exist, a traveler stopped at the home of someone he knew or knocked on the door of a villager who was considered well to do. If the traveler held an official position, hosting him was virtually mandatory.

Both Katijeh and I fulfilled these qualifications: she, a wealthy Kurdish widow whose hospitality was sought after by Turkish officers, and I, a representative of the Mudur Bey, head and master of the district.

She was about forty, and despite a face ravaged by smallpox, quite attractive. We sat opposite each other on the soft cushions of her guest room. She answered my questions in broken Turkish, murdering the grammar, but we understood each other easily. I explained that I was mudur's secretary and had come on a special mission.

"A thousand welcomes," she said courteously, although she started to torture the red apron covering her knees.

"I see I have frightened you," I said. "Do not worry, you have committed no offense and we have no legal issues. To put you at ease, let me say right off that we heard you have a young horse. I would like to see it."

"That is a lie. Who said that? Come and see my stable, search every corner, *Wallahi*, in the name of Allah, I have no horse."

"I don't know how true it is. That is what we were told."

"Who told you?" Her eyes sparked with anger.

I was sure she had the horse.

"The name of the informer is not important. We know that the horse is chestnut with white markings on its forehead and three legs. We know that it is an Arabian horse, two or three years old. We know that its mother was brought from Aleppo and that she gave birth right here."

Katijeh was astounded at the recital of details the mudur had given me. She opened her mouth to say something, but changed her mind or could not think of what to say. She put her hands up to her face and started to cry.

I stood there, confused. If the kizir had been there just then, I would have struck him. What did that reptile expect for this, I wondered? It was true that his treachery could add a wonderful horse to our stable, but at this moment I had no intention of threatening this girl for the horse.

I put my hand on her trembling shoulder and said, "Do not cry. I believe you. I will tell the mudur that there is no such horse. You might have already guessed that I am not a Turk, I am Armenian. I promise to do my best to help you keep your secret. I have not come here with evil intentions. We do not wish to seize your horse by force—no, our purpose is to buy it. The mudur instructed me to take you to him if I should fail. So if someone can watch over your home and the animals, we can go to see him. If you do not want to do that, I will go back alone and, as I said, will do my best to end the matter."

Katijeh dried her eyes with the tip of her apron, noisily blew her nose, came to me, took my hand, and despite my effort to stop her, kissed it over and over again.

"I am going to tell you something, but first you must swear," she said, smiling weakly for the first time.

"I can swear on anything you want, Allah, or the Prophet, or…"

"No, not those. Just now you said you are Armenian."

I nodded yes.

"Are your parents alive?"

"No, they were…"

"Pity, pity. I want you to swear on the souls of your mother and father that you will never reveal what I am about to show you."

"I swear."

Taking my arm, she led me to a high-roofed structure of unhewn stone and mud that formed the stable and barn. Inside was a wall with an opening that led to the stalls, also made of rough stone and mud. In this dark, damp place reeking of wet straw, she turned to me again and said: "Do not forget your oath."

"I won't forget."

She stepped to the wall and pried off a square block that had been ingeniously set in, put it down, and said in a voice shaking with pride: "Look!"

Through the hole I saw the head of a handsome horse, its sharp-pointed ears peaked up, fiery eyes, rosy trembling nostrils, the likes of which I had never seen. "*Mashallah*… God has willed it, *Mashallah*!" I was breathless with admiration.

Katijeh was crying and laughing. "He's a beauty, isn't he?"

"Beauty is not the word; he is a miracle…a miracle…a one and only."

"I hide him here, safe from the wild dogs and wolves that are always around. I creep in through this hole and feed him and keep him clean. When I miss him, which happens several times a day, I come here and talk to him."

Again her voice shook and her eyes filled.

"How long can you keep this magnificent animal stuck in here without any exercise?" I asked.

"That is my big worry," she admitted sadly. "I asked my brother-in-law for advice. He is the kizir of this village and he knows horses. He came here and looked him over, rubbed his knees and shoulders and examined him."

"What did he say?"

"He said the animal is as firm and strong as steel. He told me I have nothing to worry about."

"Is this kizir, this brother-in-law of yours, a trustworthy man?"

"Oh, yes. After all, we are related. He is my deceased husband's brother."

I ached to tell her that it was this "trustworthy" brother-in-law who had betrayed her and told the mudur about the horse to gain favor for himself, but I had sense enough to keep silent.

When we left the barn, she invited me to dinner.

"I do not have much except what God has given. But thanks to Him, I can put together some bread and moldy cheese."

"I like moldy cheese very much."

She set the table. The delicious fragrance of butter melting over an oakwood fire filled the house, and when she put the sooty pan on the table, it was sizzling with the round yellow eyes of eggs. The bread was made from wheat, and the cheese was not moldy.

As a sign of supreme respect, she did not sit with me. She remained standing, her hands tucked under the apron that hung down to her boots.

"Sit," I said. "I am not used to being served, I am uneasy. Please sit down."

She obeyed. She set her elbows, adorned with bracelets, at the edge of the table and rested her head on her hands. In this position she gazed at me sideways like a bird as I ate.

"How old was your mother when she died? Was she young?" she asked.

"Uh huh," I grunted.

"Did you have any brothers or sisters?"

"Brothers yes, sisters no."

"Did they all die?"

"Yes."

"Pity! May the homes of Turks go up in flames, may their hearths be destroyed, may fires burst upon their heads!"

"Were there any Armenians in your village?" I asked.

"There were," she replied. "They were all exiled or killed."

"Was there no one who could have saved a few children?"

"It was forbidden. Everybody had to be deported. Then later, when things relaxed, there were no children left to be saved or adopted. They all died along the way or were drowned. The witnesses wove a dirge about them:

The Euphrates River is cold and dark
For girls and brides cast in its depths,
Oh my girl, my girl, Euphrates is your end,
Become a Muslim and you will be saved."

She sang in a soft, silvery voice. As I listened to the artless song with its simple words and monotonous tune, I could not hold back tears. She was moved to see me like that and raised the tip of her apron to her eyes. From then until it was time for me to go, we did not speak, but the barrier between us was gone.

Late in the afternoon when shadows fell in the valleys, I prepared to leave. As I saddled my horse, she stood by me, hands folded across her belly, silently following my movements.

"Good-bye, Katijeh," I said, slipping my foot into the stirrup.

"Good-bye. God be with you."

"Do not worry."

She was crying.

I mounted my horse and dug in the spurs. He chomped at the bit and bounded forward. When I had gone some distance, I paused and looked over my shoulder. Katijeh was still rooted at the edge of the stream where I had left her.

I turned my horse, rode back close to her, and bending over my saddle, said: "I am a man of my word."

Then without waiting for an answer and without looking back, I rode away from Chamluja and from Katijeh.

⟶·❀·⟵

For some time after leaving her, I let my horse move ahead at will. I did not want to think of the day's events or what I would say to the mudur. My soul was at peace, and I wanted that to last as long as possible. I felt happy about my promise to Katijeh, as if I had done a good deed.

Everything around me seemed beautiful. Summer was still green in the mountains although the fields had started to yellow, and here and there was the glint of a rare scythe.

My mind went back to the wide fields of Ashkar Ova, near my homeland. On a happy day when we were on our way to the hot springs, I had passed by those fields with my family. The acres of wheat were like a sea, and the sun had not yet darkened over my people.

Already three years had passed since then, and now I, engulfed in memories, was riding in Kurdistan through fields that resembled our Ashkar Ova. That region must be abandoned now, I guessed, and my sorrow deepened. Being Armenian means having pain, I suppose. But why the need to be Armenian? How has it helped us? Has there been any advantage to being Armenian or staying Armenian? Has God, the Armenian God, ever heard us or helped us?

I remember clearly during 1915, when one of our neighbors, Vahan Palandjian's mother, after seeing the Turks throw her only son into the abyss, was taken with us into our desecrated church. Confronting the slashed paintings of saints on the altar, she screamed: "Go bury yourselves! Why do you stand there calmly, as though you have not seen anything? Didn't you see what I saw with my own weak eyes? Have you no eyes? Have you no miracles? What are you waiting for?"

My mother, standing beside her, put her hand gently over the woman's mouth, saying: "Shoosh, Mariam, my sister, shoosh. Do not sin; do not interfere with the will of God..."

Now I am starting to waver. Which one of them was right: Vahan Palandjian's brokenhearted mother, or mine?

⟿ ❀ ⟾

Seated on my horse with a pistol in my lap, I was happy to leave those memories behind, to be far from those bloody days, living as a Muslim among the Turks and Kurds. What more can I ask? I thought to myself.

But remembering my failed mission, my high spirits vanished.

What can I say to the mudur if he should hear that the horse actually exists, or if it is let out of its hiding place? What am I to do then? How can I cover up my guilt?

I am a fool. Why I was so softhearted with Katijeh? I even gave her my promise under oath. Was it because she said a few nice things about Armenians, or because of the tasty food she served me?

Worrying would not help. I decided to change course and head for a village where I could buy some raki for the mudur. Everybody bribed him that way, so why shouldn't I try? It was late when I reached the raki seller's village, so I stayed the night, thanked him, and left the next morning.

The air shone like a diamond, and the tree leaves and grass were bright after an overnight rain. My horse crossed the river without difficulty. Finally our village came into view, nestled in the foothills. As I moved up the riverbank, I heard the rattle of Haso's water mill. He was sitting on a cold stone, smoking his long pipe.

"Good morning, Haso, how are you?"

"Where do you come from so early in the morning?" he wanted to know.

"From Zeyveh. I was there for the last three days."

"Lucky you were not here."

"Did something happen?"

"Not at your house, but…"

"But what?"

"Did you know the girl, the *flah*, at the Abbass house?"

"No, I've only heard about her."

"Well, she died."

"Died? She was all right before I left."

"I found her corpse in the river."

I dismounted, took my horse's reins, and went to him.

"Tell me, Haso."

"Tell you what? I don't know anything."

"Please tell me what you know about the girl's death, even if it seems unimportant. You know that I am an Armenian and although, thanks to Allah, I am a Muslim and have accepted the true religion, I am interested in her. I would like to ask when I get home but that would cause suspicions about my faith, and I would be in trouble. So please help me and tell me whatever you know."

"Well, there is not much to say. I was sitting right here smoking my pipe when I noticed something colorful in the bushes on the riverbank. Strange, I thought. What could that be? I shaded my eyes like this"—he raised his hand above his brows to show me—"and looked again. I got up and walked over to it very slowly."

He stopped.

"What then?" I asked impatiently.

"There is no more. It was the *flah* from Abbasses' house. Dead. Turned blue. Her hair was floating on the current in black strands. I lifted her out of the water. I carried her to that oak tree and laid her in the shade, and sent word to the village. Toward evening they came and took the body....How did it happen? Believe me, I do not know. Later, I heard that Sulo's wife, Sabriye, buried her."

He paused to draw on his pipe, dimpling his cheeks.

"Haso," said I, taking advantage of the moment, "when you took the body from the water, were there any wounds—a knife, a bullet, signs of a beating or broken bones?"

"No, nothing. What I saw of her body was perfectly clear, waxen and bluish. Her belly was swollen."

"What do you mean?"

"My friend, I swear to Allah, I do not know. But it seemed to me that she was pregnant."

"Pregnant?"

"Yes, when I pulled her out of the water, her wet dress was stuck to her body like an onion. There were not many layers, and one long dress to her feet, and under it her belly was swollen and round. Just then the devil whispered into my ear that she was pregnant."

"Did you say anything when they came to take her?"

"Yes."

"Who came from the village?"

"Who do you expect? Whose duty was it? The muhtar and Abbass's son, Veli. They came with an oxcart and threw the corpse into it like a hay sack."

"Did they say how it happened, or who did it?"

"No, nothing, although I noticed that the muhtar and Veli were strained with each other."

"Why? Did they argue?"

"No, but the muhtar was cursing him under his breath."

I hurried home, heartsick. I swore to myself that someday, and with God's help, I would have the opportunity to punish the brute responsible for this.

Bozo was at the door when I got home. I handed him my horse and headed for the mudur's office. As I climbed the stairs, I regretted coming back with a negative report. Had I brought favorable news, I might have asked him, in his official capacity, to investigate the girl's sad end.

My fears were realized. The mudur was angry about my failure and called me "stupid and useless." Even seeing the bottles of raki was not enough to calm him. He ordered me out of the room and called his wife to come in and shut the door.

I went to the village to find Sabriye, the woman who had buried Asia. Sabriye was one of the largest of all women, almost a giant, but very well proportioned. When she bathed away the dirt, dust, smell, and sweat of her work and combed her ebony black hair that reached to her waist, which she did once a month, she looked splendid.

It is hard to explain why—was it her stance, her expressive black eyes, the way she held her head, her shapely curves, her feminine walk?—whatever it was, she looked as dignified as a queen, yet she was married to Sulo of Dersim.

Why she had married Sulo, I cannot say. She did not love or respect him, but she did not hate him either. She took care of him as one would do for a child. She would bathe him and try to teach him polite manners at the same time.

"Sulo, don't snort up your nose!"

"Sulo, eat slowly, don't slurp!"

"Sulo, don't wipe your nose on your sleeve."

Sulo would react as a stone. Physically and mentally he was like a bull. Comparing the size of his brain, tiny, to the size of his appetite, huge, was the topic of jokes all the way from Dersim to our village. Yet there was no one in the mountains of Kurdistan who could handle a scythe with his skill and dexterity. When he took the curved blade in his hands and spat in his palm, a vast expanse of grain would be flattened before nightfall in the path of his wide, steady swings.

And so, our kindhearted Sabriye was this man's wife. As I told you, she neither loved nor hated him; indeed, her big heart was incapable of feeling hate. I had heard about her goodness from the first day we arrived at our new headquarters.

Elmas, the Armenian carpenter's wife, pointed her out to me. "Do you see that woman? She is pure gold. Before you came, a number of Armenian boys and girls in the village died from heavy work and malnutrition, one after the other. It was Sabriye who buried them; she cared for them when they were sick and discarded by their owners."

Soon after, I invited her to our house to pick up some bread and thanked her.

"My dear sister," I said, "I am going to ask you something, and I hope you won't be annoyed."

"Ask," she said, smiling.

"Sabriye…the young orphans who died, those you took to the valley, did you say anything when you buried them?"

"Yes, of course, I prayed."

I wondered how she prayed or to whom, but did not ask.

Then she continued: "As long as someone prays for the soul of the dead, no matter that it is Sabriye's prayer directed to her Allah, I know that the souls of those precious children are protected and resting in eternal peace."

In those days it was a huge consolation for us to find anybody who cared about us, even after death. I felt grateful to Sabriye for praying for the young ones.

Arriving at her low, earthen hut, I pushed on the door and entered. No one was home. In a corner of the room, under a woven cover of black goat's hair, were several layers of rags and remnants used as bedding. An empty soup kettle and two wooden spoons were at the fireplace. The next time the Armenian coppersmith comes around, I will have him repair this kettle, I thought, eyeing the utter misery of the room.

It was the hut of a couple that worked like animals, year round. They were strong and industrious, but what did they have? What did they get for their work? Barely enough bread to keep alive, and if they were sick for a couple of days, even that bread would be gone, because the land they worked was not theirs.

I saw a pair of old torn sandals hanging on the wall. Perhaps Sulo put them there to be mended or to protect them from his hungry dog. I wondered why they kept that dog. Maybe it was to prove they actually owned something in this world…maybe it made them feel rich and happy.

Shaking off these thoughts, I left. I wanted to find Sabriye and question her, but where was she? As I walked through the village streets, somebody called. It was Elmas, the carpenter's wife.

"Brother Aram, won't you come in for a moment?" she said.

She had barely closed the door when she fell on a cushion and began crying.

"I killed the poor girl. I am responsible….."

"I don't understand," I said, going to her. "Calm down, calm down and tell me, slowly."

Amid sighs and tears, she spoke in Armenian, as we were alone: "A couple of months ago Asia came to my house, complaining of weakness and nausea. She told me that she felt like sleeping all day, that before starting her daily chores she was already tired. 'I live in hell,' she said. She cursed her fate and the day she was born. I tried to comfort her as much as I could. I asked a few questions and realized that she was pregnant, but said nothing to her. The later she finds out, the better, I thought.

"I should have gone to the mudur that very day and told him and begged him to take responsibility for her, but I did not. I misjudged. You were still new in this village…I was frightened for myself and my husband, I was afraid that they would think our conversion to Islam was a hoax, that we were not good Muslims because we wanted to help a *gavur*. I was afraid, so I kept my mouth shut and sent the poor girl back to the house of those dogs, saying words to her that I did not believe myself.

"The next time she came to visit, she knew everything. Her belly was swollen a little and her walk was slow. She told me that Abbass's wife had shouted to her face that she had crawled into their house like a snake and seduced her son and her husband. After that, the poor girl's life was hell. They beat her and cursed her every day. And she, my God, was getting more and more beautiful. She started to talk about suicide, about throwing herself into the river.

" 'Never do anything like that,' I told her. 'Wait for just a couple of months. You will be free of your heavy burden and you'll forget everything.'

" She sobbed bitterly, 'Is it easy to be free? Is it easy to wait? Is it easy to forget?' She could not stop crying and shaking.

" 'The world will not stay like this forever. Good days will come,' I said. 'You are still young and healthy. We all live on hopes…that is all we have.' I even told her that she might love the baby once it was born.

"She became terrified. Her eyes opened wide and she put her hand on her heart and stopped crying. She pressed her lips to a tight line and her face was frozen white. She spoke no more. She stood up, head high, and left without another word."

She dried her tears: "You know the rest."

"No, I do not! I don't know whether it was Abbass or his son, Veli. I don't know whether she committed suicide or if they threw her into the river to get rid of her. I don't know what happened when her body was brought to the village. Did anybody try to find out how she drowned or who was responsible?"

"The mudur was a little interested at first, but when he decided that she had committed suicide, the case was closed. The villagers met around the body and the muhtar spat on Veli's face, publicly, and called him a murderer. Veli ran home and came back with his gun to kill him. People could barely stop him. They forced the gun out of his hand. Sulo dug a ditch in the valley of willows and Sabriye buried her. What else do you want to know?"

"Were you at the burial?"

"No, I was afraid. But after dark, I went there alone and recited the Lord's Prayer over her."

"I still do not understand about the fight between the muhtar and Veli. Since when do two Kurds try to kill each other over an Armenian girl?"

"The girl was only an excuse. Their enmity is for a different reason. Everybody thinks that Veli is having an affair with the muhtar's wife."

"Then you think that…"

"I don't think anything. I don't know anything," she said.

At the edge of the village, almost secluded, was a juniper tree that the Kurdish women considered sacred. They would tie a piece of clothing or a ribbon to one of its branches to rid themselves of pain or illness. It grew on a peaceful and snug plot of land at the top of a small hill, out of sight. I went there and sat for a long time.

⟿⟿ ⊛ ⟿⟿

Only one week had passed when Katijeh, owner of the magnificent horse, arrived at our door, disheveled, dusty, and frightened.

"Why are you like this, Katijeh, what happened?"

"I am doomed. My fire is extinguished," she wailed, pounding her knees with her fists.

"The horse?"

"No, my brother. They captured my brother in the mountains."

"An escapee?"

She nodded, crying.

"Who got him?"

"Kamil Bey."

"Where is your brother now?"

"He is still in the village. They caught him last night. Kamil Bey surrounded the village with a hundred soldiers. All the boys were taken by surprise. His men swarmed down like locusts and cut off all the escape routes…not even a fly could get out. They sealed the houses, they burned the barns and stables, they searched everywhere. Beatings, threats, laments…it was something to see. They found my brother and took him away."

"And the horse?"

"The horse is untouched. My brother was hiding at Sidar's house when they found him. If he had been with me, I would have hidden him with the horse. Maybe he would have escaped."

"What do you want us to do now?"

"I came to offer my horse to the Mudur Bey. It is my gift to him if he can save my brother."

Being a Kurdish woman, Katijeh was terrified, knowing that six months before, the Turkish high commander, Vehip Pasha, had proclaimed that all military escapees and anyone helping them would be captured, strung up, and hanged.

"Wait here!" I ran inside.

The mudur and the first hanum were opposite each other in deep conversation. I blurted out everything and added: "Allah has delivered the horse into our hands."

He listened closely but did not speak.

"What are we going to do?" I asked.

"Nothing!" hastened his wife, her voice rising. "Is it worth risking so much danger for a horse?"

"Do not worry, my woman. I shall not step on a rotting branch; I've done that already. Now I am cautious. I even blow over a cup of lukewarm tea."

Then he asked me to bring in Katijeh.

She entered as one would come before a powerful king, veil over her face, hands on her belly. She went to the mudur, who was seated on a divan, bent down, and kissed the soles of his feet.

"Get up, get up," the hanum said, touching her shoulder.

"My dear Hanum, my Mudur Bey, my pashas, blessed be your souls, I am ready to sacrifice myself for your well-being. I am in your hands. I erred. I spoke a lie by saying that I have no horse. Forgive me. Let my horse and my useless life be a gift to you, a sacrifice. Charge my behavior to my ignorance, but please save my brother. He is the only hope of our home and hearth…"

She curled over the dirt floor as in Islamic prayer and started to weep.

Naileh Hanum helped her up. "We will do what we can."

"Sit and tell me what happened, calmly," said the mudur, lighting a cigarette.

She was too upset to speak, and turned to me. I recited exactly what I had heard from her.

Within a half hour, the mudur and I were riding toward Chamluja to meet Kamil Bey. I carried a purse filled with gold pieces and two bottles of good raki, the mightiest weapons of the Ottoman Empire.

We reached Chamluja in less than three hours, and stopped for lodging at the luxurious quarters of Koorshid Agha, where we learned with great pleasure that Kamil Bey was still there with twenty-one captives.

"My friend," said the mudur, "run and find that scoundrel and, in my name, see that he comes here or we go to meet him. Make it to look like we are on a routine tour, that we are here by chance."

As I rushed to leave he shouted after me, "Prove yourself, do not return empty- handed. Use your infidel brains!"

Every corner of every street in the village was thick with Kamil Bey's guards. Several of them were at the government building with Muhiddin, who was Kamil Bey's younger brother. I did not know if he remembered our last encounter when he'd kicked me. I bowed and greeted them.

"What is it, infidel son?" he said.

"I have a message for Kamil Bey."

"Can you tell me? He is busy."

"Yes, of course, it is not confidential, but I was instructed to tell him in person."

"Well then, go in."

The commander stood in the middle of a carpeted room, swinging his silver-handled whip right and left, lecturing a group of villagers. I went to a corner and waited while he spoke.

"You all are the enemies of the state! These twenty-one boys did not escape from the front just now. In fact some of them have *never* been to the front, but have remained in bed with their wives all this time! Who provided their food and shelter? Who protected them to this day? That is what I really want to know. Furthermore, I have eight other names on my list, and I am giving you two hours to bring them here. If within those two hours you do not offer a credible excuse for not delivering those eight men, I swear in the name of Allah and His Beloved Prophet that I will take your entire population like a herd of animals before the High War Tribunal. What's more I will burn the whole village to the ground, leaving not one stone on top of another! If I do not keep this oath, my name is not Commander Kamil."

The Kurds, terrified by the horror facing them, were struck dumb. I took advantage of the silence and moved out of my corner toward him.

"Kamil Bey, we stopped here on one of our routine tours, and when the Mudur Bey learned that you were also here, he sent me to invite you to join us."

"What's up?" he snapped.

"Nothing special...but we came across some fine raki along the way, which pleased the Mudur Bey, and when he heard about you, he thought you might join him and pass an enjoyable time together."

The commander paced up and down a few steps, grinding sharp and noisy turns on his heels. He shoved his whip into one of his boots.

"Let's go."

He stopped at the door, barked some rapid directions to his brother, and we left.

⊷ ⊛ ⊶

Kamil Bey was handsome. His sky-blue uniform hid a muscular, well-formed body. His light hair, beneath a lambskin cap, was almost the color of his buttons and epaulettes. His walk was sure and proud, as though proclaiming to those who bowed and scraped before him: "It is I who created these mountains..."

We soon arrived at the mudur's lodgings. Upon seeing us, he jumped to his feet.

"Welcome my commander, welcome. Come in, what an honor. I was afraid that you would reject my invitation and leave me all alone..."

"Hello, my dear Mudur Bey, you have shown me a great honor by inviting me. I am thankful."

"On the contrary, I must thank you..."

"Forgive me."

"Thank you."

"Come in."

"With your permission."

"My dear mudur."

"My brother."

"My pasha."

"To your health."

"Thank you."

"My dear *efendi*."

"My brother."…

Sitting across from each other, they drank raki, downed grilled morsels of lamb and liver, licked their fingers, and soon the euphoria rose to a height where they actually believed all their polite phrases and exaggerated compliments. Now they were ready to sacrifice anything for each other.

The mudur shrewdly led the conversation to his companion's successful mission.

"Without firing a single bullet and without any harm to my men, I captured twenty-one escapees," boasted the commander. Then, encouraged by the mudur's adulation, he added: "The Kurds are brainless, they are dumb asses."

"If they had any brains they would not be in this situation today," agreed the mudur. "Too bad they disobey the law and become enemies of the state. Yet I think it is unfair to judge them all on the same basis. Take, for example…"

At that moment, upon an almost imperceptible nod from the mudur, I left the room to get some "fresh appetizers."

"My son," the mudur had said to me one day, as he instructed me on the fine points of my duties, "no unlawful discussion or agreement should be made in the presence of a witness, no matter who is involved. All witnesses, sooner or later, cause headaches. Furthermore, because every caution must be taken, the presence of a witness can sometimes cause the agreement to fail. Remember this and conduct your negotiations accordingly. And when the situation involves me, make sure you quietly disappear from the scene."

The time had come for me to retreat into the kitchen.

Ten minutes later they called me. I ran to the room and stood, arms crossed respectfully.

The mudur held out a piece of paper, saying, "Take this message to Kamil Bey's brother, Muhiddin, and return immediately. On your way back, go to where the tribal chiefs are meeting and ask them, in my name, to give three rams and ample sacks of cracked wheat to the commander's soldiers as food for the night. Make sure that you yourself check that the rams are plump and well fed, with fatty tails."

Muhiddin was enraged to read that he was to free a captive runaway, but hearing that the finest rams would replace their usual miserable rations, he calmed down and stopped cursing and shouting. Once again he resented having to give way to Kamil, but it meant losing only one of his captives, and there was always the possibility of recapture. He ordered his aide to release Katijeh's brother.

That night, just before we were about to retire, Katijeh came to the mudur to express her gratitude, kissing his hands and feet, and praising his family.

"Your horse, my Bey, is in the stable. Take it whenever you wish. May it be a blessing for you."

"No," said the mudur, "I want to buy it."

"But my dear Bey, I promised. Let it be an offering. Let it be as blessed as the milk of your mother."

"I will pay what it is worth."

The following day, with the infamous kizir and the village muhtar looking on, we bought the horse for forty pieces of silver, threw a felt blanket on its back, and brought it home.

Chickens and trees were the most fascinating sights for him when he was first let outdoors. The horse never tired of searching the forest and the horizon beyond, spiking up his fine, sharp ears. Sometimes, when he was bored, he would start chasing a hen, or lower his head to nudge it under the porch with his nose.

"Shame on you. See how big you are, what do you want from the poor hens?"

"He is a toddler, he wants to play," the mudur would say protectively. "All his life in prison, he had no chance to see the hills or valleys. He is amazed at the sights."

"Maybe he imagines how nice it would be if he could run freely in the wind."

"He'd better forget those dreams; his days of freedom will soon be over. Anytime now he will feel a bit in his mouth and a saddle on his back, and he will have to be a true horse."

Despite our plans and his large size, though, he remained a little boy until his milk teeth were gone. He fought me when I tried to brush him twice a day, and when I bent over, he would bite my clothes. When I scolded him, he seemed to nod his head up and down, only to resume his mischief a second later. Then I would tease him and offer my palm for him to bite, but pull it back quickly when he went for it. Protesting, he would rear up on his hind legs and churn the air with his forelegs. His hooves were growing and needed to be trimmed. It was also time to think about shoeing him.

Our local blacksmith confessed that the job was beyond him. "My Bey, you need a professional farrier for this. My experience is too limited for this magnificent horse. If it was a Kurd's donkey, that would be different, but not this animal."

We learned that an expert blacksmith named Magar lived in one of the distant villages. We sent after him. He was an elderly man, about sixty, and he was frightened. He was tall, with long white hair, an oval face, and small black eyes. His hands were thin, his fingers long and waxy. Although he was wearing the usual woolen Kurdish shirt and loose pants, someone seeing him for the first time would take him for a sheik rather than an Armenian blacksmith.

When he dismounted, I shook his hand saying: "Welcome, Uncle Magar."

"Hello, my son, are you Armenian?"

"Yes, Uncle Magar."

"Where are you from?"

"Karahisar."

"Ah, they were brave people. Did anyone from your family survive?"

"Only I."

"Well, that is something, too. Why has the mudur called me here?"

"To shoe his horse. We have a wonderful horse."

"Is the mudur a good man? I've heard he is, but I could not believe it, I was afraid that again…"

He did not finish the sentence; no Armenian felt safe in those days.

I led him to the mudur and then to the stable.

"But this is not a horse. It is a marvel, a marvel. May you see the best of him, my Bey."

"Thank you. We expect you to use all your skills."

"With pleasure, my Bey."

He took several tools from his sack and waited for somebody to lift the horse's foot.

We called Sulo. We called Guelo. We also called Fasih and Ali. No use. Alone or together, it was impossible to lift the horse's foot. Finally I caressed his forehead, stroked him, spoke to him, praised him, and slowly bent down and lifted his right foreleg. He did not resist.

The old man filed and measured his hooves quickly and left, promising to return in a week.

After he had gone, the mudur said: "I am still not sure that it was wise to massacre the Armenians, but saving Magar and workers like him was definitely a smart thing to do."

With an air of having recited a profound thought, he lit a cigarette and went to the harem.

One week later, as promised, old Magar showed up at our door with four horseshoes in his toolbox. We inspected them one by one.

All of us truly loved that horse. He had brought color into our ordinary lives, and anything to do with him was important to us.

"I used two broken plows to make them," the old man explained, seeing our interest.

"Plows?" The mudur was surprised.

"Yes, Bey, where else could I find some steel?"

The mudur said nothing. Again, he had some private misgivings about annihilating the Armenians.

The blacksmith finished the job with great care and, without staying for lunch, mounted his horse and left.

Now the mudur sent word to the best riders of his province to come and train his unruly and beloved animal. They came one by one and in groups, with servants, and curiosity, and mixed expectations.

The first steps were easy. The experts placed a saddle on his shiny back. They tied the stirrups higher to prevent rubbing his sensitive ribs and hindering his stride. Days later, they added a sack of sand to his saddle. They bridled him and lowered the stirrups. The horse endured these steps well, but when one of them tried to mount him, uttering "*Bismillah*, in the name of God," he reared up on his hind feet and beat the air, his eyes fiery.

Enticing words were useless. His nostrils flared and his ears flattened back. The men stood away.

I went to him and put my arms around his neck and talked to him, saying that he was a pasha, and he was right to reject those barbarous foreigners. I put my palm on his nose and said: "Bite, if you can. Do you want me to take off your saddle?"

He lowered his head, subdued and calm. His ears were normal, and when he looked toward the mountains, the trees and the horizon were reflected in his eyes.

I patted his thick mane and went to the mudur who was standing at the door, looking worried.

"Do you want me to ride him?"

"What?"

I could not believe my daring. "Do you want me to ride him?" I repeated, turning also to the Kurds.

"Fool." It was Koorshid Agha from Kangal.

I waited for the mudur.

"Try," he said. "We have nothing to lose, but if you are disabled because of this stupidity," he warned, "I will not take you into the house."

"Don't worry, I have no intention of getting disabled."

"God willing."

"May I take the saddle off and put on a felt cover?"

"Do whatever you want."

They did not know that during my first year and a half of exile, when we took Ali Bey's herds out grazing, we would ride our horses bareback on the sand along the river, often racing with the other Armenian boys.

The servants formed a circle around the horse and me. I removed the saddle and gave it to Bozo. I took a wide woolen band and secured the heavy felt cover that I'd spread on his back, and threw the reins over him. Ignoring the others, I wrapped my arms around his neck and spoke to him.

"Look, my boy, do not shame me in front of all these big men. If you do, I won't speak with you any more. Believe me. I will not come to you or bring you even one handful of food. Up to now, we have played and laughed together like brothers, and I have taken care of you without asking for anything. Now it is your turn; do not leave me in shame."

He seemed to listen, eyes half closed, but when I took my arms off his neck he snatched my headgear.

"Give me back my hat."

Again.

He looked away as the Kurds mocked me, poking each other. I pulled the horse close to the fence. I stepped on a rail, reached his head, grabbed my hat from his mouth, and jumped on his back. He turned to see who it was. No, he was not mistaken; it was his friend, leaning over to caress his neck and whispering sweet and loving words into his ear.

"It is me, my pasha, don't worry."

He clamped down on the bit, threw his head back, stretched his neck out, and started to run against the wind, his mane streaming.

I looked back and waved to the group standing around the mudur, gaping.

Was that Kadriye watching, half hidden behind the thick curtain at the patio window?

My heart was filled.

MANNA

The lower fields of barley were harvested and the crop stored for animal feed when the muder called me to his side.

"My friend, I have arranged to have you appointed secretary to the tax collector. You can manage it, it is not difficult. In a few days somebody will come to show you how to keep books. You will do that work in the daytime and return home in the evenings. But especially when I am away on business, you must return home without fail from wherever you are, otherwise the women will be alone and terrified."

I was elated. Being the only one in the mudur's vicinity who could read and write, I would be free of the weariness of field work for a few months. I would travel from village to village to collect the payments and, who knows, I might have a chance to meet other Armenians—more good news!

I said nothing about it, but I was happy.

A few days later a man with a white pennant tied to his fez brought me a ledger. His name was Bakir *efendi*.

We settled under a shade tree and he opened the book on his knees. "It is very simple," he said. "Here you write the name of the farmer… here, the name of the village. In this column you write the name of the grain—barley, wheat, rye, and so on…and in this column, the quantity. You measure his produce and take three from every eight bushels— that means three eighths of his harvest. The first eighth is the regular tax, the second is wartime tax, and the third is for purchase by the government. After the successful end of the war, it will be paid back to the farmer."

"Shall I give them receipts for all this?"

"No, our records are considered the receipts. Do you understand?"

"Yes, I understand."

"You understand because you are Armenian. It takes hours to explain these simple things to our people."

He lowered his voice and moved closer to me. "Once in a while, do not forget to take a share for the mudur. For instance, you write 'ten' instead of 'fifteen,' and you send the difference home."

I rose up instantly: "Sir, I want you to know that the Mudur Bey never accepts illegal income."

"My son, you are inexperienced but clever," he said, stroking his gray beard. "Nazum Bey is lucky to have you in his service."

He put the ledger under my arm and left on horseback.

When I told the mudur about our conversation, his face grew serious. He said nothing as he listened, but when I reached the last part, I could see that he was pleased.

The official tax collector whom I was to assist as secretary was a Kurd named Rashid Agha—bearded, heavy, and illiterate, but a man with wide experience in record-keeping and numbers. He was close to sixty or so. He had sad eyes and big, thick hands that had felt no heavy work. He was the agha of a village that was not far from ours.

From the outset we became good friends and worked well together. We stole for the mudur, we stole for our horses' winter rations, we stole for him, and once, five bushels of satiny translucent wheat for me.

We were up in the mountains, measuring grain sacks that belonged to the wealthiest Kurd of the village. After offering us some cream and honey that had just been taken from a hive, he started chattering, obviously worried.

"I have a new type of wheat," he explained. "It is not much and I would like to keep all of it for seed. When you see for yourselves, you will agree. It is exceptional, more like rice than wheat. I want to ask you to measure it and figure the tax, whatever it is, but then let me have it back for one gold piece per bushel."

He took a sack from the folds of his sash and spread a handful of shiny gold pieces on a wooden table.

I looked at his sunburned, ruddy face and imploring eyes. Rashid Agha and I nodded to each other in agreement, and, of course, as my senior, it was his place to speak.

"We can arrange it," he said, taking a huge bite from the bread filled with cream and honey.

We went to the barn where the newly threshed wheat was heaped in a pyramid. It truly was like rice. The grains were plump, regular in size, glistening, and bursting with white flour. Our host pushed his hand into the pile and lifted a palmful up to our eyes.

"For the love of Allah, have you ever seen wheat like this?" he exclaimed, pouring the grains from one hand to the other. "Have you ever in your life...?"

We started back as the sun was sinking behind the mountains. In my pocket were five gold pieces. Now and then I would take them out, hold them up, and count them, again and over again. The coins were stamped with the sultan's seal, reddish yellow and shining as though newly minted.

When we reached the main road, Rashid Agha led his horse close to me and leaned over: "Are you satisfied?"

"Very. Rashid Agha, I am very pleased that you did not forget me. The truth is that since the summer of 1915, I have been able to save four silver coins, and a few weeks ago I used them to buy some raki for the Mudur Bey. These five gold pieces are the easiest and the most I ever earned in all my life. I am thankful to you."

He was pleased. He put a long cherrywood pipe to his lips, pulled a couple of deep puffs through his thick mustaches, and spurred his horse.

We were en route to another village in the mountains. Steep trails made climbing difficult for the horses, so we let them make their own way as they proceeded along the narrow passes, breathing slowly, deeply.

"We are headed to a place that is not a village," explained Rashid. "I don't know what to call it. Only one family lives there, and they have plenty of land and animals. They are self-sufficient and produce all they need—lentils, chickpeas, fava beans…and their honey is superb.

"The spot was settled by two brothers who found this beautiful place near a spring. They built a new house, and each brother had selected a bride when the war broke out. They were drafted into the army, but they deserted in less than six months and became escapees.

"They joined a group of bandits, fought the government soldiers, and on one bleak day, both of them were killed. Word spread through our mountains that the brothers died to save the bandit leader, Massoud. I don't know, I am telling you what I heard. Then the gendarmes came and took their old father, saying his sons had killed Turkish soldiers. He died under heavy beatings.

"When it was all over, Massoud sent word that he would personally punish and kill anybody who did not respect the widows, their home and property. Since then, the women have lived alone with only their memories. When it comes time for plowing, seeding, reaping, threshing, our boys from the nearby villages go over and do everything needed for them without expecting pay. That is what Massoud wants."

He paused. "When we measure their crops, close one eye. The government will not be any richer or poorer for what we take or do not take from them. Be polite with Emine and Besi. You are young and you might have some expectations. Be careful. Besi was the elder brother's wife, and Emine is her sister. She is a beauty. When you look at her face, the world shines."

"Isn't there some young Kurd to marry one of them and start a new family?"

"I do not know, but so far, they are not married."

The sun had lowered to the rims of the surrounding hills, and our horses were walking over their lengthening shadows on the trail.

"Is there much to go, Rashid Agha?"

"No, after this valley and a little farther."

The house stood at the base of a hill. Beside it were a large stable and barn, and a little beyond, protected from the strong sun, the beehives. A creek of sparkling water flowed all around.

Besi and Emine came to greet us. They calmed the dog and spoke in Kurdish with Rashid Agha, whom they'd known for a long time. Rashid introduced me. They smiled and led our horses away.

"Wasn't I right? Tell me, wasn't I right about Emine?" He poked me with his elbow.

Truly, she was very beautiful. She was wearing a long shirt, loose red pants, and a blue apron. Her elaborately woven hair fell on her shoulders, and her face was the color of golden wheat.

"Now I know why your mouth was watering along the way," I said to him.

"Don't try to do anything foolish!" he warned.

"Am I crazy?"

We were tired after the long journey. We sat down to rest on the wide veranda, stretched our legs, and sighed to show our contentment.

"In the morning, we will measure the produce and start back after breakfast. Now we can rest."

The women returned: "We unsaddled the horses and fed them barley."

"Our arrival is inconvenient," Rashid said, "but we have to make our rounds before the rainy season. We do not wish to cause you any trouble. We will be satisfied with a piece of bread and cheese."

"What are you saying? You are welcome, our home is yours! We are all alone here and we are hungry for company," said Besi, earnestly.

"Dear sister," I intervened, "Rashid Agha is your godfather, and I am Armenian. Although we represent the government, we come as friends. We will not go to the barn tomorrow. We will take your word to calculate the tax and record whatever you tell us."

"May God give you many long days and years, and may God not spare your shadow from our hearth. Blessed be both your lives. May God punish those who destroyed our home," said Besi, lifting the corner of her apron to her eyes.

⌁⬧⌁

"Where are you going to sleep?"

It was Emine, after we had finished our meal.

"I want to sleep outdoors," I said. "I like to lie on my back and look at the stars. My mother used to say that everyone has his own star in the sky, and when it falls, that person dies on earth."

Rashid Agha preferred to sleep with a roof over his head. "The night dew is cold and my blood is not as hot as his. My joints will ache," he explained.

His bed was prepared under the overhang in the barn, and mine was on the threshing floor. When Emine carried the woolen covers there, I tried to help her.

"Making a bed is not a man's work," she said.

"No, but I am used to it. At home I make the beds every night and put them away in the morning."

"You fix the beds of the hanums, too?"

"Yes…that is, I do the bed of the senior hanum."

Embarrassed, she covered her face with her hands.

"What did you expect? Of course I do those things! Can I say no? Can I protest?"

"I suppose not." She paused. "If I ask something, will you tell me?"

"If I know the answer…."

"Are the hanums' sheets made of silk?"

"No, they are plain white linen. They were taken from the Armenians."

"Oh, I thought all the hanums slept in silk sheets," she said.

She was quiet before starting anew. "Why do you stay with them?"

"What can I do? I am waiting for the war to end so I can decide where to go and what to do."

"You will go to your people, won't you?"

"God knows what will happen, and what ties I might have in your mountains. God knows if enough of my people will be left alive to be called a people. I can't answer you because I know nothing of tomorrow. But one thing I do know," I said. "When the day comes, I will look for my mother."

"Do you think she is still alive?"

"As long as I have no news of her death, I have hope."

"Where will you look?"

"Along the banks of the Euphrates."

"You must hate my people for what they've done to you."

"I have been living among you for more than three years, and everybody has been good to me."

"That is because you are good and you always help us. Godfather Rashid told us that you help our boys hiding in the mountains."

"He is wrong. I haven't helped your boys in this region."

"What difference does it make, here or there? They are all Kurds, aren't they?"

I did not answer. The bed was ready. She straightened her hair, said nothing more, and left.

I followed her walk with my eyes, then went over to the barn. Rashid Agha was quashing his last cigarette and had started to untie his moccasins. I bade him good night and went to my bed on the threshing floor.

The night was bright and cloudless, with a thin new moon. Stars covered the sky and peace flowed like honey from above. It was hard to believe that war was raging in another corner of the world. I did not understand why people were fighting like wild animals and killing each other. I undressed and slipped under the woolen quilt.

Far, far away, from the other side of the valley, a blinking light, probably from a shepherd's hut, pierced the darkness.

Time had stopped for me. I don't know how long I dreamed or what disturbed my thoughts. I went back to my home and my childhood. Compared to these surroundings, the mountains and sunny fields of my birthplace were sweeter. In my mind's eye I saw the creek where I had washed a boy's tireless feet, who knows how many times. I remembered my classmates and how we rushed out of the schoolhouse to race in the fields.

Where are my friends, Shavarsh, Azad, Papghen, Vaheh, Massis? Were some of them destined to be the pride of our nation? What happened to them? Are they alive? Where were our wise and enlightened teachers killed…in which valley, in which river? Which barbarous animal washed his hands with their blood? Oh, the weak, clumsy God of Armenians.

Dejected and exhausted, I was about to fall asleep when I thought I heard footsteps near the thresher.

"Who knows what it is," I mumbled, and pulled the cover over my ears. A moment later someone came to my bed on tiptoe and bent over me, breathing on my shoulder. I opened my eyes and raised my head to see Emine's smiling, sweet face.

"What do you want?" I whispered, taken aback.

"Hush!" she said, putting her little hand on my mouth. "Hush, you will wake everybody."

"What is it?" I asked, pulling her hand away from my mouth but keeping it in my palm.

"Hush, don't make any noise. Don't you see I'm shivering? Warm me a little."

She really was shivering, and her hand was cold as ice.

"How did you get so cold?"

"Besi and I went to the creek to take a bath, and we stayed too long. We thought you would have heard our shouts."

"No, I didn't hear anything. Maybe Rashid Agha did."

When I said his name she giggled and covered her mouth with her hand. Then, bending over me, she put her lips to my ear and whispered:

"Besi got into his bed to get warm."

"Well then, get in if you want to warm up."

"Close your eyes."

"Why?"

"I need to undress."

"But if you want to be warm, it's better not to take off your shirt."

"Don't you know that Kurdish women go to bed naked?"

"I know, but..."

"Shush..."

She climbed in behind my back and wrapped her arms around me.

Now it was my turn to shiver.

My sleepiness vanished.

I was lying motionless.

I felt her warm, uneven breath on my neck and the gentle pressure of two mounds on my back...

Did my pagan forefathers have a God of Patience?

What was his name...?

After a hearty and delicious breakfast, we bid good-bye to our paradise, leaving Emine with a hint of tears in her eyes.

On the road, Rashid Agha was supremely content, smiling and smoothing his thick beard. Finally, as we neared home, he could no longer resist; he leaned toward me on his horse and said, glowing: "Do you know what? Last night, after you went to sleep, Besi came into my bed."

"Really? Is that so? You lucky dog...you sly fox." I aped his voice and words of the night before: 'Prepare my bed under some shelter, my blood is cold, the night dew is not good, it causes joint pain.' And all that was because you wanted to be alone so you could take Besi into your bed, you...you sly fox."

Happy and flattered, he laughed loud and heartily.

When we arrived at the house, I rushed in and they all gathered around.

"Where were you yesterday?"

"Why didn't you come home last night?"

Bozo came in, excited, his eyes blinking fast: "Your horse is waiting for you. Every time I opened the stable door he whinnied and then, seeing it was not you, he would lower his ears."

I ran to the stable. I took his head into my arms and patted his neck. I talked to him and gave him my palm to chew on. I caressed his mane and back, and for the ultimate treat, I ran to the mudur's office, took a cigarette from his box, lighted it, ran back and, taking a deep puff, blew the smoke into his nose. He breathed it in and asked for more, stomping his foot on the ground again and again.

I felt happy that everyone had missed me. But Kadriye seemed indifferent, and hadn't a single word for me. That afternoon and until bedtime she remained cold. She was the same in the morning. By midday, I decided to wait for Rashid Agha and got on my horse to meet him.

"You seem upset," he said, running his eyes over my face.

"Why shouldn't I be?" I said bitterly. "Besides owning my life and body, these people own my feelings and soul."

"What happened now?"

"They are angry because I didn't come back last night."

"Didn't you explain that we were far away and it was not possible?"

"I explained. No use."

"Did you tell them where we were?"

"Am I crazy? So they would surely guess your nighttime escapade?"

"Hah, hah," he laughed, and stroked his beard, pleased with himself.

Toward evening I went to see the village carpenter. He was not home, so I chatted with his wife, Elmas, for a while, and turned the conversation to Kadriye.

"For the last two days she has not spoken to me," I told her.

"I've known for a long time that you had an eye on her," she said, kindling the fire.

"But it is impossible," I protested, my face reddening. "She is the daughter of a bey, and I am a servant!"

"You were not a servant in your father's house. Does she know that?"

"She knows, but…"

"Listen, my son, love does not follow rules, and cannot be bound with rules or expectations. Besides, if all the lovers in this world ended up together, no novels would ever be written."

"Then what is the use of having feelings for somebody?"

"I don't know about that, but I do know that when her father and mother find out what's going on right under their noses, they will see that a bullet gets you in the belly or skull. I do not say this to blame you. Kadriye is very beautiful, a little too beautiful. You are under the same roof, side by side, every day. You are both young and inexperienced. Even if you were saints, you would be tempted. But as an elder sister I am warning you, it cannot end well. And the bloodshed will be on your head."

I went out, troubled and still hoping for the impossible.

CHAPTER 8

The Last Year, 1918–1919

From the moment we'd settled into our new headquarters, it was clear that we'd been thrown into a poor and backward village in the deep mountains, with no shops and no markets. Unhappy at being deprived of fresh vegetables, I thought of something that was unheard of in this remote region, and spoke to the mudur about it:

"Bey, I think we should have a vegetable garden, a *bostan*."

"Who can do that?"

"I am sure we can find somebody. Lease a piece of land, order some seeds for beans, tomatoes, cucumbers, melons…"

"Do you think it would work?"

"Why not? The sunshine is as bright and warm here as anyplace."

When we proposed it to the mudur's senior wife, Naileh Hanum, she almost hugged me.

"My son, do not wait for him," she said indicating her husband. "Send somebody immediately to Zara and to Kangal to get the seeds."

That was how our vegetable garden was sown, on a smooth patch of land by the riverbank, and now it was thriving under the supervision of Keoseh Ahmed. Although we'd started late because of having to wait for the seeds, the small round heads of melons and watermelons could be seen through the wide green leaves.

One day I bent over to smell the melons.

"Those ripen late," explained Keoseh. "They won't be ready until the end of the harvest."

"By then it will be cold."

"The night frost and cold are what makes them sweet."

Bozo and I knew this, but we were impatient and went to the garden every day, peeking through the greenery, our mouths watering. Yellow-green watermelons with black stripes, and other melons of various colors and shapes, lay on the damp reddish soil while their juices were converted to sugar. They grew large, bursting through the leaves, shining by day in the sun and gleaming under moonlight at night. Keoseh was on guard continuously, chopping the earth with his hoe.

"Uncle Keoseh, cut one and let us try it! We can't wait."

"They are not ripe enough, they have no taste; you'll get a stomach ache."

"It's our stomachs, not yours. This one over here looks quite yellow, can we try it?"

"I said no. The bey will be angry."

"How will he know?"

"How?" Keoseh echoed. "He comes here every day and knows how many melons are on each plant. He won't stand for you eating anything."

"Then give us a couple of ears of corn to roast."

"How can there be corn for you? The family comes twice a day and takes whatever they wish. We were supposed to share it, but they take everything. I will not do this next year. Am I a fool?"

Bozo and I left the vegetable patch, low and dejected We got to a fence when Bozo stopped and looked at me.

"Are you with me?"

"When am I not with you?"

"Some night I am going to rob this garden. Are you with me?"

"Yes, I am."

"Swear to God, say *Wallahi*."

"*Wallahi!*"

"Say, 'If I do not keep my word, may God take my life.'"

"May God take my life if I do not keep my word!"

"Good. When the right time comes, I will let you know."

We parted for our separate duties, and I soon forgot about my promise to rob the vegetable garden.

The summer of 1918 was almost over, but not all the crops had been harvested or taken in. Now and again Rashid Agha and I were sent to measure the produce of some of the villages high up in the mountains; at those cooler elevations the wheat ripened late; trees turned yellow early, and fall and winter came immediately upon each other.

To prepare for the cold winter, we gathered wood from the forest, cut and stacked it into piles, cleaned the barley, washed the wheat that was to be used for white bread, then took the bushels to the mill and watched the milling process so that no one, including the Kurdish miller, could steal a few shovels of flour.

"The word 'Kurd' is equivalent to 'thief,'" the mudur often lectured. "If you hand your tobacco case to a Kurd to roll a cigarette, watch him closely, otherwise he will steal your box or everything in it right before your eyes." And, relishing his own wit, he would laugh heartily. As a Turkish bey and administrator of the Ottoman government, his antagonism toward Kurds and all things Kurdish was typical and accepted.

The waterwheel along the riverbank turned noisily day and night as the mild sun of autumn settled upon us. The workers hurried to finish the field work and begin the sowing. Each man rose before dawn and, with frost steaming and rising from the land, worked from early morning until dark. The workers claimed that the wind brought the smell of winter, but I could not detect it.

Milk was scarce, although it was fatty and thick and yellow as hay. In the spring, the animals returned from grazing laden with milk, their teats swollen hard and reaching to their knees. Now it was nothing like that. The rams were large and their tails were fatty and round. On the shallow mountain slope where the land was smooth, one could see the silhouettes of men leaning over the handles of their plows; it was easy to distinguish the straight lines of freshly tilled soil on the hillside, and so a Kurdish woman, hand over her eyes, watching her man in the distance, could easily tell how many hours of work remained before she would light the stove and prepare the evening meal.

"Why do you hurry to plow so much in the fall?" I asked one of the Kurds.

"Because," he replied, "once the seed is in the soil, we cannot eat it, the thieves can't steal it, and the tax collector cannot take it. Also, when the grain is planted early, it ripens earlier and has a better chance to be abundant."

Although I had lived with these people for three years, I had not heard a plowman sing in the fields. Everyone knew that Turks did not have work songs, but how to explain this on the part of the Kurds, who expressed so much in song? Love, sorrow, courage, broken dreams, longing, joy, hope—all these feelings were expressed in songs that they sang often, especially in the spring and on happy occasions. What sorrow was it now that turned these people inward and silent? Could it be the approaching shadow of winter, or some other hidden reason?

ROBBERY

The sky opened suddenly, pouring forth steady torrents, heavy and unceasing. Rains like this would prompt a typical villager to look up, beseeching: "Almighty God, let me sacrifice myself to you. Did you tear a hole in your sky?"

The field work and threshing stopped altogether, and even the animals were not taken to pasture. The misty hilltops and the sky merged into a single blurry horizon, and the rain soaked through the thickest greenery into soil that had seldom been drenched.

The village looked deserted. Every chimney was smoking. Not a single soul was in the streets except for a few cats that were searching gingerly for a dry stone to set their paws upon. The river was fierce, forcing turbid waters to churn over its banks with a mighty noise. The steady rain had dug muddy troughs in the streets, and no birds flew overhead. Night came early, and one by one the village huts started to blink as streaks of yellow light fell from their windows upon the muddy waters in thin, wavy lines.

After we fed and watered the animals and finished our house chores, Bozo and I stood in the open doorway, feeling happy to be dry as we gazed out at the rain.

"Tonight is a good time to go to the vegetable garden," Bozo whispered.

"What did you say?" I asked, not believing my ears.

"I said, now is the time to go to the vegetable garden."

"Are you crazy?"

"No. Have you forgotten your promise?"

"I did not forget, but this weather…"

"The weather will help us. Who knows where Keoseh is curled up to warm his old bones? After all, how long will it take us to collect one bagful of stuff?"

"But we'll get soaked."

"We'll wear some coverings."

"Where can we hide the bushels?"

'In the stable, under the hay."

"In our house?"

"Sure, nobody will ever suspect."

"God give us sense and protect us," I said.

"Don't worry."

Despite the rain the night was pale, like diluted ink. We waited until it was dark and everyone was asleep, then left.

Stumbling and sliding on the muddy road, slipping, falling, we reached the garden and saw that Keoseh's hut was pitch dark; the roof had collapsed and no one was within. We fell into the garden. It was impossible to see anything. We were dripping, water running down our necks, over our shoulders. We had to wait for short flashes of lightning to see anything.

"Be damned, Bozo…"

"Shut up. Don't utter my name. Pay attention to what's in front of you," he snapped.

"It is too dark. I can't see a thing."

"Squat down and feel around with your hands a little above the dirt. When you find something round and hard, cut it off and put it in your bag."

"Here, I found three watermelons, that's enough. Let's go."

"After coming all the way here and getting soaked, go back with only three watermelons?"

Finally we filled our bags and got to the house wall, panting under the heavy load. We crept in noiselessly to make sure that everybody was still asleep. All the lights were out and the bedroom doors were closed. The mudur's snoring was audible from the guest room, where he was sleeping.

One by one we carried the bags in and hid the melons and watermelons under the hay.

"What do you say, Bozo? Shall we eat one?"

"Of course, we can eat one and more."

"Won't we get stomach aches?"

"So what if we do, who cares?"

"What about the rinds?"

"We'll give them to the cow, she'll devour them."

That night I slept so peacefully that when I awoke in the morning, I was surprised. My conscience was not upset, nor was my stomach.

─╼─◉─╾─

While we slept a strong wind had swept the clouds away and cleared the sky. The morning sun was so bright and warm that no one could imagine it had ever been hidden by a storm.

Now happiness, real and tangible, infused the air. Mist rose from the ground and almost instantly disappeared without a trace. Trees and plants smiled, and the village dogs, their eyes half closed and noses pointed upward, sniffed at the sun. The river, though still churning, had receded almost to its former boundaries. Villagers were collecting the fish that floundered in the cane fields and calling to each other to gather them up in baskets.

I glanced sideways toward the vegetable garden and my heart sank. It was wrecked. Nothing was left intact or alive. All the plants were strewn flat on the soil or buried in the mud. Keoseh, bent from old age and sorrow, wandered through the garden, shaking his head.

A while later, tired and moving slowly, he crossed the path to our house and stopped at the door.

"Good morning," I greeted him brightly.

"May I see the Mudur Bey? My news is not good. Last night, between the storm and thieves, my vegetable garden was destroyed, ruined."

"Really? The melons and watermelons too?"

"Everything."

"You know, Uncle Keoseh, the other day when Bozo and I asked you for a melon, you refused. Now God has punished you."

"How could I know, my son? If I had known what would happen, I would have given you more than just one melon."

"You say that everything is destroyed?"

"Come and see for yourself. The thieves took whatever they could, and anything they left was smashed by the storm."

"Do you have any idea who they might be?"

"I know who he is."

"He?" I asked, somewhat fearful.

"The one with the biggest feet in the village."

"How would I know who has big feet?"

"If you don't know, I know. It is Abbass's son, Veli."

"Veli?" I cried, bewildered.

I ran to the mudur. He was just out of bed, and his wife Naileh was helping him dress.

"The gardener is here, he wants to speak to you," I burbled. "He says thieves robbed the garden last night."

"He is lying. He took the vegetables himself and hid them somewhere or sold them."

"I don't think so, he is really upset."

"Does he suspect anyone?"

"He suspects Veli. He says the footprints in the garden are the size of a baby's coffin, and the only person with such big feet is Veli."

"Our Veli?"

"Yes."

"I don't think he could have done anything like that," said Naileh Hanum, commenting for the first time.

I ran back to Keoseh.

"Wait until the mudur gets dressed and has some coffee," I said. Then I whispered, "You had better insist on Veli's guilt, otherwise he is going to suspect you!"

"Thank you," the old man replied, sadly. He looked anxious and started kneading his hands.

The mudur was sitting on the divan in the guest room, about to light a cigarette, when we entered. Poor Keoseh had nothing to add to what he had told me, but he said more about Veli.

"My Bey, call the men of the village to stand in a row and look at their feet; then you will believe me."

The mudur pointed to me: "Get the village head, the muhtar."

I rushed out and in minutes was at the muhtar's threshold. I was about to push open the door when I heard loud voices.

"I will break all the bones in your body, crush them, turn them to flour," the muhtar was threatening. "If you don't behave like a faithful, loyal woman, I'll kill you like a slut. Your adultery is enough! You have shattered my honor. Shame on you, bitch!"

"What have I done?" his wife shrieked.

"What more is there to do? You cheated me. By Allah, I will kill you both if I see or hear that you are together again. The son of a bitch, after he finished molesting the Armenian girl, he did the same thing under my own roof! Does he think I have no honor? Am I blind? By Allah I will—"

I pushed on the door and went in. The windowless hut was dimly lit by a single opening in the roof. In the middle of the room, sitting on a scrap of sheepskin, was the muhtar's wife, weeping. When she saw me she cried louder and noisily blew her nose.

She was at least twenty years younger than her husband. Her fiery eyes darted about continuously. Her long black hair was tied with a band of gold coins circling her forehead. and her large breasts bulged under a blouse of bright woven cloth.

"He wants to kill me! Save me from his hands," she wailed, running to me.

"Is killing somebody that easy?" I asked sarcastically.

"See what she is doing?" the muhtar exploded. "It wasn't enough to disgrace me before all the villagers! Now, in the presence of a government official, she dares to accuse her husband of being a murderer… she has the gall to open her mouth!"

He ran toward her.

"Muhtar, muhtar," I reached him. "Calm yourself. What happened?"

"What could happen? The whore turned me into two cents!" he howled, snatching his headgear and slamming it to the floor. "She cheated me. She was out with that son of a bitch Veli again last night.

She didn't come home! When I asked where she was, she could not answer."

"Come with me," I said, taking his arm and easing him out the door. "Muhtar," I murmured, "God heard your prayers and has come to help you."

"What?"

"Keoseh, our gardener, is with the mudur right now, accusing Veli of robbing the vegetable garden in the rain last night. And since Veli was not home…"

"What if that whore of mine testifies that he was in bed with her the whole night?"

"She will never do that, but if she does, it will be worse for him."

"How?"

"They would say that Veli robbed the garden to please his sweetheart."

The muhtar nodded wearily.

We went together to see the mudur, who was very angry.

"Where have you been?" he demanded. "All of you—Bozo, Keoseh, Muselim, Muhtar—go to the garden immediately and measure the tracks. They will prove who is the thief."

We were at the door when the muhtar turned back: "Bey, we can measure the footprints, but Veli is not here."

"Where is he?"

"I do not know."

"Ask your wife. Go home and ask your wife! Go home and break her cursed bones. Have you no pride, have you no shame? Kill that dirty slut! Crush her bones under your heel. Do not fear, I am the judge and the ruler of this area, I represent the government and the law. I will not let you be hung for that."

The old Kurd no longer heard. Someone had plunged a knife into his wound and was turning it mercilessly. The entire village knew about Veli and his wife, and he was already suffering for that. But nobody had shouted it so cruelly to his face, nobody had spit the adultery squarely upon his beard. Up to this moment, he had hoped that the mudur and his family did not know about his disgrace. Now all hopes were smashed, his heart broken. His back rounded a little more, and his arms hung uselessly at his sides.

"You go to the garden," he mumbled to Keoseh. And then to me, "I am going home."

I wanted to stop him, but instinct told me to let him go. Ten minutes later he was back. I looked at him questioningly, fearfully. He understood. In a weak voice, shaking from shame and emotion, he said:

"No, I did not kill her. She is not home, she has escaped."

After wandering around the demolished garden for a long time and taking measurements, I myself almost believed that Veli was the thief. Despite last night's drenching rain, Bozo's and my footprints remained intact in the red clay soil. Of course this was due to the properties of clay, but I saw the finger of God there. How our footprints had grown enough to match Veli's feet was easy to explain after seeing them. The clay sticking to our moccasins made them larger, and since we slipped with every pace, the outlines had become huge. Fortunately, such reasoning would not occur to the simple men of the village.

By now the situation had reached a point that would be devastating for somebody. And that somebody was Veli. If I had wanted to, I could have spared him the disaster. But I was not crazy. I had looked to the heavens when, unexpectedly, on earth, I found a way to avenge the death of the innocent Armenian girl whom he had defiled and made pregnant.

With my naive belief in fate and destiny, there was only one explanation for this: the finger of God. Although somewhat late, God wanted Veli to be punished for his crime.

Four of us returned from the vegetable garden to report to the mudur. The evidence left no doubt.

The mudur sent us to look for Veli, but he was not at home. "Sooner or later he will return," he said, cracking his whip. "I know how to deal with him."

We tried for hours to find Veli. Finally I gave up and went to care for the horses. The mudur was on a stool in front of the barn, watching as I worked. Fortunately, his eyes could not penetrate the thick layers of hay we had piled over the melons and watermelons from last night, or else Veli's fate and mine would trade places.

"After you feed the horses, go and see if the bastard has returned," he said, rising from the stool.

"I do not think so," I replied. "Muhtar's wife has run off, and he is probably with her."

"I will show him what it means to rob a *bostan* and take somebody else's wife."

"I don't understand why anyone prefers somebody's wife when our village is full of young girls."

"Otherwise there would be no theft," the mudur hastened. "Haven't I told you that a Kurd is not happy unless he steals?"

Each time he spoke I shook with anxiety. I kept going in and out of the barn. My eyes focused continually on the stack of hay covering our loot.

I was afraid that he would try to investigate further. Several times in the past when pursuing major crimes, he had turned to mysticism. He would call Farieh, his youngest daughter, or any young girl from age eight to ten, and draw a triangle in her palm and a circle within the triangle. Then he would write some numbers and recite verses about mystical beings, and question her at length about the images she saw in her palm. He boasted that he had learned the ritual from an old dervish in Constantinople who had supernatural powers.

Now, recalling all this, I was afraid that the dervish's powerful ritual would help him identify Bozo and me. How could we escape if Farieh, or another child, were to widen her eyes in discovery and shout, "The stolen goods are in our house!"

All day I stayed close to the mudur and tried to keep his mind off the theft. Finally, when the sun disappeared behind the hills, I took a deep breath. I grilled a sizable fish over the fire and, with raki that I cooled in icy water, took it to him on a tray.

"Welcome, my friend."

He gulped down the raki and wiped his mouth.

"Give me my saz."

I lifted the saz off the wall and handed it to him. He put it under his arm, adjusted it on his belly, and started to play—always the same simple and monotonous tune. After struggling with it, he stopped.

"Where is Bozo? Call him, I want him to sing for me."

I went out to get him.

Bozo tilted his head and sang in an untrained but sweet voice, and it was quite late when he stopped, having exhausted his repertoire. I urged him to continue, pointing out that if the mudur was drunk, he would not dig into the details of the robbery. "Don't forget that it was your idea to rob the *bostan*."

The mudur opened his eyes.

"Muselim, hey, Muselim!"

"*Efendim!*"

"Go and bring Veli here. If he is not at home, get on your horse and find him. Do not let me see you without him."

"I'll do it, Bey."

"Take your gun with you. If he gives you any trouble, kill him on the spot like a dog. I give you permission."

"Yes, Bey."

It would be easy to shoot Veli for any reason, but tomorrow, when the mudur was sober and reasonable, he would blame me, and I would never escape his anger. Taking vengeance is fine, but keeping your head on your shoulders is better, I thought.

"Take my ten-shooter hanging on the wall and put it in your belt."

I took it and left. When I reached Veli's doorstep I saw a light within and pushed open the door. Veli was hunched over, mending his moccasins.

"Veli, Mudur Bey wants you."

"Now? At night?"

"Yes."

"For what?"

"I don't know."

He rose from the fireplace, glanced at the corner where his parents were sleeping, and headed out ahead of me. When we arrived at our house, he looked worried and smoothed his clothes.

"Bey, Veli is at the door."

"Bring him in and call the muhtar."

After grumbling about having to leave his bed at this hour, the muhtar joined me. I prepared him along the way.

"Something important is up. Veli is there, and the bey is drunk."

When we entered the room, the mudur was threatening Veli, his whip in hand.

"Tell me the truth. Where were you last night?"

"Bey, I kiss your feet, but I've told you over and over that—"

"I heard you, I am not deaf, but I want the truth, not a lame story that you went to Sovouk-Sou."

"What can I do if you don't believe me, Bey? What can I do?"

"What can you do?" the mudur was raging. "You can ruin this man's life," pointing to the muhtar with the tip of his whip, "by wrecking his house, by taking his wife. In the darkness you can sneak into my vegetable garden and rob it, and who knows what else..."

"My Bey, my Pasha," pleaded Veli, "I have not been in your garden, I have stolen nothing. I was not here last night."

"Where were you, scoundrel? Who were you with? What were you doing? Do you have witnesses?"

"I have, Bey."

"Who is it? Name who it is!"

Veli flicked a side glance at the muhtar and said nothing.

"You are lying, you Kurdish ass," the muhtar intervened. "Do you think we are fools? Is there anybody in the village with feet as big as yours?"

"What does the size of my feet have to do with all this?" cried Veli, startled.

"Don't pretend, don't hide your guilt!" shouted the mudur. "It was not I who measured them, it was these boys, this muhtar. Do you want me to call Keoseh also? You bastard. The man worked for six months to grow that vegetable garden, and you ruin it in one night!"

Raising his whip, he attacked him viciously. The blows landed on his shoulders, back, head, waist, buttocks.

Veli was moaning in pain and fear.

"I didn't do it, my Pasha, I did not rob the *bostan*, believe me, in the name of your children, in the name of God, I swear…"

"Shut up, you scoundrel, swearing means nothing to a Kurd. I will teach you about robbery, I will beat you until you confess or die, and I will leave your body unburied so the dogs and jackals can chew on your bones."

He stopped for a moment.

"Muselim, get me some raki."

I took it to him. He swallowed it and turned to the muhtar and Bozo: "Lay him down!"

We three looked at each other but did not move.

"Lay the dog down, I say," barked the mudur again, and lunged toward us.

I went to Veli and said softly: "Veli, lie down. It is better to receive the blows on your feet than on your face. I promise," I lowered my voice, "I won't hit hard. Cry out very loud to convince him you are about to die. Then we will let you go."

Veli looked at me but said nothing. He stared at the open door of the room. Perhaps he was considering escape. I took the ten-shooter off the wall, kicked the door shut with my foot, and put my finger on the trigger.

"Lie down, Veli. I do not intend to get beaten in your place."

"But you will kill me!"

"Nothing will happen to you; your evil soul is very strong," the muhtar sneered.

"Lie down."

Veli put his hands over his face and started to weep. I tried to turn away from that huge man crying.

"Tie his feet and hold them up high!" ordered the mudur.

We did.

"Muselim, bring the cane."

Veli howled and his body twitched like a spring when the first blow landed on both his feet.

"Shut up, you ass of a Kurd, aren't you ashamed?"

The mudur was getting angrier amid the screams. He was breathing hard but continued to strike. Veli tried in vain to escape the blows by moving his feet right and left. Bozo and the muhtar were holding the ties. The mudur was panting.

"Are you ready to confess?"

"My Bey, my pasha, I kiss your feet, in the name of your children, in the name of God, in the name of the Prophet, believe me, I did not go into your *bostan.*"

"Continue," said the mudur, handing me the cane.

I took my position beside his feet and, leaning over, whispered: "Veli, it is to your advantage if you confess."

"What should I confess? I did not do it."

Bozo's face was ash white.

"Start!" ordered the mudur.

Blow...blow...blow.

"Confess!"

Blow…blow.

Veli's feet.

I stopped. The muhtar and Bozo put his feet down very carefully.

"What is it? Why did you stop?" the mudur demanded, trying to stand up.

"Bey, he is bleeding."

"Let him bleed, let him die."

"Bey, it will cause trouble later…"

"Nothing will happen. Continue."

"But he is unconscious."

"So what? Throw some water on his face and when he comes to, continue."

"He will die, Bey, it is enough."

"Let him die, it will be one dog less."

Pretending to get some water, I ran to Naileh Hanum.

"Hanum, he wants to beat him to death."

"What can I do?"

"You can intervene. We will have trouble tomorrow. I know that when he comes to his senses, he will blame me."

The mudur's voice was calling me from the next room.

"Go back and do not beat him any more," the hanum advised. Find a way to get the muhtar out of the room so that I can go in and try to calm him."

I took a bowl of water and rushed in.

Muhtar and Bozo had untied his feet; Veli was lying flat out on the dirt floor like a log.

"Do you want some water, Veli?"

He did not answer.

The mudur threw the water on his face.

"Get up, bastard. Aren't you ashamed?"

He hadn't the strength to open his eyes.

"Get up, I say. Do you hear?" He pushed him with his foot. "Why are you lying there like an ass? Do you think this is a dog's den?"

Veli did not move, did not hear, did not feel the tip of mudur's shoe kicking his side. Yellow-faced, forehead wet, eyes closed, he was motionless as a cadaver on the ground.

I pitied him. I had started to feel sorry for him earlier, but had not accepted it up to now. I tried to shed my feelings and revert to my former hatred for a thousand reasons. I tried to remember those black days, the inhuman acts suffered by my people at the hands of the Kurds, the slaughter of my relatives. No use. I tried to remember the oath I made over Asia's grave. No help. I felt like crying, and crying, and never stopping. For what? For whom? I did not know.

The mudur's voice roused me. "Muselim, get me a raki."

I filled the cup and gave it to him. He was sitting on the couch, panting. He looked calm, almost sober, but the brutishness in his Turkish soul had not abated. He swallowed the raki and whipped the cup back to me.

"I will teach these Kurds that everything has a limit! Murder, prostitution, adultery, robbery, all have their limits. For the last three years, so busy killing the Armenians and raping the girls, they forgot that it is against the law and religion. Stealing properties from the *gavurs* and then from each other, they forgot that stealing is forbidden by the Koran and by the Prophet. I will force these truths into their stupid heads or my name is not Nazum. I will beat them and put all the Kurds in jail until they understand! Fill me a raki."

I gave him half a cup.

"What is this half?"

"My hand is shaking and I don't want to spill any."

"Do you think I am drunk?"

"No. I have not seen you drunk."

"Bozo, you bastard, sing me something in Turkish."

While he was distracted, I beckoned the muhtar to help me.

Together we lifted Veli's limp body and dragged him outside.

"What the hell are you doing? Where are you taking him?" the mudur shouted after us. Just then, the door of the next room opened and Naileh Hanum appeared. She walked into the mudur's room silently and closed the door behind her.

Muhtar and I pulled Veli away from the house and, when we were far enough, let his limp body sink to the ground. The cool night air brought him around. He raised his hands to his head and started to moan.

"Why didn't you let the dog die from the beating?" the muhtar berated me.

I did not answer. He was seething with vengeance and hatred. How could I confess that I was afraid for myself, and that my troubled conscience was also part of it? How could I explain to that relentless husband that if Veli died under the beating, the mudur would blame me for not preventing a fatality, and threaten me when he recovered from his drunkenness in the morning: "If you cannot help and cannot control a critical situation, why do I keep you in this house?"

And if, God forbid, it ever came out that Bozo and I were responsible for all of this, then our lives—especially mine—would be worthless.

Still, I had to answer the muhtar.

"He has been punished enough for looting the vegetable garden… and as for his other sins, let God punish him. Now take his arm and let's get him into his house," I said.

It was easy to say, but doing it was impossible. Veli could not use his legs, and his body was huge and heavy as lead.

"Wait," I said, to the muhtar. "Wait here until I bring the stretcher so we can carry him on it."

"All right," he said, as he straightened up.

Two minutes later, when Bozo and I returned from the barn with the stretcher, we saw Veli's long body stretched out motionless on the ground, with no sign of the muhtar.

"Where has he gone?" I thought aloud.

"Who?"

"The muhtar."

"He has probably gone around the corner to piss."

We moved closer. We stood frozen. I covered my mouth with my hands to stem a cry. Where Veli's head should have been, there was a big round stone, heavy, black, smeared in blood.

Bozo leaned over to look, screamed, and fled.

I stood, horrified, trying to figure out what had happened.

Months before, when we were digging to build our fence, Bozo and I had found a large stone. We washed it and set it by the wall so that when our work was finished at the end of the day, we could sit on it and rest while listening to the sound of the river.

Obviously the muhtar had managed to lift up that heavy stone, as high as he could, and with a venomous curse dropped it on Veli's head.

THE BRIDE TO BE

It was late night when a knock came at the door. I took my pistol, finger on the trigger, and stood to one side: "Who is it?"

"It's me, open the door," a voice answered.

It was Khudur's son, Haso.[8] "Hurry, open the door."

On the porch flooded with moonlight, with a long-barreled Mauser rifle in hand, rows of ammunition across his shoulders, and a knife in his belt, stood Haso. At his side was a small human being with a colorful turban on her head.

"Here, I brought you a sister," he said, pushing her toward me.

He asked that we "take her in for now" and said he would explain later. He was about to leave when he turned: "Guard her well, and

---

8 For some time Haso lived as a bandit in the mountains. The Ottoman government, unable to cope with his kind, passed a law saying that if such outlaws surrendered and engaged in agriculture, they would not be punished for their ill deeds and would be exempt from conscription into the army. After that law was enacted, Haso came to the mudur, saying: "Vehip Pasha has pardoned me." From that day on, he was a friend to the mudur and his home.

don't let anybody know she is here."

He leaped on his horse and disappeared.

I understood what was going on. Haso had carried the girl off from her father's house and brought her here for safekeeping.

When the sound of hoofbeats faded, I turned to her. "Come, come in, make yourself at home. Haso is our good friend."

"I know," she said, entering.

I lit a candle made of goat fat and held it high to see her. Under the bright turban circling her head, a young face appeared, angelic and innocent.

"Where are you from?" I asked.

"Chorakh."

"Do you have mother, father?"

"I have my parents and three brothers."

"How old are you?"

"Sixteen."

"Do they know you love Haso and that you ran off with him?"

"Only old Birwa. She raised me, I grew up on her milk."

"Does she know that you ran away?"

"Do not tell anyone, but she helped me."

"Birwa must be a good woman."

She nodded vigorously. With every move, the coins in her hair, hanging about her neck and arms, jingled and jangled. She was wearing an elaborate embroidered dress that had been made for festive occasions.

"I will wake the hanum and she will take care of you," I said.

"Wait, please, I beg you," she replied. "I am afraid of the hanums."

"I am sure they will like you, especially the elder daughter. She is just about your age."

"But…"

"But what?"

"How do I behave with them?"

"Just as you do with me. It's true that I am not a bey or a hanum, but they are people like me, you can be sure of that."

"Can I act like a normal person with the big hanum too?"

"You will see her tomorrow morning. She will be like your mother. Now I will take you to Kadriye Hanum to care for you. But tomorrow morning, when you see the big hanum, kiss her hand—they like such gestures. Do you understand?"

"Yes." She smiled sweetly and nodded. Then she grabbed my hand and took it to her lips.

"What are you doing? Do I look like a big hanum?"

She covered her face with her hands and laughed, then straightened up and smoothed her hair.

I went to Kadriye's room and softly knocked. When she came out, I quickly explained everything and took the girl's hand and put it in Kadriye's palm. "Here, I deliver her to you; she is yours."

"You mean she ran away from her father's house to get married?" she gasped.

"Uh huh."

She reached out and hugged the girl. "Oh my little fool, come in."

There was nothing more for me to do. I went to my corner and got into bed with my clothes on.

I was sleepless for a long time. It was not hard for me to put myself in Haso's shoes, and Kadriye in place of his young fiancé. But when I imagined lifting her onto my horse to flee, I could not think of where to take her. In the whole wide world there was not a single place, nor any friend, whose door I could knock upon at night, and say, "Here, I brought you a girl. Please take care of her and do not tell anybody."

Morning came peacefully. The animals streamed out of the stable and were led to graze with Shepherd Ahmet striding ahead of them, staff over his shoulder. Thin, bluish smoke rose from the chimneys and the pleasant aroma of frying eggs filled the air. Young goats scrambled and climbed over the low roofs, and half-naked children tumbled into the streets, munching on pieces of buttered bread, calling for their dogs and friends.

Suddenly, from the east, a cloud of speeding horsemen ruptured the scene. Even before the dust settled, they pulled up in front of Haso's house, firing Martinis (rifles) in the air.

"Hey, Haso, you scoundrel, where are you? Come out!"

"Come out so we'll teach you what happens to abductors!"

Haso appeared with his father and brother, thumbs dug into his belt, looking fearless, scornful, measuring them up and down.

"By Allah," he sneered, "these breast-feeding babies dare to call me a scoundrel?"

Then, to the older leader of the group: "Why do you give firearms to children? They can get hurt!" He stopped for their reaction and continued. "Come in and see for yourselves that no girl is here. You are knocking at the wrong door."

"Kidnapper! Then who ran off with our girl?"

"A brave man. If you had locked your doors securely, the roosters could not have snatched your hen," he laughed mockingly.

"Believe him, he is telling the truth, *Wallahi*. I swear by Allah there is no girl in our house," his father hastened.

They did not believe him; who would believe the sworn word of a Kurd?

It was just then that our new village head, whether planned or by chance, appeared. He listened to both sides and raised his arms, now as arbitrator and disposer of justice. He asked them to get off their horses, put down their rifles, have a yogurt drink, and cool off. "Wherever your girl is, we will find her," he assured them.

"You son of a bitch, bastard, why don't you confess that she is here?" shouted the girl's uncle to Haso's father. Several others grumbled but slowly dismounted and, bending their heads down, stepped through the low door of Haso's hut.

Several hours of bargaining and negotiating brought no agreement. Passions were still inflamed when it came time for lunch, and it took some coaxing before they sat at the table. But full stomachs tended to calm them, and the conversation became more reasonable. They hung the Martinis on the wall and put away their other arms.

"This place is too hot. Let us go to my office," said the new muhtar, as he rounded up both sides and led them off. The office was a wide and spacious room that had been built by skilled hands. Long wooden planks lined the walls and wood-carved decorations were everywhere. On one side was a fireplace large enough to barbecue a whole calf. Along the walls were low banks of seating covered with rugs, and above the fireplace was a prominent display of arms.

Toward evening, an agreement was reached. The groom would give a dowry of six sheep, four goats, and one cow to his father-in-law, who in turn promised to bless the couple on their wedding day.

"And now, let us see our girl so we can return home in peace," said the father.

"Your daughter is not here in this village."

"We can make you tell," said one of the young boys, reaching for his dagger.

"Stay where you are; there is no need to start up!" ordered the father, and turned to his future in-laws. "Let it be as you wish. We will see our daughter in fifteen days on the day of the wedding." And they left.

The villagers, who had been holding their breaths while they followed the negotiations, were relieved and happy.

"There has been no wedding here for three years. We can't wait for the celebration!" someone shouted. A moment later several young men mounted their horses and left for the plains, eager to start training for javelin-throwing and other competitive games on the big day.

The week before the festivities, Haso appeared to officially invite the hanums to his wedding. "The roof of our house is low, the door narrow, and the floor earthen. But our food is *halal* [permitted] and our hearts are open. We will be most pleased if the hanums would honor us by coming to my wedding."

The mudur politely explained that for "obvious reasons," the older hanums could not attend, but Farieh, his youngest daughter, would be there throughout.

Haso asked, "With your permission, we hope that the bride may start the procession from your house. That would be a great honor for us and, I believe, would strengthen my father-in-law's respect for me. And we also thought that the procession should tour the village a couple of times. Naturally, your little hanum, as maid of honor, would accompany the bride."

"Of course, of course," the mudur grunted impatiently, bored with such details.

Pleased that everything had gone well, the groom paid elaborate respects and left. I went to the harem to tell the women.

"You are all invited to the wedding, but only Farieh Hanum may go. The others cannot attend 'for obvious reasons.'"

"What about me? Why can't I go?" Kadriye said, rising from the settee.

"Are you crazy, tomboy?" her mother chided. "Farieh is permitted because she is a child."

"If she is a child, then I am a grown-up!"

"That is exactly why you may not go," replied her mother.

"I will wrap myself completely in my *charshaf* [covering garment] from head to toe. Please, mother."

The case was presented to the mudur. He listened to each side like a reasonable judge until, faced with his daughter's pleading looks, he gave way: "All right, let her go too."

Happiness filled the house, because Kadriye was loved by everyone. Her joy was everybody's joy, and her sadness was everyone's.

In the evening, when Kadriye had a chance to be with me, she asked: "Which horse do you think I should ride?"

"The red one, of course. Red."

"My father might object."

"If you were able to persuade your father to let you go to the wedding, you will manage this too. And I will be at your side."

"Infidel!"

She was very happy, and fled into the house.

The next day, as I neared the stable, the horse recognized my footsteps and started to stomp and neigh. I opened the door and went to him with soothing words. His sharp, fine ears pointed up and he looked at me. I held his beautiful head in my arms and caressed him. I untied him and we went out together. He took deep breaths, looked toward the distant forest, and pulled at the rope in my hand. He started digging at the ground impatiently.

When I lifted the noose from his neck he stood for a moment, unbelieving, took a few steps and then, certain that he was free, raised his head and ran to the field. His mane and tail streamed behind him, and the rays of the sun glistened on his hide.

Mudur, watching admiringly, was concerned: "I hope he does not overdo it."

"I don't think so. When he comes back I will massage his knees with cold water."

Kadriye, seeing us from the window, emerged.

"What is it, my daughter?"

"Papa, which horse will I ride to the wedding? The one running out there?"

"A beautiful girl like you should have a horse that becomes you, but that one is dangerous."

"But Papa, Muselim will be with me."

"There is still time, we will think about it," he said, and turned away.

Kadriye and I looked at each other and laughed. We had won!

When the subject came up the next day, the mudur was annoyed: "My infidel son, I know that you put the idea in her head to ride the red horse. If anything happens to my daughter, Allah is witness, you will not escape my hand. I will have you skinned!"

"If anything happens to her, as Allah is my witness, I will donate my skin to you," I replied fervently.

Hearing that, he stopped and looked directly at me, unblinking. I did not turn my eyes away. He shook his head and went into the house. It was the first time, I believe, that he suspected that my feeling for his daughter went beyond the proper bounds of a servant.

Finally the wedding day came. Kadriye was busy and excited as she prepared the bride. She fussed, dressed her, adorned her with jewelry, and fashioned her hair. Her mother lost patience: "That is enough. Now come here so I can make you ready, too."

"What's all the fuss about?" I heckled, poking my nose in. "Who's going to see anything under her *charshaf*?"

"Mind your own business!" Kadriye snapped.

"Forgive me," I bowed in mock reverence and went out.

When I returned they were ready, and the mother was instructing her daughter. "Do not lift your veil when you look around to see this or that. Remember, you are not a child, you are old enough to be married. It is a sin for a Muslim girl your age to show even the tip of a single hair to the opposite sex."

"Muselim sees my hair…"

"That does not matter; he is a family member. Do not dare to forget my words. Let them be earrings upon your ears."

"Yes, Mother, I will."

"If you see her feeling dizzy on the horse, take her down and let her walk," the mother said to me.

"Yes, Hanum, do not worry. When I am with the horse, he obeys. He is gentle as a lamb."

"I know. Otherwise, do you think I would allow you to put my little chick on that animal?"

The groom's party came to our door with drums and pipes, leading a heavy, gentle, white horse for the bride to ride. Before mounting she flung her arms around the Naileh Hanum's neck and bid her farewell, crying. Naileh Hanum was touched; she kissed her and put a gold piece in her hand, saying: "My wedding present for you."

While the noise of the celebration continued, I went to the stable for Red. I put my face close to his head and whispered: "I am going to give you the most beautiful girl in the world. This is a big honor for you, so behave yourself; do not jump, do not race with passersby, and do not try to play with other horses. I warn you."

I led him to the mounting stone, and Kadriye, with help from her father and Bozo, climbed up. The horse lifted his head and chewed his bit. A maid covered Kadriye's ankles with the tips of her black outer garment so that no eyes could penetrate.

"If you are afraid, it is not too late," I said to Kadriye.

"I am not speaking to you for eight days!"

Most of the wedding party had already passed, so we moved forward and joined the last of the group. There was no order. Spirited horses were trying to pass each other. Men were firing rifles to the sky, and dogs and children ran about in all directions. It was chaos, movement, and noise. Now and then a rider would move away from the group and empty his Mauser into the air, spinning his horse around, or pull off its saddle and hold it up high, or pry a heavy stone from the ground and raise it up to display his strength.

Before long Bozo and I managed to advance, one of us on either side of the bride, and the girls had a chance to speak to her, saying they hadn't seen such a nice wedding party in all their lives.

Just before we crossed the mill canal, the drummers and pipers approached our group. They maneuvered in front of the lead horses and laid down their instruments, a sign of asking for gifts.

"We have no money with us, and we will be disgraced if we don't give them anything," Kadriye cried, flustered.

I had a gold piece in my belt that I'd kept for an emergency. I took it out and pressed it to the forehead of one of the pipe players. "Share it among all of you."

Kadriye extended her fingers to me from under the *charshaf* and thanked me.

"I will tell my father that you saved our honor, and he will return it to you."

"That is not necessary."

"Tell me truthfully, how long did it take you to save that much?"

"About a year and a half."

"And you gave it to the pipe player without hesitating?"

I said nothing.

"Speak."

"What am I to say? I thought that an honorable person gives honorable gifts."

Nothing more was said until we reached home and I helped her off the horse. "Too bad you were born a *gavur*," she said, and went in.

Toward evening the muhtar came in person to invite the mudur to dinner, since he was Haso's godfather and the feast was to be held in his guest room. When the mudur hesitated, he coaxed: "Don't worry, Mudur Bey, we will serve you very well, and we have ample raki."

Hearing that, the mudur gave way and joined him. Naileh Hanum was concerned, and asked me to see that he did not drink too much.

"Yes, Hanum, I will keep an eye on him." I said it, but I was not sure. If he got drunk, how could I stop him from doing anything? Who was I? On what authority could I supervise the mudur?

It was dark when he came home. He almost fell in the hallway, and as I took his arm to help him, he lunged at me.

"What, you think I am drunk?"

"Forgive me, Bey, of course you are not."

When we got to the door, he ordered me to spread a rug in the garden so he could have some snacks with the raki he had brought from the dinner. Bozo and I unrolled a carpet under the old apricot tree in the center of the garden, and he collapsed on it.

"Bring my saz," he ordered.

He hung over it and started to play. Soon he was bored.

"Hey, Muselim, Bozo!"

We stood ready before him.

"You asses, where were you? One of you go and get three hundred bullets to celebrate Haso's wedding. Fire all three hundred into the air while I watch you. Two hundred ninety-nine is not acceptable. I will count them one by one. But wait, better than that, call my daughter Kadriye to count for me."

Bozo went to get the bullets and a gun. I went to Kadriye's room.

"Your father wants you."

"What for?" she asked.

"Don't you know? When he gets drunk, he feels affectionate."

"I hate those times. What can I do?"

"Nothing. He is your father. We're firing three hundred bullets in the air and he wants you to count them. But you know that is an excuse to keep you close to him."

"Haven't I told you I hate that?"

"You've told me, but I feel jealous. It is not good."

Now it was her turn to be silent.

Finally we went to her father. He was happy to see her, and asked what had kept us.

"I am tired, and I was getting ready for bed," Kadriye replied.

"It is too early for bed. Now come over and give me a kiss."

Kadriye approached and put her cheek to her father's reeking mouth.

I turned my back and moved behind the shrubbery where I could not see what was happening.

It was dark enough now for the first stars to appear in the blue-green sky.

"Muselim! Hey, Muselim, did you get lost?"

"Here I am," I said, going to him.

"Why do you stand there like a log? Fill me a raki."

I poured one and gave it to him.

"Do you know this daughter of mine?" he said, poking Kadriye, who was sitting on his knee. "She is the most beautiful of all the beauties of the world."

"Yes, Bey, she is the most beautiful…"

"I said that. Did you see how elegant she was on the horse this afternoon?"

"Of course I did, I was walking at her side."

"Ass, what can you see from the side? To see her, you have to look from the front."

"Yes, Bey, from the front."

"All right, I'll deal with you later. Fill me a cup of raki."

He took it and swallowed the fiery fluid, twisting his face in pain. He dried his mouth with the back of his hand and said: "My daughter, my dear daughter, a little appetizer, please."

Kadriye took a piece of cucumber with a fork and raised it to his mouth.

"No, no, you don't understand…something from your cheek."

When he kissed Kadriye with his hot, foul-smelling mouth, I felt sick and backed away again behind the bushes. I put the Mauser on my knee (we had to carry a rifle when we were out at night) and buried my head in my hands.

I was jealous and blamed Kadriye.

I do not know how long I had stayed that way when suddenly I heard Bozo's frightened voice calling me: "Muselim, come fast!"

The village was being raided by bandits, I thought, and with my finger on the trigger I ran toward the alarm.

It was dark, but I was able to see the mudur embracing his daughter, trying to unbutton her shirt. Leaning on her, he was murmuring unintelligible words.

Taking hold of my Mauser, which was almost the length of my body, I raised it high with both hands to smash it down on the mudur's head. Then I realized his brains would splatter and fall over the girl.

I dropped my arms. The rifle fell on the ground. I threw myself at the mudur, twisted the arm that was around Kadriye's waist, and punched him hard with my other fist. He fell on the carpet, motionless.

Kadriye, freeing herself, ran toward the house without looking back. I bolted and caught her.

Sobbing, ashamed and shaken, she was crying, her head down.

"Kadriye, please, please don't cry. And before you run home, straighten out your clothes and wash your face. You must do that so your mother will not suspect anything. Do you understand? Your mother must not know anything about this, it would kill her, it would send her to her grave. If somebody sees you before you get cleaned up, put the blame on me. Say that I did it, say that we had a fight…I can straighten it out tomorrow, I'll find some good excuse. But your mother must never hear anything about this."

The next morning the mudur did not comment or hint in the slightest way about what had happened the night before. Was he so drunk that he forgot? Did he remember but was ashamed? Did he feel grateful that I had saved him from the sin of incest?

Who knows? Perhaps God does.

TWO WOMEN

On an afternoon when he felt warmly amorous, the mudur entered the bedroom of his second wife, Merouze, and closed the door behind him.

Merouze was his uncle's daughter, whom he had married the day before we moved to our new headquarters. She was an emptyheaded woman, big and fleshy, with a magnificent and lusty body, just the opposite of her rival, Naileh Hanum, who was slender as a lily with the air of a dove, a Turkish lady with some formal education.

During the three years of her married life, Merouze had barely been alone three times with her husband. She was more unseen and disregarded than a slave.

One day, when we were alone in the kitchen, she confided that she wanted me to write to her father (I was the only servant in the village who could read and write) to allow her to return. "Ask him to come here and take me home," she cried. "Tell him I vow not to be a burden to him. I can sew and knit, I will earn my keep. All I want is for him to come and rescue me from this hell."

I wrote the letter, and she sent it to her father with a reliable servant. But her father did not come, nor did he show the slightest interest in his unfortunate daughter.

And so the young woman lived for years under the sovereignty of Naileh Hanum, subject to her contempt, insults, episodes of jealousy and hate. She suffered silently, collecting venom in her soul. Even her name was not uttered by other members of the household; they scorned her as "the woman" instead of "hanum," and everybody knew whom they meant.

On the day that the bey went into Merouze's bedroom, Naileh Hanum, pale and grieving, withdrew to her room. Her pride and love were wounded. She sat on her divan for hours, hurt, lost in deep thought, eating nothing.

Kadriye and I were worried, and watched over her all day, until bedtime came and passed. Then the hanum quietly told me to get some sleep. "My son, you have a lot of work tomorrow, go to bed and rest. Your being here does not help. You need not suffer with me."

I wanted to say something to comfort her; she was Kadriye's

mother, and had influenced her husband more than once to help me out of a difficult spot. But I could not find the words…what could I say? Finally I bid her good night and went to bed.

I had barely closed my eyes when I jumped. Somebody was leaning over me, calling, "Muselim, Muselim! Wake up!"

It was Kadriye. "It is my mother, hurry!"

"Let me put something on."

She waited for me in the hall. "Hurry up!"

We ran down the hall and outside. We turned the corner of the house and stopped at the wall of Merouze's bedroom. There on the ground was Naileh Hanum, lying motionless in the dust.

"What happened? What is your mother doing here?" I asked, bending over her. I pushed aside something with my foot. "What is this…?"

"The stool for milking the cows."

"Why is it here?"

"My mother brought it."

"She wanted to get on it?"

"Yes, so she could reach the window. She wanted to listen."

"It seems she listened well."

Kadriye started to cry.

"Don't cry. Your mother is all right; she just fainted. Help me get her inside."

I bent and lifted the hanum's thin, light body.

"Go ahead of me. Open the door and hold it until I get through."

"Be careful; don't make any noise so we won't wake anybody."

We put her on her bed and sprinkled water on her face to revive her. No use. I burned a scrap of cloth in a dish and held it to her, blowing the sharp fumes toward her nostrils. She opened her eyes and tried to push away the smoking plate. We rubbed her arms and temples with raki and gave her some water. She was barely able to take one gulp. She was weak and pale. I could see her pulse through the delicate skin of her neck. She tried to speak.

"Stay quiet and rest," I said, putting my hand on her arm. "Rest."

"I am ashamed."

"There is nothing to be ashamed of. It is all over now. If you hadn't sent me to bed, I would have been at your door and not let you go out."

"Promise that you will not tell anyone; no one is to know about this," she implored in a barely audible voice.

"I promise. Do you want me to swear?"

"No, no need for that. Go to bed, it is almost dawn, and I am well."

"I want to stay here and watch over you with Kadriye Hanum."

"Listen to me. The bey might wake up and come out. If he finds you here, how can we explain?"

"Do you want me to sit outside your door?"

"No, I have had my lesson. You needn't be afraid. Go to sleep."

Soon after I closed my eyes, somebody was calling my name again: "Muselim!" I jumped up.

"Muselim, please get me some water. I want to heat it so the bey's bath will be ready when he wakes up." (Islamic religious practice requires men and women to bathe after sexual intercourse.) This time it was Merouze asking for help.

I dressed and went out to the riverbank. As I sank my buckets into the water, a school of tiny fish escaped. How lucky they are, I thought. I washed my head, neck, and ears with the icy cold water and left.

It was already light. Birds were singing. The village had also awakened, the smoke of newly lit fires rose from the chimneys along with the tempting smell of eggs frying in a sea of butter.

When I got home Merouze had lighted the fire and was waiting for me to start up the kettle. Seeing her now in full daylight, I did not believe my eyes. On her right cheek was a dark round bruise that faded gradually to her nose and eyes.

"Your face is bruised. What happened?" I asked, concerned.

"........"

"Did you bump into something?"

"......"

"You don't know how it happened?"

"Yes, I know."

"Well then?"

Her voice grew loud. "What is it you're after? If you absolutely must know, here it is. My husband desires me so much that he bit me, so now do you understand? Are you satisfied? You can go and tell the others too, especially my *kuma* [the other wife], may she crack with jealousy! Her days are past; now it is time for me to reign. Do you want proof? Here is my face and here is my breast…" She lowered the scarf from her head. "You take a look, and the others can see it too. My husband bit it because he was longing for my love. I am not imagining all this; he was in my bed last night and he said all these things. And if God helps me and grants me a boy, your big hanum can throw herself into the river!"

The cat was baring her claws. Where was the neglected and helpless woman who, a couple of months before, had tearfully asked me to write a letter begging her father to take her back home? Yes, the cat's claws had flared, and she was hissing.

All day long, barely ten words were spoken in the house. Everyone was solemn, going about their chores silently. Naileh Hanum stayed in bed, and Merouze did not leave her bedroom to exhibit the "proof of her husband's fiery love."

Night came.

Early the next morning it was Naileh Hanum who woke me to fetch some water, with a happy lilt to her words: "Muselim, my son, light the fireplace and put the water on." Then, leaning toward me, her voice hushed: "Last night my husband asked for forgiveness."

⌐•⊗•⌐

Around noon, I had the luck to meet Kadriye alone in the hallway. She smiled and said, her eyes sparkling:

"Did you see my stepmother yesterday morning?"

"Yes, what about it?"

"Did you see her face, with the black cheek and eye?"

"You shouldn't stick your nose in such matters. You are a young girl."

"Do not speak to me." She lifted her chin and walked off.

Two days later, deciding that I'd been punished enough, she came to me looking conspiratorial. "I know certain things."

"Anything of interest to me?"

Like one divulging a great secret, she whispered: "Yes. My mother is going to cast a spell to purge that woman's influence over my father."

"Do what?"

"Cast a spell. Do sorcery."

"What is sorcery?" I said, pretending I did not know.

"If you want two people to love each other, or hate each other, or make a woman barren so she cannot have children—things like that—sorcery is needed. And the expert in that is my mother."

"Tell me, is the same sorcery used for every problem?"

"Don't be crazy. Is every meal cooked the same way? Do you think the same sorcery would work for everything?"

"I assume your mother intends to stop your father from loving the other wife, and make her infertile so she can't bear a child."

"Yes, because if 'the other one' has a son, my mother will fall to number two rank."

"And what do I have to do with this?"

"You will bury an item of the sorcery in a grave."

"Where?"

"In the grave of a man who has just died."

"Who says that I am not terrified of the grave of a man who has just died?"

Silence.

"I suppose if no man dies naturally, you also expect me to kill somebody," I said.

"This is serious. My mother will speak to you about it."

"When?"

"When the time comes."

Some days later, while the mudur was at one of the neighboring villages on business, Naileh Hanum called me to her room. She closed the door very carefully and, in a barely audible voice, asked if I knew anyone who could make a spoon.

"Of course. There is Salman's father, who makes spoons, utensils, combs, everything."

"Have him make two spoons. I will give you the money."

"It won't cost much. I will pay him whatever it is."

"Bless you, my son, but make sure that the spoons are not used."

"Of course, they will be brand new, unused, the smell of wood still on them."

"No one must know of this."

"Yes, Hanum, nobody."

"I need something else."

"What?"

"In a moment." She was trembling. We were sitting on the divan close to each other, and she moved even closer, our knees almost touching, and whispered in my ear, "The nail of a black mule."

"Is that all? That's easy. The muhtar's black mule is always in the field or on the streets. Someday I'll make an excuse to ride him and lead him to our stable. The Armenian blacksmith can trim his hooves, and I will bring the pieces to you."

"But the blacksmith must not know it is for me."

"Do not worry about that."

"May God give you many days and keep you from harm, my son."

I was touched by her blessing. "Anything more?"

"That is all for now. Later, when everything is prepared, I will need your help again and will call you."

She could not know that little more was left to tell me because her blabbering, charming daughter had divulged it all. To make sure I had it right, I got hold of Kadriye the next day and asked her to review the steps needed for the sorcery.

"Let me see," she started thoughtfully, folding her fingers, one by one, into her palm: "Spoon, oilcloth, the nail of a mule…"

"Black mule," I corrected.

"…and from my second mother, a strand of hair and pieces of her fingernail. That's all."

"I see. And how do you plan to get those things? Are you going to ask her: 'We want to make your husband shun you and dry up your womb, and my mother will do this with witchcraft…therefore kindly let us have some of your hair and a fingernail'? Let's assume," I continued, "that you get a strand of her hair while she is asleep. How will you manage to cut her fingernails?"

"Are you finished? Getting those things is very easy for us. My stepmother, after taking a bath, sits down to comb her hair and cut her nails. Then she gathers the nail clippings very carefully and gives them to the servant to put in a crevice in the wall. Being a *gavur*, you do not know that those things are helpful to followers of Islam on the day of resurrection."

"I understand now," I remarked. "By removing those things from the crevice, you actually harm her in two ways…first with your sorcery, second by denying her what she needs for her life after death."

"Do you joke? Don't you believe in all this?"

"Of course I believe in all of it, I swear by Allah."

"Your mouth says it but your eyes say something else."

"May I go blind, I believe it!" I said, trying to look as serious as possible.

She believed me. "Do you want to hear the rest?" she asked.

"Yes."

"My mother will write my father's name, Nazum, in one spoon, and that woman's name, Merouze, in the other. She will place the spoons face-to-face, but first she will fill them with the nail...uh, the pieces from the black mule, my stepmother's hair, her fingernails, and press them hard and tie them together, very tightly. Then she will wrap them in oilcloth and tie them again."

"Then?"

"Then you take them and bury them in grave of —"

I interrupted: "—a newly dead man. You and your mother, of course, expect me to do the job secretly, at night. And what if, while I'm digging to bury the spoons, the ghost of the dead man rises and grabs my arm and asks what I am doing, how am I to answer him?"

Kadriye's eyes dimmed. I was afraid she might faint.

"Do not fear," I assured her. "Ghosts will not touch a man born of Christian parents."

Whether or not she believed it, she managed a weak smile and said, in a very low voice, "You frightened me."

When all the items required for the witchcraft had been gathered, we waited for somebody to die.

Ali, the only son of the widow Khatoon, was a wan and skinny boy who had barely reached the age of adolescence. One day he ate some mushrooms in the mountains and died. The villagers found his body, brought it to the village, and buried him the next day in a small grave-yard that was separated from our house by a valley. I was at the burial. They dug very deep and covered the grave with a mixture of clay and hay to prevent rainwater from seeping in.

That night, after we had carried the drunken mudur to bed, Naileh Hanum came to me, hand on her bosom to calm her quivering heart. "Muselim my son, you are to bury this in Ali's grave." She handed me a small packet. I knew it was for the sorcery.

"Yes, Hanum, I will bury it," I said, taking it from her.

"Aren't you afraid?"

"Of what?"

"Going to the graveyard after dark."

"Do I look like a scared chicken?"

"How am I to know? People ten times older than you will not go near a cemetery at night."

"Do you remember a few years ago, when somebody had to go to Huni for your sick brother-in-law [Ali Bey], and the Kurd servants would not go at night, so I went there on the road that passes between the two graveyards?"

"I will not force you, but if you do it, I will be eternally grateful."

"Do not worry, I will do it," I said, looking confident.

"May God lengthen your life. Let him cut days from my life and give them to you."

She was trembling. The tears on her face and chin shone in the candlelight. Seeing her distress, I pitied her.

"Go in and rest. I promise to bury this tonight exactly where you want it to be," I said.

"Thank you, my son. I will pray until you return."

After she went into her room, Kadriye appeared. "Did you speak with my mother? Did she give it to you?"

"She did."

"Do you want me to come with you to the edge of the garden?"

"No, go to your mother. I do not need help." She went in.

The logs and branches that we had brought in from the mountain were stacked in the hallway for firewood. I chose a log about the same diameter as the witchcraft bundle, sharpened one end of it with an axe, and put it under my arm.

It was a little past midnight when I started out. The light from the thin crescent moon barely touched the ground, and the village huts were dark and peaceful. Not even a cat was around as I walked.

Engrossed in my thoughts, it seemed only a moment later that I neared the graveyard, although I had crossed to the other side of the valley. The cool night wind whistled through the tall grasses sprouting between the tombstones, and I, as if seeking atonement, started to recite the last part of the confession. I debated long before deciding on those lines as the most appropriate, since they asked for the help of every saint, every martyr, spirit, angel, patriarch, and the Virgin Mary, for redemption.

I set the sharp point of the log on Ali's grave and struck the top of it as hard as I could with my axe. It sank easily into the soft, damp earth, and when I pulled it out, a dark hole about the size of my fist remained. I stuffed the packet in, filled the hole with dirt, covered it with the mixture of clay and hay, and packed it down. My job finished, I took my axe and, without rushing and without looking back, started for home.

Kadriye, watching for me from behind the window curtain, hurried out. "Thank God you are in one piece."

"Why shouldn't I be?"

" If anything happened..."

"Shush, you see that I am back safely. No need to worry anymore."

We went in to see her mother. The hanum was on folded knees, still praying.

I turned away so as not to interfere with her prayer. She remained on her knees until she finished the verse she was reciting from the Koran. Then, hands across her bosom, she came to me. "Praise Allah, you have come," she said, her voice happy.

"Why wouldn't I have come?"

Seeing that she hesitated to ask the question so important to her, I said with great assurance: "I swear on the soul of my father that I did everything exactly as you wish and as you told me to do."

She put her hand, white as marble and icy cold, on mine, and said, "Thank you, my son."

ESCAPE

World War I rolled over the land until, on October 30, 1918, Turkey admitted defeat and put down its arms. I do not remember how many weeks after the surrender a courier brought the news to us, but I do remember the exact circumstances.

The day was wet and cold. The mudur and I were at the home of the village elder near Zara when a Kurdish boy, sodden and obviously having traveled far, burst in shouting: "Good news! I have good news, but I want my reward first!" as he handed the mudur an official-looking document: Turkey had agreed to an armistice with the Allies, and the war was over for us.

We were all at once jubilant. I think the mudur was happy because his country had come out of the war without being completely dismembered. The Kurds were happy because they would no longer be used as pack animals to carry food, arms, and other military equipment to the front. I was buoyant because somehow, some way, I would manage to escape captivity and return to my own people. For more than three years I had lived as a serf without human rights and, worse, as a Musluman Turk. I could not speak or pray in my mother tongue. Had anyone known that every night after lights were out, I secretly prayed to the Christian God of my forebears, my head would have been cut off.

The mudur, who was drunk when the news came (was there ever a time when he was not?), ordered me to give the messenger forty silver coins, a generous sum that brought loud praise, as well as resentment, from bystanders. Festivities were ordered, and drum and fife players were summoned from the nearby village. A ram was slaughtered. Guns were fired into the air, and a celebration with fanfares began.

After the feast, when the courier came to me for his promised reward, I placed two silver coins in his palm: "Be satisfied with this," I said. "One, I do not have forty silvers to give you, and two, even if I did, the mudur would punish you tomorrow for accepting that amount and leave your mother weeping."

He grudgingly took the coins and then, resigned, thanked me and departed.

The next day, we mounted our horses and returned home, where toasts and drinking continued for days until not a drop of raki was left anywhere in the village. Horsemen were sent to neighboring villages to buy more, but, fortunately, could not find any, which gave us a chance to have a rest.

Meanwhile, winter was already upon us, bringing massive snow-storms from the mountains. For four months we were cut off from the rest of the world, until warm winds thawed the snow and ice. By then the rivers were overflowing and were impossible to cross, as bridges were unknown in that part of the country, and so our isolation lengthened.

Our only comfort in those days was to mark time as we awaited the gentle hint of spring, and when it came, men and animals drank in the honey-sweet warmth of the sun with yearning and love. Field work did not begin because the soil, though steaming, was too soppy, and patches of crusty snow still lingered over much of the landscape. But the long and awesome winter was over.

I have seen many springs since 1919, but no spring anywhere has seemed more sweet and beautiful to me as that year in the mountains of Kurdistan.

Seeds and insects awakened from their earthen slumber, beetles and sparrows darted through the newly washed blue sky, rivers and creeks rushed down from the mountains and valleys, breezes caressed the flowers, and all were singing. Shepherds returned from the pastures, their arms heavy with new kids and lambs and flowers. Women gathering vegetables in the fields sang songs of love and longing. Petals fell like snow from the tips of fully blossoming trees, and wispy white clouds rode on warm winds overhead. Everything was sweet, alive, growing, stirring and flooding. Sweet too were the young girls of the village, with their dreamy eyes and their gently swaying hips.

How good it was to be alive, healthy and nineteen years old, and not serving as a feast for worms underground. True, my blood was not any more worthy than the blood of thousands of my dead countrymen, but it was mine and precious to me.

Spring must have come to my Armenian homeland by now, I imagined, and the storks and swallows had probably returned.

The other day, when one of the Kurdish servants delivered a packet to us from the county seat, he told me in secrecy that the Armenians in Van had fought against the government, winning a victory and declaring independence.

I had heard many impossible rumors, but this? I did not believe such a big lie. How many Armenians were left anywhere in the world to be able to fight the Turks? Except...yes, except perhaps in the Caucasus. It was true, the Turkish sword would not extend to there. And Van was close to the Caucasus. How stupid I was. Yes, of course the Caucasus Armenians must have helped the people of Van win their freedom and proclaim a *beylik*, as the Turks called it, an independent state.

I was almost beside myself, but my joy was short-lived. If I ran away to join my compatriots, how could I leave Kadriye behind? No. But if I stayed here and put down roots, I might never return to my people. I would live as a Muslim slave serving the Turks forever, licking their boots like a beaten dog.

There are some who are worse off. Yevkineh, an Armenian girl with two chubby babies from her Kurdish husband, wept bitterly when I told her about the independent state in Van and that I might soon try to join them. I had barely finished my words when she burst into tears.

"What has happened? Why are you crying?"

"Why shouldn't I cry? If you go, I will be alone here, all alone with them."

"But who said that we would leave you here? I'll get the other Armenian boy from the village, and we will take you with us. Or we will come back later and rescue you, maybe with an organized group. We know where you are!"

She shook her head and continued sobbing. "That is impossible."

"Why impossible? Did you hear what I just said?"

"You do not understand, my brother, you do not understand."

"I don't understand what?"

"I cannot leave this house. I have children. True, their father forced me into his harem, but the children are mine, my own flesh and blood. I carried them inside of me for nine months, I nursed them; I love them, don't you understand? I love them!"

She shouted, "I love them!" at me as though I blamed her for loving them. I lowered my head and left, unutterably depressed. I did not understand such matters, but I was glad that the news of the victory had come to me before I was married and had children.

What an idiot! Whom would I marry? I could never have Kadriye, so why worry about putting down roots?

Still, leaving would not be easy for me. But to hell with it, one morning I would cross myself and go. The important decision was whether or not I should tell Kadriye. How perfect if she could come with me. I knew that was an impossible dream, but it did not stop me from dreaming.

I knew that I would have to leave her behind.

The Armenians in Van have formed an independent state, and I have not slept since hearing the news. It is my nation calling me now. How can I sleep?

The only way is to cast off the chains of her heart.

Wrong. Wherever I am, whatever I become, I will be happy or

unhappy with her sweet memory, always.

Just as birds exercise and test their wings before migrating, I started to walk one morning with all my belongings in my pockets, but had not gone a half mile when I returned.

"Wait, think it over," I told myself. "What's the hurry? You're not going to be proclaimed king of Van. They hardly need your help to solidify the foundations of Armenia there. Besides, where do you think you're going? What excuse can you give if you are arrested? And suppose somebody on the road skins you alive for the shirt on your back? It happens every day."

When I could think sensibly for a moment, I admitted that all these arguments were mere excuses not to part from Kadriye and the life I knew. But what was more important than returning to my own people? How to decide? I spent sleepless nights weighing the pros and cons. What to do?

Rains started in May. I stood on the porch, staring out endlessly... silver threads in the gray air. No harm in waiting a few more days.

Finally the sun blazed in a crystal-clear sky.

If the sun shines like this for three days, I will escape, I thought, and so as not to weaken, I swore on my father's soul.

After two sunny days and only twenty-four hours left to act on my vow, I went to the Armenian carpenter in the village—his life had been spared because nobody could do his job—to say good-bye to him and to his wife. He insisted that I inform the mudur and thank him for his hospitality.

"After all, he protected you from harm for all these years, didn't he? Tell them you are leaving the household, and thank him for everything."

I was angry.

"I?—I must thank him? Or is he to thank me? What kind of logic is this? For all this time I have slaved for the mudur and his family for a bellyful of bread. I was his secretary, I groomed his horses, I was his servant, I collected bribes for him, I cleaned his stable. I cut firewood for his hearth, I carried water on my shoulders from the river for them to drink and bathe in. I stood guard at his door like an obedient dog and watched over his family. What more do you want me to say? You saw it all with your own eyes. Tell me, was there any service that I did not provide? Was there any demand they did not make? And now you want me to be grateful? For what?"

"You did all that, we know, but I repeat, give him a reasonable excuse for leaving his household and thank him for his patronage."

"What reasonable explanation can I give? Can I say that I am tired of him and my Turkish name, which I carry like a dirty shirt on my back? Can I say that I am tired of lying and pretending and praying in secret?"

"Nobody is asking you to say that."

"What then?"

"You can say that you are going to search for your mother."

"Their people threw her into the Euphrates! They know I cannot try to find her... even her bones have disintegrated by now."

"All I know is, it is right to tell them you are leaving."

"And I know if I tell them, they won't let me go."

"They will."

"They won't. Who knows them better, you or I?"

He was silent. "Is your decision irrevocable?"

"Good-bye," I said, giving him my hand.

"Good-bye. God be with you....with us, too," he added dejectedly, and hung his head.

At the time I did not understand his concern, but months later, when I was in Sivas and a free man, I met a woman from our village who told me that the mudur had flogged the carpenter unmercifully on the night that I escaped.

My heart sank. "Why? Why did he do it?"

"He wanted to know where you were going—in what direction."

"The carpenter could have said anything, anywhere."

"Are you mad? Whatever he said would mean he knew about your escape, and he would be condemned as an accomplice. He swore he knew nothing about it."

"What's the difference? He was flogged anyway."

"If the hanum and Kadriye had not interfered, he would have been beaten to death."

"How is she?" I asked, hiding my feelings.

"Who?"

"Kadriye."

"She is grown up and self-assured."

Then, looking straight at me: "Everyone was surprised."

"Surprised at what?"

"That you went off and left her."

"How are the Armenian girls, Yevkineh, Mendoohi, Mariam?" I asked, changing the subject.

"They are all right. They manage one way or another."

She was somber, quiet. And with "God be with you," she walked away.

I did not see her after that day.

Back to my escape. It was the last week of May. More than by calendar dates, time in Kurdistan was measured by the seasons. The rains had ceased. The days were hot and nights were pleasantly warm. I knew that if I had to, I could sleep outdoors for several nights during my flight. I took two loaves of bread that Mendoohi had pilfered from the storeroom and put them in my goatskin sack, along with my awl, a shoemaker's needle, several yards of waxed cord, and nothing more. I hid my sack under a pile of stones near the path so I could pick it up the next morning, and returned home.

I spent an anxious night of worries, unknown fears, and night-mares. Daylight came. We sent the herd out to graze and went about our daily chores, cleaning the stables and the grounds. Two hours later the animals were brought home and milked, and after the milk was poured into tubs for cheese-making, our breakfast was served. I don't know how I ate. I was not hungry, but I managed to swallow the watery soup that was placed before us. "I am going to be on the move with no chance to buy food. Whether or not I want to, I must eat now so I can endure the journey," I told myself. Kadriye stood at the door chatting with her mother, unaware of anything.

"If she only knew," I thought, without taking my eyes from her.

"Come, can't you wait?" I asked myself. "Wait just a little, until you can see her alone. Then you can tell her that you will always be grateful to her for bringing sweetness to the days when you were an orphan and slave....Yes, wait until you can tell her. Surely you're not afraid that she would betray your secret.

"But if she starts to cry and says: 'Please do not go,' then what about returning to my people...the independence of Van, my Armenian nationality, my oath. Won't I turn into another Yevkineh if I stay and put down roots here?"

I went outdoors, looked around, and picked up a flat stone. I spit on one side and threw it up in the air as high as I could. "If the wet side comes up—no more back and forth—I will set out immediately," I promised myself.

My heart was pounding as I bent down to see how the stone landed.

The decision was clear. I went into the stable, got the horse, told the boys standing around that I was taking him to pasture, led him out, and leaped on his bare back. At the side of the road, I stopped at the pile of stones, picked up my sack, tied it to my waist, remounted, and rode to the pasture. I tied the horse to a wooden fence that I had spotted some days ago and took his head into my arms. I stroked him, bid him a lingering good-bye, blessed him and the people I loved, the orphan servants back home. My eyes were wet. We separated.

I started my journey on foot. True, I would travel faster and tire less on horseback, but I would be pursued relentlessly for stealing a horse and, if caught, my punishment would be merciless, perhaps fatal. Too, with a horse, I would easily be seen—how could I hide under a thicket or in a hollow if I had to? And more, what about the swarming brigands who would happily shoot me for this beautiful animal?

I prayed, "Lord, let me not rue this day," crossed myself, and started to walk.

By now it was almost noon, a pleasant spring day. I looked back toward the village. My heart ached. How many loved ones and close friends I was leaving behind, with no chance to ever see them again.

Had I run or walked for hours? I could not remember. I had to get as far as possible before my absence was noticed. The narrow, rutted clay road was choked with travelers. Famine prevailed. People were moving from village to village to beg friend or kin for a handful of flour or some grain to mix with grass for food. If somebody I knew—after greeting me respectfully and inquiring about my health—asked where I was going, I would say that I was en route to a nearby village on business for the mudur.

Hours passed. The shadows at my feet lengthened until I was walking over them. Birds hastened toward their nests. I came to a creek in the valley. I was tired. I stopped and washed myself in the clean, cool water. I drank until I could drink no more and was refreshed. I took a half loaf of bread from my sack and ate it slowly, wondering which one of the young servants had baked it. What were they doing now? Had they realized that I was gone…that they would never see me again? Did the mudur regret that he had not settled my fate some time ago? I gave him many reasons to do so, knowingly or unknowingly. If I decided to go back, would he pardon me or punish me to the ultimate? I knew that Kadriye and her mother, Naileh Hanum, would side with me as always, but what about this transgression?

Filled with these thoughts, I started to walk again. Faint stars appeared as the light dimmed. "Dear Lord, it is almost dark and there are not even any trees in sight where I can sleep tonight. Merciful God, strengthen my legs and footsteps to help me reach someplace." I started to run. I had to find shelter. To the left of the road, far off at the side of a hill, a light flickered. I turned toward it, a yellowish dot. A dog barked and birds soared overhead. As I neared the light, an old woman, veiled to the top of her nose, came toward me.

"*Abla,* sister, I said, my voice weak and tired, "will you give me a place to sleep the night? I am traveling and I do not need anything more, no food or drink. I have already eaten, and, thanks to Allah and the Prophet, I am not hungry."

I used words to show that I was a believer and devoted to Islam because, except for her eyes, she was totally covered in the mode of strict Muslims.

She listened to me closely and asked, "Are you a religious convert?"

"Yes, I am."

Witch! I said to myself, it's none of your business whether or not I am a convert. What's it to you? How on earth did you guess that I was a religious convert? If you guessed it, that means others can guess it as well, which is not good.

"I do not have a place for you. I am a lone woman, I am afraid of strangers, and I have only my dog to protect me. But if you go around that hill you will see a big village in the valley. The village chief—Khalil Agha—is a rich and hospitable man. His door is open to all travelers. I am sure he will have a place for you to sleep."

"Is Khalil Agha a bearded man with three wives and two boys?" I asked.

"Yes, how do you know?"

"We are friends. I did not know that his village was so close. Thank you and good-bye."

"If you go past the greenery and around that hill, you will see the lights of the village."

I was renewed. I had not lied when I told her that I knew Khalil Agha. Years before, when the mudur was moving his family to Bey Punar, we had stopped overnight at Khalil Agha's house. Much later, after the mudur had settled into his official duties, the Agha paid us a visit in return. We honored him, and I served him at table and in his room. Surely he would remember. He had no way of knowing that I was a fugitive, since radio and telephone were unknown in this part of the world. I would simply go there and knock.

One of his sons came to the front door.

"Is Khalil Agha at home? I am a friend."

"Come in. He is in the parlor with guests."

The room I entered was dark because the fireplace, which was used for light as well as heat, had not yet fully kindled.

"Good evening, Khalil Agha, do you remember me?" I asked brightly, taking his hand and lowering my head over it in supreme respect.

"Your voice seems familiar, but the room is dark and I do not see well. Who are you?" the old man asked.

"I am Muselim—Nazum Bey's secretary and servant. I once wrote a letter for you."

"Of course, of course, welcome. How is the bey, how are his wives and children? Has the last wife given him a son?"

"Unfortunately, no. They are still with two daughters."

"Do you know these *efendis?*" he asked, nodding at the two men sitting on cushions.

"I have not had the honor."

"One of them is the tax collector Dirbas *efendi*, and the bearded one is the chief of the gendarmes, Captain Tevfik Shukrue *efendi*."

Then he introduced me: "Muselim...the servant of Kujorzade Nazum Bey."

"Is he a convert?" asked the chief.

"Yes, but he is a good convert. The Mudur Bey is very pleased with him."

Then he turned to me: "Where are you coming from, son, and what is your destination?"

"I come from home and am bound for Bayburt (this was opposite my destination, but the mudur had relatives there). The bey is so busy, he sent me to represent him about an inheritance," I lied unhesitatingly.

"May God grant you success in your mission."

"Thank you."

Soon, dinner was brought in, and what a feast! A huge platter piled with bulgur pilaf and lentils topped with fragrant bits of lamb roasted in butter, wafers of white bread, and bowls brimming with yogurt.

The rich food and the day's journey overwhelmed me. I started to nod. Khalil Agha noticed and called a servant to prepare a bed for me. I thanked him and went outdoors to see about the next day's weather. It was cold. Bright stars as large as my fist gleamed in the dark velvet sky. A light breeze came from the west, and a yellow moon played over the rippling wheat fields.

All was quiet, with the promise of a clear morning. I felt optimistic. Anyone pursuing me could not reach this far tonight, I thought, and went to bed. Before falling asleep I fantasized about what the mudur's reaction would be when he heard that I was a guest, in his name, at his friend's house, and had dined on lamb and pilaf in the company of the chief of gendarmes, no less. Who knows how much he would curse me, the *gavur* infidel! I slept peacefully.

I was up before dawn. The tax collector and the police chief were still in deep sleep. I dressed quickly and tiptoed out. The overcast sky was about to unveil a bright day. A servant passed through the hall and a rooster crowed. I was fastening my moccasins when I sensed Khalil Agha standing over me.

"You are up early."

"I should be on my way before it gets hot," I explained, and asked how far it was to Zara.

"If you start now you will reach there before the sun is as high as a poplar."

"Very good. By then the district head will be in his office and I will be able to see him," I said, adding another lie.

"What do you have to do with him?"

"I need a letter, like an identity confirmation."

"The roads are bad, very bad, thieves and lawlessness everywhere. With God's help, you will go and return safely."

"And with thanks to you and deepest gratitude for your prayers."

He was standing above me, his hands tucked into the wide sash wound several times over his waist. I wanted to ask him for some bread to take with me, but did not dare.

"Good-bye, Khalil Agha," I said, with utmost politeness. "I will recite my debt to you with each step as I walk along the road. Deep thanks for your hospitality. And one of these days, when you see the Mudur Bey, tell him that I was your guest, and spent the night here as he instructed."

"You are the guest of God, my son. Stop here again on your way back. Take the road to your right after your cross the water, it will lead you directly to Zara; after that, ask again for directions."

What he called the "water" was a rivulet, somewhat deep and cold, formed from mountain streams and not yet warmed by the sun. I sat on the bank and hurriedly started to loosen the ties of my moccasins so I could remove my pants to cross. But I changed my mind. The sun would be up soon and dry me off, so why waste the time? Who knows, people looking for me might be close by. After all, they would be on horseback, and I was on foot.

I waded into the water in my clothes. It did not seem cold; it felt more like burning. I bent, cupped some water in my hands and washed my face, forehead, mouth and neck, and began to pray.

"I am the last and only survivor of an Armenian family, Lord, please keep me and guide my footsteps along the right path." Only after I crossed myself did I realize that the last part of my prayer was from the Koran.

When I reached the opposite bank and shook off the water, I felt relieved and almost happy. The world seemed more beautiful to me. The sun was over the mountains. Skylarks soared like arrows through the fields, goldcrests hidden in the thickets accompanied them with song, and droplets of dew on the poppies sparkled like fallen stars before disappearing in the sunlight.

"Dear Lord…you put this head on my shoulders, please help me to keep it there," I prayed fervently. "Do not let other humans mar your personal creation…"

Soon the outskirts of Zara lay ahead, and as I moved closer the air was filled with the distant buzz of the awakening city, an unmistakable sound that I had not heard in years. On one side, women in the pasture were gathering beets and herbs, and on the other side, a shepherd was with his flock. Facing me was the mountain peak hovering over the city. I swelled with emotion as though, after a very long absence, I was returning to my home and to my loved ones. I sank to the ground and wept.

When I got up, my heart had cast off a heavy burden. I hummed to myself, remembering the words of a Kurdish song: "If they gather all the people in the world who have suffered, my troubles would be more than all their troubles put together." I sang it in a singsong, almost pleasurably, and continued on my path.

I knew from the mudur's past trips that the owner of a coffeehouse in Zara was an Armenian named Saduk. When I reached the city, I asked around and found the place.

A man forty to fifty years old, bright-tasseled fez on his head, was preparing coffee in a long-handled brass pot, moving it to and fro over the fire.

"*Efendi*, is your name Saduk?" I asked in Turkish.

"Yes, they call me Coffee-maker Saduk."

"I am Armenian," I told him, this time in Armenian.

He looked around cautiously and nodded.

"My name is Muselim," I said. "My Armenian name is Aram. I was Nazum Bey's secretary. I have escaped."

"Which Nazum? The one I know? Kujorzade?"

"Yes."

He clasped my hand: "Welcome."

"Thank you," I replied. "I hear that the Armenians in Van have declared independence. Do you know this? Is it true?"

"It is true," he said, laughing, and asked where I'd heard about it.

"The Kurds in our village told me."

"That news is three years old…."

"Never mind that. But it is true, isn't it?"

"Yes, yes it is true."

"Thank God."

"Did you run away from the mudur because of that?"

"Yes, why else?"

"So you can go to Van?"

"Yes!"

"Why? Are they waiting for a king?"

"I know nothing about that, but I can tend the finest horses belonging to any king," I replied naively.

"Well, what is it you need now?"

"A place to sleep for the night."

"My place is unsuitable. Too many policemen and officials come and go. Let's go up to the roof and I will show you where an Armenian family lives. They can take care of you."

We climbed to the roof.

"See that house across the way and up? Go there."

"What is their name?"

"Setrag, but he changed it to Hilmi. He is known as Craftsman Hilmi. He is a furniture maker."

I was so happy my words tumbled out.

"Does Craftsman Hilmi have a mother, a wife, and sister-in-law?"

"Yes, how do you know?"

"I know them," I shouted. "I know them!"

I explained how we met. "It was a very bad time. We were in the town of Karaja Veran, the mudur, his family, and I. There were some wealthy young Turks hanging about, posing as soldiers to avoid going to the war front. Hilmi and his family were also there. One of the guys was after his sister-in-law; he followed her day and night, he was crazed, threatening to take her away or kill the whole family. They turned to the mudur, begging for help. You know, when you say to a Turk, 'I've fallen into your furnace,' meaning 'I am at your mercy,' they tend to soften. He offered protection by saying I was engaged to the girl. Of course this was only a pretense, but it served its purpose. The mudur summoned the pursuer and told him that the girl he wanted was his secretary's fiancée, that he was to stop and cause no more trouble. So it became my duty to visit them a couple of times a week to have dinner, and occasionally, to appear in public with my "fiancée." I am not a stranger to the Hilmi family—I had delicious meals with them back then."

"Small world," said Saduk, smiling. "Now you might truly become engaged."

"That is not possible. It is dangerous for me to stay here, and for them too. Besides, I am nineteen years old, what's the rush?"

"Fine, son. Go. They will probably be happy to see you."

I ran there and knocked. The old mother, whitened and a little unsteady, opened the door.

"Mother!"

"Wait. Let me see...who are you?"

"Don't you recognize me? I am Aram."

"May I go blind! How did I not recognize you?" And taking my hands, she held me out before her outstretched arms.

"You have grown and become a young man, my child," she said, and started to cry.

"Why are you crying, because I grew up?"

"Come in, come in, your brother and the girls will be overjoyed."

Her daughter-in-law came to the stairs.

"Come down and see who is here," said the old woman, wiping her eyes.

They took me upstairs and fussed over me. We rejoiced. We cried a little and laughed a little. They heated some water and washed my hair and feet.

"Setrag will be here any minute," the mother announced. "My child, how are you, what has happened to you, how did you find us?"

I told them everything, including that I was a fugitive and had to leave in haste before my tracks were found. They fed me unsparingly and surrounded me with loving warmth.

When Setrag arrived and heard my story, the situation changed.

"Why go?" he asked. "It is free here, and the annihilation of Armenians is ended. Your mudur's dog teeth can't reach here. Stay and we will start a business together. If nothing else, we can operate a merchant warehouse or commercial building. We will make your pretended engagement to my sister-in-law a reality. You will be married and be happy with us."

The sister-in-law, who was a beautiful, plumpish girl with shining eyes, looked down, embarrassed.

"Setrag, my sweet brother," I said, moved and bewildered, "do not be annoyed but there are things I cannot tell you. I am here for only one night. I have been running for three days and I am tired. Let me stay here tonight and leave tomorrow."

"Where do you intend to go?" the mother interceded.

"To Sepastia [Sivas], for now. I must go tomorrow without leaving any trace behind. Make sure that nobody knows I spent the night here—I do not want to cause you any problem by staying. Even if Saduk the coffee-maker happens to ask about 'the Armenian boy I sent you—did he find your place?' you must say, 'Who was that? Nobody came here...'"

They were convinced.

That night, sitting in the candlelight, we talked about past memories, good and bad.

"May those black days be gone and never come back," said the old woman, wiping her eyes.

It was the prelude to the inevitable conversation when survivors came together.

The dead...sudden partings without return...the lost...those drowned and those shot... those put to the sword or hacked by axe... those thrown upon fires or into bottomless chasms...the emaciated and dead from hunger or one thousand ills. This was the eternal nightmare, the unending sorrow for anyone left alive. We could not forget them because we witnessed it all with our own horrified eyes. How, then, were we to forget?

Finally, we went to bed. The old woman covered me with a quilt and was the last to say good night. "You will be traveling tomorrow, my child. Sleep well so you'll be strong."

I awakened at dawn and dressed. Soon the family was up and breakfast was prepared. The warmth and intimacy of the evening had disappeared, to be replaced by formality. It was as though I was a stranger. I slyly glanced at my "fiancée" and could see that she had not slept the night, and had been weeping. My heart sank. I regretted escaping and was sorry for finding the coffeehouse. If only I had not knocked on

Setrag's door... if only I could undo it.

Lost in these thoughts, I was straining to down my food when the young girl rose from the table, covered her face with her hands, ran into the next room, and slammed the door behind her. I was ashamed and wanted to disappear under the floor. I was responsible for all this. I had unwittingly caused serious upset to this family and the peace it had miraculously found. I opened my mouth but could not speak. The old lady saw it all and decided to intervene.

"Do not worry, my son, this too shall pass, she will forget. Do not be troubled. She is young and inexperienced, and her heart will mend."

"If I had known..." I said, raising my bowed head. "If only I had known."

"There is nothing to know or not to know, my son, God has wished it so. What is written on our foreheads is our destiny. Apparently this was not your destiny."

Go to hell, Aram. Better you had escaped to hell than to have set foot in this house, I berated myself. Why? Why did you shatter the comfort and peace of this family?

I thought of going to the girl's room to beg her to open the door, to take her into my arms and explain lovingly that it was not because I did not want to stay and be married, but there were overpowering reasons that prevented it, that could ruin my life and her family as well. My courage failed. I could not do it. But Setrag came over and asked me, openly, "Are you satisfied with what you've caused, what you have done to my family?"

I could no longer hide it. I pulled him aside and whispered: "Setrag, listen well. You knew Gazin, the Kurd from Karaja Veran, right? You and I were together when he boasted that he had killed the tinsmith of the village, an Armenian, by putting the muzzle of his gun into his ear and firing so precisely that the bullet came out his other ear...You remember, don't you? And he took the man's white woolen waistband after killing him. I am not imagining this, he bragged about it to both of us. Then, after that, whenever he had a chance, he bragged about killing nine other Armenians in unspeakable ways.

"We worked together for two and a half years while I was the mudur's servant. We were rivals and I hated him. Last summer, when all the hills and valleys in the region were thick with bandits and army deserters, we were both on watch near the house when a stray bullet hit him and he was mortally wounded. The mudur heard the sounds of fire and ran out in his nightclothes. Gazin was on the ground, trying to push his intestines back into his body with his hands...and with the mudur bent over him, in his final agony, he had the breath to gasp, 'Muselim did it!' Of course I denied it.

"The following night, three of us took the corpse to the woods and buried it secretly because Gazin was an army deserter. The mudur could not risk the military finding out that he had shielded him for years in his household—it was a serious crime against the government. And more, there was the risk of discovering me—keeping an Armenian of my age would have meant disaster for him. Time passed, and I thought that everything was forgotten. But one night two months ago, when he was drunk, the mudur was angry with me and raged: 'Some day I am getting rid of you the way you got rid of Gazin.'...After that I knew my life was worth nothing. Now do you see why I cannot stay anywhere near the mudur's reach, and also not endanger your family?"

"My brother, why didn't you tell me?" Setrag grew anxious. "You are right, go as far and as fast as you can. Do you have any money? Here, take this letter of introduction to our representative in Sivas. God be with you. The name and the address are there; he is in the office of Ibranossian Trading."

It was a sad good-bye. I again urged him not to mention my overnight stay to anyone—never, not even to the coffee-maker.

Setrag and I walked along the streets as though we were strangers. I stayed behind him until we came to the square. He pointed out a road: "This will lead you directly to Sivas."

We parted.

After he disappeared, I stopped at a bakery filled with fragrant breads and bought two pitas. From another shop I bought some raisins and put them in my sack. Who knew when or where I might find anything to eat again?

I was barely past the town border when I ran into a peasant mule driver. I greeted him in Turkish:

"*Merhaba, hemsheri,* [hello, fellow citizen], where are you bound?" I asked, adjusting my pace to his.

"I'm going to Yeni Koy. I sent one of my wives to her father, but they sent word that they are starving, so I am on my way to bring her back. We do not have much to eat either, but I have a milking cow and two goats, and some vegetables in the field. One way or another, we will manage until the harvest."

I tried to be companionable, and we exchanged pleasant conversation. The road was crowded with people on the move. I tended to his animals and their loads as we went along, hoping that others would assume that the Turk and I were together. As we were passing a lush green meadow, he said, "It must be noon. What do you say, shall we stop and eat? The asses can also graze a little."

We stopped and combined whatever food we had—my raisins and white wheat bread, his cheese and black bread. "*Bismillah,* in the name of Allah," I said, raising the first piece of bread to my mouth.

The man looked at me, surprised: "I thought you were Armenian."

"Do I look like a *gavur?*" I retorted, as though offended.

"I do not know, but your face, your clothing…" (Setrag had given me a shirt.)

"What about my clothing? These days we wear whatever we can find."

He was convinced. We walked together until evening, when our roads separated.

Before dark I reached Kochisar, but now I worried: How to find shelter in this village that was totally strange to me?

I walked around the marketplace, eyes and ears scanning the new surroundings. I saw a shopkeeper with a round face and light skin in a small retail store. When a little girl with big black Armenian eyes, clenching some money in her fist, went into the store, I moved close. The door was open, and I heard a young voice:

"Uncle Kaloust [an Armenian name], my mother sends regards and says that…"

After she left I went in to see "Uncle Kaloust," who was sitting cross-legged on a tattered scrap of carpet, and said: "Sir, I am Armenian, I have just escaped from Turks and am going to Sivas. I have no place to stay tonight."

"My son, if you go to the shop across the street, order a cup of tea, and pay a penny for it, they will let you sleep the night there. The place is warm, and they are good people. You have nothing to fear."

I did just that, and slept with a number of strangers, side by side in a row, which lengthened with newcomers during the night. True, the place was warm, but it was also a haven for lice. When I awoke in the morning my whole body itched, with caravans crawling up my back.

I was on the road before sunrise. This time I joined a soldier who was on leave and heading for Sivas. He served as a guide, and toward evening, as we climbed to the top of a red clay hill, the panorama of Sivas was before us. I separated from him and ran as fast as I could to the outskirts and into the city, alone.

Any Armenian who survived seemed to have gone to Sivas. Once there, I found relatives and countrymen that I did not know were alive. I felt happy. I stayed there a few months. The American missionaries had turned some former college buildings into orphanages and vocational schools, and I worked in the carpentry shop in the district known as the American Center. However, the Kemalist movement [for Mustafa Kemal] was gaining strength and visibility throughout the country, including Sivas, which led many Armenians to decide it would be wise to leave or to head for Constantinople (Istanbul), where the Allied Coalition Forces were in charge.

It was during that time that I found myself in bed one day in the American Hospital. I do not know how long I had been ill— days, weeks—but when I opened my eyes, a woman dressed in black was sitting beside my bed, stroking my fevered brow with a gentle hand.

"I am your auntie," she said, her voice shaking with emotion. "Aunt Aghavni from Zileh, do you remember?"

How could I not remember? She was one of my father's sisters, and was away with her children during the massacre. How else could she have survived after the annihilation?

I nodded.

She kissed me lovingly, achingly.

She did not ask about my father, who was her one and only brother, nor my mother, nor any of the others in our large family. Why open more wounds? She, too, for four long years, had grown to know the length and breadth of living in hell.

"I came to take you to Constantinople," she said, wiping her tears. "When I heard that you were alive, I left my children and came to take you back with us. Yes, Constantinople, too, is ruled by dogs, but it is relatively safe. The Coalition Army of the Allies is there, and the Armenian Dashnags federation…Maybe someday…the sea…eh, who knows?" In her dictionary, "the sea" meant freedom.

It was the fall of 1919 when the train made its way through Kayseri, Konya, and Eskisehir, and I arrived in Constantinople. I did not know anybody there except Victoria, my aunt's oldest daughter; she worked in a pharmacy that was operated by the Armenian Patriarchate, and she had no way of knowing that I would arrive. The other Armenians and relatives who started out with me from Sivas had all separated; some missed the train, others debarked along the way, including my aunt, who stopped in nearby Izmit where her two younger children awaited her.

Unfortunately I had no identity papers or verification of good health—documents that were mandatory for entry into Constantinople, as I later learned. But good luck smiled upon me because a Greek soldier, serving in the Allied Coalition Army, took me under his wing.

I met him on the train. He and his men—all in uniform and carrying military equipment—boarded in Izmit. My compartment was packed with travelers. The other passengers and I instantly made room for them, and once settled, they started celebrating. Out of their lunch bags came raki, then a slab of bacon that they cut into squares. One started playing his saz; soon they were all eating and singing Turkish songs, and before long the bacon was gone and nothing more was left.

At one of the stations en route, I had bought some apples arranged in rows on strings. I took one full string from my sack and offered it to them. They tried to pay, but I refused, saying that listening to their music was my reward. Their commander asked where I was from and where I was going.

"I come from Sivas and I am going to Constantinople."

"Do you have your papers, identification, travel permit?"

"No. When we stopped along the way, my relatives missed the train and my papers were with them."

"Do not worry. I will see that you and your friend get into the city safely."

My companion, who had traveled with me from Sivas, was Megerdich Kazandjian, who like me had recently escaped from

Turkish captivity and was hoping to join relatives in Constantinople.

When we reached Haidar Pasha terminal, the commander, who was Greek, formed his men in lines, two by two, and put us in the first row.

"I have permits for ten men," he announced. "Two of my men stayed in Izmit with their families. You take their places; you are my soldiers now," and he winked.

Outside the train station, when we were on the European soil of Constantinople, the commander asked me: "Where will you go now? Do you have an address? Do you know your way?"

"I do not have an exact address, but I can ask somebody and find it. My aunt's daughter works in a pharmacy in the district called Kum Kapu."

"Hm. Come with me."

We entered a bar. He ordered three beers. When the glasses of the yellowish frothy liquid were put before us, Megerdich looked at me questioningly and I, without lifting my glass, pushed the glasses toward our host.

"You are not drinking?"

"My friend and I are afraid of getting drunk."

"Have you had beer before?"

"No, we have not."

"Try it, one glass won't hurt. Sooner or later you are going to drink, and you will get used to it."

It was a hot day. He slid the glasses toward us. The foamy liquid tasted somewhat bitter but it was cool. Again, gingerly, I put the glass to my lips and, carefully and slowly, drank half of it. He finished his glass and ordered a second one.

"Are you still there?" he asked jokingly. We both smiled and nodded.

When we were outdoors, he led us to the Sirkeci train station, put us on a train to Kum Kapu, and also paid our fare.

As the train was preparing to depart, he went to the conductor:

"Conductor, please do not forget to let these boys out at Kum Kapu station; they are from Anatolia. They are orphans, and inexperienced."

We had told him nothing. How on earth did he know we were orphans? He disappeared into the crowds before we could even thank him.

It was growing dark when we reached our station and got off the train. We asked directions and found the Patriarchate. The doorkeeper explained that the pharmacy was closed and that "Miss Victoria goes home at five o'clock." He clicked open his silver watch: "It is seven o'clock now," he said, but if we waited a few minutes, he would lead us to her.

We had all the time in the world, so we waited until he was ready. Talking continuously, he led us through narrow, dark streets, pausing to direct Megerdich to his destination before he and I walked on to the house. He knocked on the door, and when it opened, he told my cousin that he had brought a guest, bid her "Good night," and left.

I was not going to tell Victoria who I was. I planned to make up a little joke, that I had met her mother on the train and we rode together, that she got off in Izmit and invited me to rest for a night at their house before going on. But when I saw Victoria's bright, open face, I melted. Emotion flooded over me at seeing a family member, and I could not restrain myself. "I am your uncle's son, Aram," I bawled, and flung myself around her neck.

We were bewildered: should we laugh or cry? I think we did both.

That night, before going to bed, Victoria heated some water and washed my head. I remembered the old days, when my mother would stand me in a wooden tub and soap my hair several times, and pour the hot, hot water over my head and body while I howled and threatened to jump out of the tub.

The next day my cousin took me to my first movie. I still remember it: a nobleman killed the villain and threw him over the wall of a fortress into the sea below.

MY AUNT

Several days later my aunt arrived from Izmit. I would have been overjoyed to be with her if she had not decided to send me to school.

I had already spoken to the owner of a shoemaker's workshop who'd agreed to let me join him to learn the craft of shoemaking when my aunt interceded and disrupted my plans. One way or another, she managed to persuade me to go to school. I do not know whether it is correct to say that she "persuaded" me, but it happened like this.

In the single room where I lived with my aunt and her three children, she sat me at her knee one afternoon for "confession," her word for having a talk.

"Eh, now that you have been here a while and are rested, tell me, what are you thinking of doing?" she asked.

"I am going to learn a craft. Back home, before the deportation, during summer vacations from school I used to help my brother make sandals at his place. Now I can learn how to make real shoes. The son of one of our in-laws has a shoe store in the city. I spoke to him, and he is willing to take me on as an apprentice."

"What did you say?"

"I said that I am going to be his assistant so I can learn how to be a shoemaker."

"And I will permit that?"

"Why wouldn't you? Is there something dishonorable about shoemaking?"

"No…no handicraft is dishonorable, but you are going to school."

"My school days are long past," I protested.

"No, they are not past. The time for school never ends. I did not go all the way to Sivas, to your feet, to see you become a leather chewer."

"Fine, my dear aunt. I am truly grateful that you found me and brought me to Constantinople, but what's the point of even thinking about school for me? After four years of working as a shepherd and servant, I've even forgotten the little I knew! At this age, what business do I have in school?...Me? My age and height in a classroom? My knees will not even fit under a desk! After all, there is a limit. It's shameful!"

"Your age and size have nothing to do with it. What is shameful is not to know anything...the shame is to remain uneducated. Your teachers will understand—after all, they too are Armenian. I admit, my son, that your education is a little delayed, but not past."

"It is past, not delayed."

"Listen to me. Delayed, yes...past, no!"

"Past."

"Delayed..."

"But Aunt..."

"For your sweet father's sake."

"Don't bring my father into this!" I was upset. "I am not a student. Besides, you alone are carrying the burden for all of us here. You work fourteen hours a day to keep us alive, and you come home exhausted. How bad would it be if I, as the elder son of the house, earned a few pennies to bring home? That way, I'd have the satisfaction of contributing part of my debt to you."

"You do not owe me, or anyone, anything. I do not need help. You will go to school, it is not for you to say," she said in one breath.

"What you say or I say is not the point," I said.

"Then what is it? It will be my word!"

We were silent. Seeing that I was not going to give way, she started again. "It will be as I say, I am telling you. Do you understand? My word! Otherwise...otherwise I will renounce you. I will say that I do not have a nephew. Just as Peter denied Jesus, I will deny you."

"But Aunt..."

"I will put you out of this house!"

I was wounded. I thought of saying, "Then I will return to the Turks. I managed to keep my head on my shoulders when I was with them, now I can do even better," but I said nothing, because her voice broke. She was still arguing, but she had taken my head in her arms and was pressing me to her warm chest.

She was crying, pleading with a wet voice. "Do as I say, my child, do as I say…For your father's sake. Otherwise you will regret it later…"

Tears dropped on my hair.

"I will go, Aunt, I will go….Do not cry, I will go. I'll go to school or anywhere else you wish, wherever you say. I will go, only don't cry… don't cry. I'll go…I'll go…I'll go…"

That was many, many years ago. Now my aunt is gone; she has long since turned to ashes. But before she died, she was delighted and pleased to see me become a "writer" in the United States. When my name was mentioned at a gathering, she would say, with great pride, "He is my brother's son."

May heavenly light shine upon her grave.

1919-1920: Author's Aunt Aghavni (center) with her family of survivors. At top, her daughter Victoria and niece Zabel in white nurse's
shirt. Seated and flanking her are Aram Haigaz (left) whom she found
in Sivas and rescued, and her son Sumpad at right. Seated in front is
her daughter Ardemis.

ABOUT *the* AUTHOR

A ram Haigaz was the pen name of Aram Chekenian (1900–1986), who lived through the Turkish genocide of Armenians in 1915. He was a young boy when his town of Shabin Karahisar was attacked, which he wrote about in his first book, *The Fall of the Aerie*, often cited by historians as the sole eyewitness account of that struggle.

Following the surrender of his people, Aram Haigaz was taken by Turks, converted to Islam, and lived for four years as a Muslim until he was able to escape. That experience was recounted in *Four Years in the Mountains of Kurdistan*, which appears here for the first time in English translation.

In 1921 he arrived in the United States and settled in New York City. He studied English at night, worked as an apprentice at the newspaper *The Daily Mirror*, and read avidly the great world and American classics, from Kipling and Balzac to Poe. Within a year he started writing for the Armenian publications, and chose a pen name in remembrance of his youngest brother, who had been killed. At twenty-two, Aram Chekenian became Aram Haigaz.

When he died at age eighty-five, Aram Haigaz had published ten books that were read by Armenians throughout the world. Except for his accounts of the genocide that he experienced in his early years, much of his output was in the form of humorous short stories and vignettes of contemporary life in the United States that were immensely popular with readers. He also wrote many essays and articles for Armenian newspapers and magazines. He received several prestigious Armenian literary awards, and in 1972 the jubilee of his fifty years as a writer was celebrated with programs and tributes in a dozen cities in the United States and Canada, and in Beirut, Lebanon.

In 2010 his 110th birthday was commemorated in New York by Hamazkayin, the Armenian Educational and Cultural Society. In recent years, several new volumes of his work have been published in Armenia, the first in 2009, *Aram Haigaz, Letters*; in 2012, a volume of short stories, *A Living Tree*; and from 2010 to 2014, four volumes of essays and articles, *Forgotten Pages*.

BOOKS *by* ARAM HAIGAZ

IN ENGLISH TRANSLATION
The Fall of the Aerie 1935

IN ARMENIAN
The Call of the Race, vol. I 1949
The Call of the Race, vol. II 1954
Shabin Karahisar and Its Heroic Struggle 1957
Four Worlds 1962
Hotel 1967
Yearning 1971
Four Years in the Mountains of Kurdistan 1972
Live, Children! 1973
Happiness 1978

BRIEF FACTS *about* ARMENIA

The ancient Armenians, one of the world's oldest civilizations, lived in the highlands surrounding Mount Ararat, where Noah's Arc is said to have rested. Early Sumerian inscriptions from 2700 BC and later hieroglyphs of the Hittites refer to the Armenian people. By the first century BC, the kingdom of Armenia had reached its height, stretching from the Caspian to the Mediterranean seas and from the Caucasus to Palestine. Throughout its long history, however, it was invaded and conquered by a succession of foreign powers, including the Romans, Persians, Byzantines, Seljuks, Mongols, Arabs, Ottoman Turks, and Russians.

Armenia was the first country in the world to adopt Christianity as its official religion, in 301 AD, and its alphabet was created in 405 AD to translate the Bible. The first words written in Armenian are said to have been from Proverbs: *To know wisdom and instruction; to perceive the words of understanding.*

The threat of domination by foreign forces never abated, and in the sixteenth century, major portions of Armenia fell to the Ottoman Turks. From that time through World War I, the Armenians experienced continued oppression and armed attacks. Under Sultan Hamid a series of horrific massacres took place in the 1890s, a portent of the systematic annihilation of 1915, which took the lives of 1.5 million and is considered the first genocide of the twentieth century.

After World War I, in 1918, Armenia was briefly independent for two years, until it was absorbed into the Union of Soviet Socialist Republics (USSR). In 1991 Armenia again gained independence when the Soviet Union was dissolved. Today Armenia is a country slightly larger than the state of Maryland, bordered by Georgia, Azerbaijan, Iran, and Turkey. It has a population of about three million, and was admitted to the United Nations in 1992.

TURKEY *in* WORLD WAR I

Allied Powers: British Empire, Russia, France, Italy, United States
Central Powers: German Empire, Ottoman Empire (Turkey), Austro-Hungarian Empire, Kingdom of Bulgaria

1914 Turkey enters war on the side of the Central Powers. Russia, Great Britain, and France declare war on Turkey.

1915 Armenian intellectuals and leaders are arrested in Constantinople and later slain in prisons or en route to exile. Armenians throughout Turkey are massacred.

1916 Turkey is in fierce conflict with Russia.

1917 Bolshevik revolution ends the monarchy in Russia.

1918 Turkey surrenders to Allies in October. Armistice is signed on November 11. End of the Austro-Hungarian, German, Russian, and Ottoman empires.

1918-1923 Allied troops occupy Constantinople.

1923 Republic of Turkey is declared.

ACKNOWLEDGMENTS

Much of the work for this book was done at the corporate office of George L. Lindemann, former chairman and CEO of Southern Union Company, who provided generous office space and use of the facilities for several years after my official employment with his firm had ended; I owe him special thanks and appreciation.

Carol Rusoff Kogan and her husband, Stephen Kogan, read an early and lengthy version of the manuscript. They returned the pages to me with thoughtful comments and insights, even marking the passages where they did not agree with each other. Their help is reflected on every page of this book. I will never forget their commitment and support.

Other readers during the first years were Elizabeth Seitz, Kenneth Wallace, and my cousins Anahid Keosaian and Diran Seropian, all of whom shared valuable perceptions. I am especially indebted to my late cousin Christine Najarian, who researched old family documents for me, and whose caring involvement continued up to a few days before she died.

Jorge Abellas-Martin was on the scene from the beginning, and gave me his time and expertise, willingly and patiently, to navigate the difficulties of the digital world. Aside from his computer and technical knowledge, his sincere interest and impeccable taste helped me through the years of bringing this book to completion.

Aimée Brown Price was a meticulous critic with an artist's eye for detail and nuance; as an author herself, she helped me immensely in the later stages and taught me some new things about my father's writing.

Herand Markarian, playwright, poet, critic, cultural and educational leader, went through the final draft to make sure that I did not stumble in the translation of idiosyncratic Armenian expressions. He had read the book years ago in the original Armenian, and I am more grateful to him than I can say.

My thanks also to these organizations and individuals: Hamazkayin Armenian Educational and Cultural Society; The Zohrab Information Center at the Eastern Diocese of the Armenian Church of America; the Eastern Prelacy of the Armenian Apostolic Church of America; the National Association for Armenian Studies and Research (NAASR); Karl Doghramji and his wife Laurel; and above all to Jane Porter for her ongoing support. Jane and her sister Laurel are the great-granddaughters of the aunt who is described in the last pages of this book.

I am indebted to Chris Jerome, my copyeditor, who vetted the manuscript with expertise and understanding, and took the time to explain the fine points.

Marly Rusoff was on hand from the outset with her much-needed voice of experience, along with encouragement. Her belief in this memoir, and what it said, was unparalleled. Her love of the printed page has been an inspiration for me in today's electronic world. My deepest thanks to Marly and to her wonderful staff at Maiden Lane Press.

GLOSSARY *and* DEFINITIONS

Abbas – Kurd servant of Ali Bey

Abbasses – family in Bey Punar

abla – elder sister, sometimes madam

Aga – title for leader, master, lord

Agha – Turkish title of respect for important official, chief, man of wealth

Aghvanis – military crossroad

Aghul – short for Aghullar

Aghullar – Ali Bey's village, where Muselim and other orphans lived

Ahmed Bey – the Black Captain, Turkish

Ahmet – an escapee with Hasan's bandit group

Ak-Dagh-Maden – locale

Ako – Shero's younger son, (Ako and Zeki are brothers)

Ali Bey – Turkish master who adopts Aram, changes name to Muselim

Ali – servant to Almas

Ali – a widow's son

Alishan Bey – Kurdish bey, arrives with a group of beys to hunt

Allahum – my God!

Allied Powers in WWI – Russia, British Empire, France, Italy, United States

Almas – Zeineb's daughter-in-law

Anatolia – Asian part of Turkey, large area comprising most of the country

Anoush – Kamile's Armenian name; Ali Bey's young bride

Aram – author's Armenian name changed to Muselim

Arev – Osman's Armenian wife, name changed to Gulizar

Asia – Armenian girl, real name Kohar

Aydzbuder – Armenian village

Ayishe – Guelo's wife

Bado – Kurd servant

Bahsen – a place

Bakir *efendi* – tax administrator

Besi – widowed sister of Emine

Besy – office janitor's daughter

Bey – title of respect for government officials, military officers, ruler; equivalent today to "mister"

Bey Punar – a region

Birwa – old nurse

Bismillah – in the name of Allah

Bogar –Ali Bey's dog

Bogaz Veran – a village

bostan – vegetable garden

Bozo – young Kurdish servant

Buffalo Village – famous for yogurt

caravan – groups of Armenians on forced deportation march

Central Powers in WWI – Ottoman Empire (Turkey), Germany, Austria-Hungary, Bulgaria

Chako – Kurdish servant

Chakur – goat's name

Chalum – Ali Bey's dog

Chamluja – a village

charshaf – long black outer garment that conceals the entire body of Muslim women except for the eyes or face

chavush – chief guard, sergeant

Cherkes or Circassian – Caucasus Muslims under Ottoman rule, with their own language

choban – shepherd

Chobanle – a town

Chomar – Abbasses' dog

Chorakh – a village

Constantinople – modern name is Istanbul

dayee – uncle, Turkish

Dersim – Kurdish city, Musto and Sabriye's hometown (site of Turkish massacre of Kurds in 1937–1938)

Deylem – Muhtar Deylem in Kabak Chevlik

Dibo – Zeineb's son and Almas's husband; Izzet's brother

Dirbas efendi – tax collector

divans – placed around walls for seating, also used as beds

Divrig – city that Almas visits

Dohan – name of an ox

Dursun Bey – Kurdish bey, arrives with other beys

efendi – title of respect, sir

efendim – my master, sir, or a polite way to say "Pardon me?"

El Hamdullah – praise to God

Elif – Kurdish girl

Elmas – wife of Armenian carpenter in Bey Punar

Emine – a widow

Erzinjan – city in eastern Anatolia

Erzurum – important city in WWI (Garin in Armenian)

Eskisehir – stop on train route

Farieh – Mudur's youngest daughter and Kadriye's sister

Fetiye Hanum – Ali Bey's senior wife

fez – cap worn by Turkish men, usually red with a tassel

flah – Kurdish for an Armenian converted to Islam, though still considered an infidel

gamper – Caucasian shepherd dog or mountain dog

Garin – Armenian for Erzurum

gavur – infidel in Turkish, also written as *giavour* or *giaour*

Gazin – Mudur's Kurd servant who hates Muselim

Geig – goat's name

Giresun – city on coast of Black Sea

Giresonian – native of Giresun

Guelo – Kurd servant

Gulizar – Arev's Islamic name

Hadji Bey - Kurdish bey

Hagop of Malatya – an Armenian in the workforce

Haidar Bey – Kurdish bey

Haidar Pasha – train terminal, Istanbul

Haji – Islamic name for Khoren

halal – lawful and permitted within Islamic religion

Hamid – young Turk who is killed

Hamo – son of Abbas

Hamza – a guide

hanum – lady, title of respect for Turkish women or girls

Hasan – leader of guerrilla Kurds who is killed

Hashim *efendi* – mudur of Yelijeh who is replaced by Nazum

Haso – tends water mill

Haso – a young Kurd, Khudur's son

Hekar – Kurd office janitor and Besy's father

Hilmi – Armenian family, name Islamized to Hilmi; father is Setrag, a furniture maker

hoja – Turkish wise man, minor cleric who travels around villages, a popular character in folk tales

Hozan – a servant

Huni – Rufet Bey's village, also home of Ali Bey's father

Hussein – Osman's father, also called Uncle Hussein

Ibo – a servant

Ibrahim Bey – Ali Bey's father, he is Kujorzade Ibrahim Bey, and lives in Huni. Two of his four sons (Ali and Nazum) become Muselim's masters

Ibrahim – Muhtar in Bey Punar

Ibranossian Trading – Armenian trader in Sepastia/Sivas

Ihsan Bey – Kurdish bey

Inshallah – God willing, if God wills

Islam – religious faith of Muslims

Islamized – converted to Islam

Ismail – a *kizir*, aide to the muhtar

Izmit – city in Turkey, about 62 miles from Istanbul

Izzet – Zeineb's son

Izzet Bey - Kurdish bey

Jibo – Ibrahim Bey's dog

Kabak Chevlik – village where mudur is reassigned

Kadriye – Nazum Bey's elder daughter

Kaloust – Armenian store owner

Kamal – name of servant

Kamil Bey – *Cherkes* (Circassian) captain

Kamile – Ali Bey's bride and third wife, age 15; Armenian name is Anoush

Kangal – county seat, Sivas province in central Turkey

Kanlutash – a village

Karahisar – short for Shabin Karahisar, Muselim's hometown

Karaja Veran – a large village

Katijeh – Kurdish widow from Chamluja, owns a fine horse

Kayseri – stop on train route

Kayu – a village in the mountains

Kazanjian, Mgerdich – Muselim's friend

Kel Dag – mountain locale

Keoseh – caretaker of vegetable garden, the *bostan*

Khalil Agha – friend of Mudur

Khalil *Chavush* – Sergeant Khalil

Khatoon – a widow

Khavak – Hasan's native village

Khoren – Armenian servant renamed Haji, Muselim's close friend

Khrimian Hayrig – Father Khrimian: patriarch and later catholicos of all Armenians

Khudur – Hasan's brother and father of Haso

Kiamil Bey – Turkish lieutenant, head of Ali Bey's region

Kiazum Bey – Ali Bey's brother

Kiraz – dancing girl in Izzet Bey's quarters

kizir – village headman's assistant, muhtar's aide

Kochisar – a village

Kohar – Armenian girl, name changed to Asia

Komo – Muselim's dog

Komushdoon – water buffalo village

Konya – stop on train route

Koorshid Agha – from Kangal

Koran – word of God, the central Islamic religious text, parallel to the Bible

Krikor – Armenian boy servant, converted to Shukri

Kujorzade – tribal affiliation or clan; identifies Ali Bey's father and family

Kujorzade Nazum Bey – Ali Bey's brother and Muselim's second master, the mudur Nazum Bey

Kum-Kapu district – Armenian quarter in Constantinople (Istanbul)

kuma – second wife

Kunjul *Oghlu* – Kurd bandit leader, Hasan's aide

Kurdistan – "Land of the Kurds"; straddles parts of Turkey, Iraq, Iran, Syria, and other countries inhabited by Kurds

Kurds –largely Muslims; an ancient tribal culture with their own language but without their own country. Since 2003 they have had an autonomous region in northern Iraq with a constitution, parliament, and president.

La Ilaha Illallah – part of Islamic creed

lavash – flat bread

Laz – region in northeast Turkey on shore of Black Sea

Lutfiye Hanum – Mehmet Bey's wife

Mad Shero – Turk

Magar – Armenian blacksmith

Mahmoud Bey – Kurdish bey

Makbule – converted name of Armenian girl

Malatya – city known for good raki

Mariam – Armenian girl servant converted to Melike

Martini – rifle, from 1880s

mashallah – God has willed it; praise for something much admired

Massoud – bandit leader

Mehmed Ali – one of Hasan's men

Mehmed *Chavush* – (sergeant)

Mehmet Bey of Rooskü – Ali Bey's uncle, husband of Lutfiye

Melike – Muslim name for Mariam

Mendoohi – Khoren's sister, name changed to Minireh

Merchan – Michig's daughter

merhaba – hello in Turkish

Merouze Hanum – Lutfiye Hanum's daughter, the second wife of the mudur Nazum Bey

meze – overall Turkish word for appetizer or selection of appetizers

Michig – Kurdish shepherd from Huni who marries Armenian girl, Siran

Minireh – Haji's sister, Armenian, her real name is Mendoohi

Moris – Ibrahim Bey's dog

Mudur – district officer, Turkish; an appointed, mayorlike governing official of the Ottoman government who oversees a small town and its surrounding villages in a district

Mudur Nazum Bey – Muselim's second master

Muselim – Aram's Islamic name

Muhammad – founder of religion of Islam

Muhiddin – Kamil Bey's brother

muhtar – village head man, elected by the village council of elders; a position under the mudur

Murad – young Armenian "doctor"

Muslim – follower of Islam, meaning submission to Allah and the Prophet Muhammad

Musluman (Müslüman) – Muslim

Musto – short for Mustafa, a Kurdish servant

Naileh – Nazum's first wife and the senior hanum

Nazum Bey – Ali Bey's youngest brother, and Muselim's second master

Nedim Bey – Turkish lieutenant, head of Ali Bey's region

Niazi – young Armenian servant from Ordu

Nokhudpert – village, Kiazum Bey's home

oda – guest room, parlor

oghlum – my son, Turkish

oghlu or oghlou – son, or son of

Ordu – port city located on the Black Sea coast

Osman – Turkish head shepherd for Ali Bey

Ottoman Empire – late 13th century to 1922; the Turkish Republic was proclaimed in 1923 with Mustafa Kemal Ataturk as its first president

Ottoman writing – before 1928, Turkish was written using the Persian-Arabic alphabet, with texts reading right to left; replaced with the Latin alphabet by Mustafa Kemal in late1928

Pasen – a locale

pasha – honorary title given to officials

of very high rank both civil and military, like governors and generals

peej – bastard

Prophet – refers to the Prophet Muhammed, messenger of Allah and prophet of Islam

raki – strong alcoholic spirit, national drink of Turkey, sometimes flavored with anise

Ramazan – Turkish for Ramadan, Islamic holy month

Rashid Agha – tax collector

Red – Muselim's horse

Roosku – Ahmed Bey's village

Rufet bey – brother of Ali Bey

Rustem – black servant in Ali Bey's household

Sabriye – Sulo's Kurdish wife

Saduk – Armenian coffeehouse owner in Zara

saz – long-neck stringed instrument, member of lute family, very popular in Turkey

Sedat – a Kurd

sedir – bench covered with carpet for seating, a divan

Sehel – Rustem's wife

Sepastia – Armenian for Sivas

Setrag – Armenian carpenter, Muslim name is Hilmi (Hilmi family)

Shabin Karahisar – author's birthplace, a town attacked by Turks in 1915

Sher *Oghlu* or Shero – Kurd with four sons

Shero (Mad Shero) – Turkish gendarme

Shevku – Kurd servant

Shukri – Muslim name for Krikor

Siran – Armenian girl, marries Kurd Michig

Sirkeci – train station, Istanbul

Sivas – capital of Sivas province in East-central Anatolian region of Turkey

Sou Sheri – site of military court and prison

Suleyman – Kurdish servant

Suleyman – Ahmet's helper

Sulo of Dersim – Kurdish servant of Ali Bey

Tamzara – Armenian village near Shabin Karahisar

tan – yogurt and water drink

Tekke – a place, village

Tevfik Shukrue *Efendi* – Turkish captain of gendarmes

Tumeker – village

Vartuhi – Armenian girl, youngest of the Norikanian children

Vehip Pasha – high commander

Veli – son of Abbass

Victoria – cousin of Aram in Constantinople

vilayet – an administrative division of OttomanTurkey, a province

Wallahi – In the name of Allah; I swear by God

World War I – July 1914 to November 1918; Central Powers against the Allied Powers. Turkey fought with the Central Powers

Yayla – refers to the highlands

Yelijeh – a remote village

Yeni Koy – Turkish village

Yevkineh – Armenian mother married to a Kurd

Zara – county seat

Zeineb – widow in Karaja Veran; her sons are Dibo and Izzet

Zeki – Sher *Oghlu*'s older son, brother of Ako

Zeyveh – a town

Zileh – a city

Zindi – Kurd servant of Ali Bey

An Excerpt From
Aram Haigaz's
The Fall of the Aerie

"At the beginning of this month all the inhabitants of Karahissar were pitilessly massacred, with the exception of a few children."

—*The New York Times*
AUGUST 18, 1915

SIGNS OF THE STORM

Christmas of 1915 [January] was extremely sad. Rumors had already reached us about a campaign that had begun in mid-December. The Turks were orating about the victories and the thousands of men their armies had slain. They said that an advance of the Russian Caucasus army towards Erzerum and the frontier had been repelled and forced to retreat in November. We all heard and did not want to believe it. We anxiously awaited the Constantinople newspapers for reliable information. Our faith exaggerated the power of the Russian army into legend. Our sympathy was unreservedly with the Allies. I do not know how it came to be so, I only know that a Turk had wittily observed that the face of an Armenian was a barometer of the war: sadness indicated a Turkish victory, while happiness meant Turkish reverses.

The Turkish army passed through the villages and towns, leaving destruction and ruin in its wake: "Barbarians have passed this way." The government began to confiscate supplies for the soldiers. The Turks would unexpectedly surround a store or an entire street and, in the name of the army, commandeer shoes, clothing, fabrics, leather, food, and anything they could use. Unfortunately, they usually confiscated their supplies from Armenian merchants. The officers determined the price of the goods at their discretion, and handed out receipts which nominally promised to pay after the end of the war.

In an effort to escape this official robbery, many businesses and services moved out to the residential sections. The all-but-empty marketplace took on a desolate appearance. The number of profiteers and exploiters multiplied. The price of all European goods went up as never before. Taxes increased and incomes dwindled and disappeared. And misery, which already was not unfamiliar to the people of Turkey, reigned everywhere.

Before the snow began to melt, several of our young men who had gone to war returned home, secretly, and went into hiding. They told us that Armenians in the army were not at all trusted. They were denied rifles, and the Turks had tried to break their spirits and kill them by using them as laborers, digging trenches, building roads, and doing other hard and degrading work on short rations, in malaria-infested regions.

These escapees were followed by others who confirmed their stories. They told of comrades who had been shot or clubbed to death. They had asked only for rifles and the same rights as the Turkish military. Had they not been called to defend the same fatherland?

When the story of these escaped soldiers reached the ears of the Turks, the distrust between Armenians and the government escalated still more.

We had to be cautious not to be taken by surprise. Many of our men carried weapons. The probability of a bloody encounter was in the air.

One spring day, the news came that a high-ranking clergyman had been killed by the Turks on the road to Erzerum. Thereafter, no doubts remained about a clash in the near future.

The Armenian Revolutionary Federation and the reorganized Hunchakian party (the two political parties in Karahisar, both of which dreamed of reform and an end to the periodic massacres), were invited to a conference by the Prelate. In short order, they agreed that a clash was inevitable, and we must prepare for it at once. It was decided that the Armenians should not be the aggressors, and should not furnish the Turks with the least excuse to open an attack upon us.

If and when the fighting should begin, our men were to fortify the wards bordering the Turkish section of the city, and to resist until death or deliverance. Already, the principal barricades and their garrisons had been determined. The rivalry between the two political parties gave way to solidarity and cooperation.

Runners were appointed to carry messages between the wards, and spies were chosen to observe the movements of the Turks. Women and boys took charge of these responsibilities. To their credit, it must be said that they carried out their duties with wonderful courage and devotion.

If ten gendarmes started out from the guardhouse in a certain direction, our entire ward knew about it within five minutes. A housewife would shake out a sheet on a flat rooftop, as she did for her usual dusting. The observer, on a roof in the next ward, picked up the signal and passed it on to the next. Groups of small boys scattered swiftly through the streets and carried the warning to houses where men were in hiding.

I can positively say that without these early precautions, the future defense of Shabin Karahisar would have been impossible, as the Turkish government would previously have hunted down all those who organized and led the fighting.

The government's first, and supreme, objective was to seek out the young men who had fled from the army and returned home. Some brought with them army rifles that they had somehow managed to pilfer. When the police failed to apprehend the deserters, they tried to seize our political leaders, but they were already in hiding.

As a final resort, the government prohibited all communication with the outside. The people of Karahisar could not write to anyone or go to the nearest villages. The city was isolated.

Messengers, who secretly entered the city at night, told how an army of ten thousand had raided, looted, and smashed every Armenian village that it passed through en route to the front. Resolutely and purposefully, it had destroyed the prosperous Armenian villages of Poork and Andreas, which were rich and well organized.

In Dziberi, a detachment of gendarmes killed one of several boys following a skirmish, and brought his pitifully mutilated body to the city center, leaving it at the door of the government house. There, it was exhibited for twenty-four hours, until his relatives and a group of professional women mourners arrived and, praising his courage and youth, took away his remains.

In Poork, the persecution had begun toward the end of May. Through unspeakable tortures, the Turkish gendarmes had succeeded in getting hold of a number of weapons and making a photographer, named Shahnazar, reveal the names of the men who owned and distributed rifles. Needless to say, they were the political leaders of the city. Fortunately, the police did not have time to act.

One night, a limping Shahnazar, weak from loss of blood, came to his comrades. Warning them, he confessed how he had betrayed them and asked the Party to punish him for his treachery. Considering that he had made his confession under the most horrible tortures, and reached here ahead of the gendarmes, Shahnazar had all but repaired the harm. The Party did not punish him at all. But he had no peace of mind, and about eight or ten days later, he died as a result of the beatings he had received.

Thereafter, messengers came every night from all directions. Young men and even boys of twelve to fifteen, disguised as Turks or Kurds, staggered into the city, exhausted and broken, with mourning and revenge in their hearts for their murdered loved ones. They came to tell of the like fates of Mishaknotz, Kirthanotz, Aydzbidir, Sevindik, Arghavis, Aghvanis, Chirdikh, Puseyid, and Anerghi. All of these villages had been destroyed and plundered. Father Sophonia Karinian, the valiant priest of Anerghi, was exiled and all his parishioners had been murdered.

It was most wonderful that these boys, who warned us with the news, came not to save their own lives or for the sake of a reward, but only to serve.

After putting the Armenian population of the villages to the sword, the government centered its attention on our city. One day, it unexpectedly rounded up a number of our citizens who, in spite of the peril, had come to the marketplace, pretending to be occupied with business so as not to arouse suspicion.

Encouraged by the success, the police began new searches the next day. Families and neighbors who were searched learned that they were out after Himayak Karagheozian, Vahan Husisian, Shabouh Ozanian, and Ghoogas Aghbar. Fortunately, these pivotal men had gone to stay in the Fort Ward, in the heart of the Armenian section, where they were safe from searching parties. The government arrested Husisian's father as a hostage and, pretending to take him to a military court martial, shot him outside the city. Then it called the head man of the ward and openly demanded the surrender of Khosrov of Divrig (a member of the City Council), Medzadourian, Bidza, Shabouh, Karagheozian, and Himayak. Already it had gotten hold of, and imprisoned, at least a dozen men, only one of whom was able to escape and fight in the Fort later on.

AN ATTEMPT TO DISARM

After arresting certain of the prominent and influential men of our community, the government attempted to strengthen its position by disarming our entire population. The order published for the occasion proclaimed a state of martial law and demanded all weapons from all citizens, apparently without discrimination between Greeks, Turks or Armenians. The day the order was posted, the government also called for Turkish volunteers to enlist as home guards. Twenty or thirty men answered that call.

A corporal drilled them in right and left turns, how to step forward and back, and then marched them in file around the marketplace and through the streets, carrying on their shoulders the rifles given to them at the armory. The parade was followed by Turkish tramps, street urchins who had been born and lived in the gutter, and half-wild pariah dogs with tails curled high on their backs.

On the second day, in the center of the marketplace square, they began to chant a march:

> *The infidels have placed church bells on our mosques,*
> *Let us throw bombs, and*
> *May the Turkish people spread from sun to sun.*

Immediately after the demonstration, the police began a search. This time, they were looking for arms.

Our prelate, after a brief conference with our elders and political leaders who were still free, went straight to the government house and announced to the mayor that he, as the prelate and representative of his people, would undertake, within a day or two, to collect all of their arms and hand them over to the government.

Women and children began to work feverishly after this promise had been given. From house to house, and ward to ward, they carried rifles, knives, pistols, old and useless double-barreled shotguns, and sabers. Any good weapons they collected were saved and replaced. Firearms that were broken and useless were repaired and put in working order, then sent to the churchyard. The pile was hauled on an oxcart to the government courtyard and delivered to the mayor, together with a bribe of several hundred gold pounds. I do not know whether the Turks believed that we had really disarmed. But the government put a damper on the search for weapons.

Twice each day thereafter, the Turkish home guards, now expanded to one hundred men, marched through the marketplace, singing the song about "the crosses that rose above the mosques," so as to incite the wrath of the Turkish villagers who came there, armed.

A storm was certainly about to break, but when, or at what signal, no one knew.

A telegram to our Prelate, from the Patriarchate in Constantinople, advised obedience and faithfulness to the government. We, however, had our doubts about the source of the message.

In order to gain time, our political leaders managed our people with an iron hand, hoping to prevent any incitement or provocation for the coming fight. Our preparedness was a precaution only for self-defense. We did not propose to commit treason against the state, or stab it in the back.

In our city, where there were no newspapers, the government issued bulletins of war news every day. The Turks bought the sheets for ten pennies each and spelled out the reports:

"The Russians have been defeated and are in disorganized retreat… the invincible Ottoman army is advancing." Despite these announcements, all of officialdom had long faces, and all the telegrams had come from cities far from the front.

OUR PRELATE IS ARRESTED

The frequent searches resulted in a calamity towards the end of May. The Turkish police had beaten women and children, trying to wring confessions from them. When this, too, yielded no concrete results, they called our prelate to the government house one night for a "conference," and detained him there. The news spread through the city as fast as lightning. Some young men wanted to attack the government house immediately and free our spiritual leader. Fortunately, our far-sighted prelate, before departing to the Town Hall, had called Father Megerdich, the aged priest, and appointed him locum tenens, specifically ordering that the boys should not try any "wild schemes" for his sake.

This unselfish clergyman had leaped into the fire knowingly, hoping that, perhaps, his own death might avert the fate of his people.

The very next day, twenty-five armed policemen escorted our prelate out of the city toward an unknown destination.

His death warrant rode with him.

The Turks killed him a little beyond Andreas village on a sand drift, where his unburied body remained until it decomposed under the summer sun.

I mention this here particularly because nearly a year after this tragedy, I met his murderer, Kujorzade Kiazim Bey (it was this wretch's father who destroyed the Armenian village of Chirdikh). The monster proudly told several Turks, and me, how he had shot the prelate in the back, how the victim had fallen, rolling and pale, from his horse, and how, later, his remains had decomposed under the sun and oiled a large oval area of white sand.

"I did not know there was so much fat in one human body!" he chortled, as others in turn began to tell about their "deeds of valor." Helpless and unable to do a thing, I had to listen to these details of the crime, digging my fingernails into my palms. The hero of this masterpiece of vileness had shot an unarmed man in the back, and had come to boast about it before the crowd.

Even today, I can remember all the details of our prelate's departure. A group of boys my own age, and I, had been detailed to watch the government house and the prison. We relieved one another at frequent intervals so as not to arouse suspicion. If one of us was obliged to keep watch more than once a day, he changed his clothes before going back.

In the early morning, when I got there to relieve another boy, horsemen appeared in the walled courtyard inside the prison gate. A little later, our worthy prelate walked proudly and steadily out of the prison. Under his black hood, his face was extremely pale. 'He probably did not sleep the whole night,' I thought. Then I remembered those boys who, rifles in hand, were ready to give their lives to save the holy prisoner. Tears filled my eyes.

The prelate mounted his white horse without help. The entire party moved toward the gate.

From the windows of the government house, fezzed heads watched this humiliating parade until it disappeared behind the trees of the streets.

The hoof beats of that swift cavalcade echoed for a long time in the morning calm, and still ring in my ears.

A deathly quiet reigned throughout the day in the larger courtyard of the prison. It was customary for the Turkish criminals, in chains, to be brought out there. Peddlers were permitted to enter and sell their wares to the prisoners. Usually there was shouting, swearing, and the clash of chains. But today, the prison yard was entirely deserted. The sentry paced steadily up and down before the gate, carrying the rifle and fixed bayonet on his shoulder.

Where were the hundreds of prisoners?

That evening, my father told us that the Turkish volunteer company had grown very large that day. When it was drawn up in line, one could not see from one end to the other, he said.

My brother, to whom I had spoken about the empty prison yard, looked at me and, with signs, made me understand that we must keep that a secret between us.

After supper, he took the news about the murderers and bandits being released from prison, to a place I did not know, and returned very late at night.[1]

THE KNIFE REACHES THE BONE

On June second, Wednesday afternoon, without warning, policemen and soldiers surrounded the two markets called the Old and New Tashkhan, which were publicly owned by our people, and where nearly three hundred of our merchants conducted their businesses. All the shopkeepers and their customers were taken at bayonet point to prison.

The two markets were in separate buildings, where only our prominent merchants could do business. Each building had two ironbound doors, one on the first floor, and the other on the second. This made the government's work very easy; it had only to put several squads of men, with bayonets, outside each door. Resistance from within was impossible, help from the outside improbable. Then too, the seizure happened so quickly that there was no chance to prevent it.

This mass arrest broke the back of Karahisar's Armenians in the fullest sense of the word.

While this was happening in the marketplace, a notorious criminal Turk named Kel Hassan, who had been released from prison, had come down to the Central Ward with some fifty armed men and a public crier. At his command, the poor crier had to shout that Armenian outlaws must surrender themselves within twelve hours, otherwise the government would burn their houses and shoot their families – fathers, mothers, wives, children and infants.

Because no one heeded his threat, Kel Hassan seized every old man he could find, and forced a group of them to Sibon's coffeehouse, which was located at the boundary of the marketplace and Church

---

1 Editor's note: In 1915, "butcher battalions" made up of violent criminals released from prison, were recruited throughout Turkey to brutalize and "kill without mercy" as many Armenians as possible.

Ward. There, sitting and drinking whiskey, he began the torture of his victims. The men, whose confessions he sought, were hung, head down, from a specially-built beam while their bare soles were burned with cigarettes. If the victim did not talk under this torture, a glass of whiskey was poured over his soles and ignited.

Eight or ten young Armenians surrendered in a futile attempt to save their fathers from this torture. But Kel Hassan was not yet through. Until dawn, the coffee house echoed with screams, deafening blows, swearing, and lewd Turkish songs.

Except for Fort Ward, the situation for the Armenian population of the city was not any better. Forcing the head men of the wards to guide them, the police continued to search through homes and make arrests.

There was not a single light in any house that night. House dwellers stood hidden behind curtains, watching the streets.

Occasionally, the dim light of a lantern appeared around the corner – then footsteps, muffled sounds, sudden and clanging noises, the steel of bayonets and sabers gleaming in the darkness. The impact of the soldiers' heels on the cobbles was so loud that it echoed within the house. Whose door would they stop at? How loudly their boots clashed on the stones! Were they striking the door with a saber hilt or an ax?

The window of a house down the street glowed red. A man in nightclothes opened the door and, holding the lamp high, stared at their faces. They shouted commands at him. He made motions as though saying, "I don't know," and "I haven't got it," gesticulating desperately and shaking his head. Silence for a while. The number of shadows at the door seemed to fade. Had they gone? Ten minutes... fifteen minutes. Now they all emerged again; the aged master of the house, who had dressed, wearily followed his guide, two policemen walking behind him, the dim light of the lanterns glinting on their brass buttons.

Another lantern stopped before a house on the opposite street.

"In the name of the law!" a voice shouted, and the knocker crashed down on the door. Not a sound, not a sign of life from within. It was a strong, stone house. Two valiant brothers lived there. The policemen hesitated. Then they went away.

My father, who was a good and peace-loving man, carefully oiled his pistol.

"My heavens!" questioned mother, wringing her hands. "Have our men been captured tonight?" My father, without interrupting his work, answered:

"Are the Turks so many that they can go near the Fort Ward at night? They are brave here, where our houses are so far apart, and at the marketplace, where they are close to the Turkish ward. Do they dare try to threaten the Fort Ward?"

That June night proved to be the most terrible and critical of any so far.

1920: Aram Haigaz (front left) with fellow orphans from the
Central Armenian High School (Getronagan) of Constantinople,
which established an orphanage to house young boys who had
survived the deportations and were attending classes.

"The past is never dead. It's not even past."

—WILLIAM FAULKNER

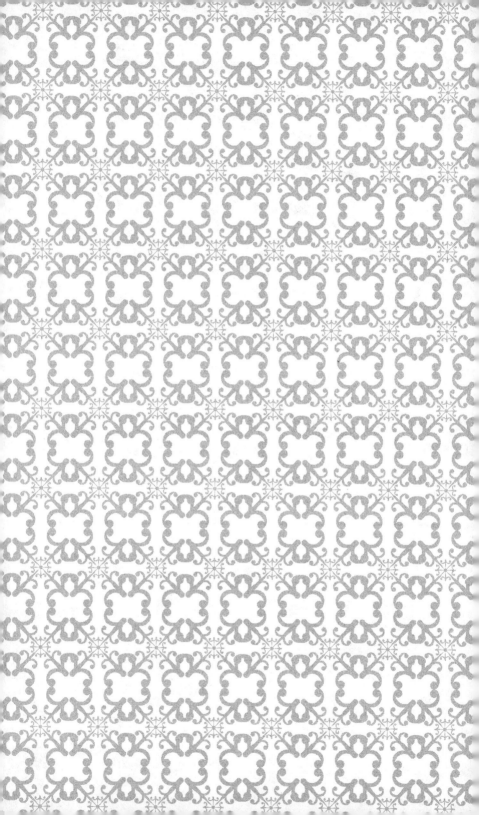